THE
COMPLETE MAGICK
CURRICULUM
OF THE
SECRET ORDER
G.·.B.·.G.·.

Lisa Novak

Carl Llewellyn Weschcke

Chairman of Llewellyn Worldwide Ltd., one of the oldest and largest publishers of Metaphysical, Self-Help, and Spirituality books. He has a Bachelor of Science degree in Business Administration (Babson), studied Law (LaSalle Extension University), worked toward a doctorate in Philosophy (University of Minnesota), has a certificate in clinical hypnosis, and honorary recognitions in divinity and magical philosophy.

A life-long student of Metaphysical, Spiritual and Psychological subjects, he variously studied with the Rosicrucian Order, the Society of the Inner Light, and Aurum Solis. After corresponding with Gerald Gardner and several of his associates in the late 1950's and early 1960's, he holds a carbon copy of Gardner's own Book of Shadows, known as the "Weschcke Documents".

He is a former Wiccan High Priest and Past Grandmaster of Aurum Solis. He played a leading role in the rise of Wicca and Neo-Paganism during the 1960's and 1970s. Author Donald Michael Kraig refers to him as "the Father of the New Age" because of his early sponsorship of new understanding of old occult subjects. In the fall of 1973 Weschcke helped organize the Council of American Witches and became its chairperson and drafted "The Thirteen Principles of Belief", one of the corner-stones of modern Wicca. While no longer active, he retains ties to the Wiccan and magical communities.

Still actively associated with Llewellyn, he is engaged in studies and practical research in parapsychology, quantum theory, Kabbalah, self-hypnosis, Tantra, Taoism, Tarot, Astrology, Shamanism, Wicca, Magick, and World Spirituality. He is also actively writing, and has co-authored three books with Dr. Joe Slate *(Psychic Empowerment for Everyone, Self-Empowerment through Self-Hypnosis,* and *Self-Empowerment & your Subconscious Mind.* He and Dr. Slate are planning several more co-authored projects.

THE
COMPLETE MAGICK CURRICULUM
OF THE
SECRET ORDER
G∴B∴G∴

Being the Entire Study, Curriculum, Magick Rituals,
and Initiatory Practices of the G∴B∴G∴
(The Great Brotherhood of God)

A Shortcut to Initiation & the Most Efficient Program
for Union with the Holy Guardian Angel

LOUIS T. CULLING

EDITED, REVISED, AND EXPANDED BY

CARL LLEWELLYN WESCHCKE

Llewellyn Publications
Woodbury, Minnesota

First Hardcover Edition, 1969
First Trade Paperback Edition
First Printing, 2010

Cover art © Artville: Weathered Backgrounds
Cover design by Lisa Novak
Editing by Tom Bilstad
Interior photos and art courtesy of the authors

Llewellyn Publications is a registered trademark of Llewellyn Worldwide Ltd.

Library of Congress Cataloging-in-Publication Data
Culling, Louis T.
  The complete magick curriculum of the secret order G.B.G : being the entire study, curriculum, magick rituals, and initiatory practices of the G.BG. (The Great Brotherhood of God). — 1st trade pbk. ed.
      p.   cm.
  Includes bibliographical references and index.
  ISBN (invalid) 9780738719 (alk. paper)
  1. Magic. 2. Great Brotherhood of God (Secret order) I. Title.
  BF1621.C86 2010
  133.4'3—dc22

                                                                      2010021070

Llewellyn Publications
A Division of Llewellyn Worldwide Ltd.
2143 Wooddale Drive
Woodbury, MN 55125-2989
www.llewellyn.com

Printed in the United States of America

Forthcoming Books by
Carl Weschcke and Louis T. Culling

Contents

About the Book
and About the Authors

This is a new book, and it's an old book. It's a new and expanded edition of a modern classic that has been out-of-print for nearly forty years.

But as a combined editor and "co-author," I am trying to do something unique.

The author, Lou Culling, died in 1973. When Llewellyn published the first edition in 1969, I was so interested in it that I edited and designed the book and even did the cover art for the dust jacket and typeset the entire book on the IBM Composer system that was a technological breakthrough at the time.

1973 is a surprising long time ago in an era of rapid change and innovation, not merely in science and technology but in psychological understanding and spiritual growth that Lou Culling has missed. Otherwise, he would be writing this new edition himself. It's not that the "Ancient Wisdom" is no longer valid, but the modern understanding of it has to change with the times to facilitate an increasingly wide application of it, and an ever-increasing need for more people to understand, apply, and grow mentally, emotionally, and spiritually.

We no longer see the Universe as a machine-like mechanism (somewhat like a wind-up clock) but more as an organism based on complex interactions of energy and matter guided by "intention," which is another name for "Will" or for "Divine Plan." And we no longer see a person as merely a biological wonder with—perhaps—something called "my soul" attached to it.

In today's global civilization we are far more integrated than ever before—despite the traumas of economic challenge and cultural conflict—and the human person is likewise far more integrated and aware of his depths of consciousness and heights of spirit.

Why produce a new edition of an old book? Because it is a good book made better, and it is a better book than most new books. It was a pioneering book at the end of an age that helped usher us into the New Age. This new edition helps demonstrate that transition and clarify its meaning. At the same time, the message and the technique of "A Shortcut to Initiation" is forever valid.

"As Above, So Below"

That phrase was written long ago with "Above" representing the Macrocosm—the Cosmos as a whole, and "Below" representing the Microcosm—Man in his total self. What is being said is not merely that Man and Universe are part of a single whole (a glorious realization itself) but that each human being is a miniature cosmos, complete in every detail even though those details may exist in more potential than current fulfillment.

In our new perspective, this means two things.

First: Each person functions through the same laws, principles, formulae, etc., as does the Universe as a whole;

Second: Each person has the potential to become successively greater representations of the Universe in all its glory.

We are "gods in the making!" Each of us is in process of becoming more than we are. The life purpose of each person is to grow in our wholeness, developing innate powers into actual skills.

It means that the "laws" of the universe—the systems by which it functions everyday from the beginning to the end of time (if there is such a thing)—are the laws of magick, and through the study and practice of magick we grow into the Whole Person we are intended to be, uniting our Lower Self with the Upper Self. In psychology that is called "integration." In magick it is called "Initiation." *It is also known as*

Self-Empowerment because the process heals the divisions of Self, enabling the Whole Person to draw upon all the Knowledge, Powers, and Skills of the entire Consciousness.

"A Shortcut to Initiation"

That is the promise of this book. The founding concept is that the whole operation of Ceremonial Magick can be reduced to a few very efficient steps.

It means that, acting upon the premise that the goal of Magick is the integration of Lower and Upper Selves, we may remove all excesses commonly found in other Magickal Orders and Esoteric Societies—those robes, fancy trappings, complex formulae, long drawn-out rituals and extensive speeches, secret handshakes and unnecessary acronyms, and the necessary everyday "busy-ness" of groups functioning as lodges or covens or organizations.

It isn't that those things don't have genuine values, and those organizations do serve as communities for mutual support and enjoyment, but a shortcut calls for single-minded pursuit of the personal goal of Initiation and these other things can divert attention and energy from our chosen destination. If we are travelers with a detailed map, we look for the shortest route from where we are now to where we want to go: from our current condition to psychological and spiritual integration.

On our map, we could write "Start Here" and circle "Final Destination."

You're the Captain of your own Ship!

Yes, of course, should you wish you can bring together a small group of like-minded people and follow the same instructions given in this book—but like the journey of the Fool in the Tarot deck, the esoteric path is ultimately personal and solitary even when you are surrounded by others in a "Lonely Crowd."

On the solitary path, you are the one in charge, you are the one responsible, and you are the lone actor on the stage of life even though it is the same path and the same stage we all eventually traverse. You don't have a teacher to lean on, you are not apprenticed to a "master," and your only True Guide is your own Higher Self—your own Holy Guardian Angel!

Of course you have resources—like this book, and others—to draw upon that were previously unavailable to sincere students. There was a time when only the teacher/student relationship was the reliable way to go, but that is no longer true. There are hazards you will encounter, and you alone will meet and defeat the challenges to your success. Even with the help and guidance of others, you alone must crown yourself, just as Napoleon crowned himself emperor of the French empire.

The Only Mysteries are the Inner Mysteries

That's what I hope to accomplish through my editing and through the additional "Commentary" and the "Definition and Discussion Points" I've added at the end of each chapter. In some cases I've simply substituted common words for the abbreviations and acronyms used in the original; in other cases I have newly defined words within the context of their use in the text and in relation to the times.

I don't want you to shake your head in confusion or to abandon the ship because you can't readily understand a particular word, phrase, or concept. I've also tried to add to your interest with a few stories and explanations.

I've tried to remain true to the intent of the Order itself and to Lou Culling's authorship. Even though Lou is long gone and I don't claim to be in actual communication with his spirit, I do hereby state I sense his approval of what I'm doing.

And it is in that regard I want to tell you a little about Lou and then a few words about myself.

About Louis T. Culling

Lou Culling, 1894–1973, (born February 12) was a fascinating and beloved person. I knew him for only a few years before his passing, during which time we communicated and visited, and published four books.

He was born in St. Louis, Missouri, of a prosperous family owning their own business, the Carondelet Foundry.

There's a lot we don't know about Lou.

His daughter wrote in 2009 that Lou was never interested in the foundry business, which disappointed his father.

"Instead, on graduation day, from high school, he got on a mule and took off for the South to make money on 'white pine.' At a later date his parents took off for the South to rescue him from the people there who saw him as an invader & stranger.

"He was brilliant on the pipe organ and was the sole organist at the Emmanuel Episcopal Church in Webster Groves, Missouri."

Lou was married and had a daughter, Georgine, born August 24, 1925, in Florence, Kansas. He was in the navy during World War I, and then they moved to California where he had a job playing the organ in a small theatre in Encinitas. In the era of silent films, his profession was a moving picture pipe organist. Lou wrote, "In playing music for the fifty-six varieties of emotions, I developed a deep interest in human psychology which destined me to become the sole disciple of psychologist Dr. Clarke Walker. He was my mentor for six years until his death in 1940."

For a time Georgine was in a private school (the Rosicrucian Fellowship). "I hated it and tried to run away!"

In 1929 he homesteaded eighteen acres in Rainbow Valley at the base of Vallicitos Peak near San Marcos, and they lived there until 1935. He dug his own well, grew grapes, planted trees, and milked goats for his daughter's needs. She writes that they mostly lived on quail and rabbits. "Later they moved to San Diego and Dad had a terrible time finding work. For a while he worked in book stores, but the Depression was too tough."

In June 1927 he attended the first national astrological convention in Los Angeles where he met Llewellyn George (founder of Llewellyn Publications), then known as "the Dean of American Astrologers," and was invited to do a week of astrological lecturing in San Diego where he outdrew the better-known Manly Palmer Hall.

Georgine still owns the ranch, and her oldest son lives there, managing a nearby nursery. She has four children who were always proud of their grandfather and his books, but neither Georgine nor her children shared in his interest in the occult. Her mother likewise was not interested in the occult but went to meetings with Lou and met Crowley and Regardie, and others involved in the A∴A∴ and O∴T∴O∴ She did not like any of them.

Wanda Sue Parrott, forty-one years his junior but sharing the same birthday, then a young student who often shared coffee with him, wrote: "Many people look upon Louis T. Culling as a spiritual or occult master. Perhaps he was, but to me he was a kind, perhaps eccentric, unforgettable human being—an Aquarian like myself—who adventured into psychic territories because he was born to do so. Perhaps Lou's greatest, most misunderstood message was that ALL human beings are demigods and demi-goddesses and he tried to help them see this truth that was the true light that shone in his young-old eyes."

He was a man whose mind had tremendous reach and vitality, whose life was one of adventure and fulfillment, and whose contributions to modern Occultism are unique.

In 1931, Lou joined the Magickal Order G∴B∴G∴, and soon became head of its southern California section. In connection with the dream techniques of the Order and his work with Dr. Walker, he helped many people learn to "dream correctly and significantly." He worked with many patients of Dr. Walker, applying the G∴B∴G∴ techniques, and sometimes was able to help a patient dream "the dream that actually resolved the case" within two days.

In addition to this book on magickal initiation, Lou wrote several other books on the I Ching, Dream ESP, Nature Magick, Psychic Self-Defense, Sex Magick, and other shorter papers that we may be able to combine in an anthology of his writing and thoughts. There's much here to explore, some in this book and more in the others. In the yet-to-be-published books *Dream ESP*, *The Magick of Nature Worship*, and *Psychic Self-Defense*, Lou, and myself, develop themes less known but more effective than other better known techniques.

The same is true of the forthcoming new editions of *The Manual of Sex Magick* and *The Pristine Yi-King*.

Lou Culling was involved with many of the southern California esoteric leadership during approximately forty years, and had friendships with many of them, including Israel Regardie, Grady McMurty, L. Ron Hubbard, Jack Parsons, and others. He also was in communication with Aleister Crowley who issued him a chart for an autonomous O∴T∴O∴ lodge which he turned over to Carroll (Poke) Runyon of the O∴T∴A∴, which claims to possess the "secret rituals of the Ordo Templi Orientis in Crowley's original holographs."

About Carl Llewellyn Weschcke

My intent in this new edition is not only to "bring back a CLASSIC" but to take this as an opportunity to get rid of the misapprehension and misunderstanding of what is communally called "Ceremonial Magick." Much of the complexity found in the rituals and practices of the Golden Dawn and other orders should be understood as voluntary—to be used as needed in the same way a symphony director can call upon more musical instruments to enrich the presentation, or a good chef can add other seasonings to please different pallets.

The object of ceremonial magick is to stimulate the senses, to power-up the emotions, and to firmly conceptualize the purpose of the operation—which is to create a transcending experience to unite Personality with the Divine Self.

To this end, rituals, symbols, clothing, colors, incenses, sound, dramatic invocations, and sacraments are selected in accordance with established "correspondences" of one thing to another to transport the magician towards a mystical reality.

While some groups and individuals insist on "rich recipes," I suggest that you can strip them down to what works for you. Even more, I suggest that sometimes all those extras can get in the way of your intended goal, just as too much incense can cause an asthma attack. The G∴B∴G∴ rituals in this book are pretty much "bare minimums" just as the whole intention is "A Shortcut to Initiation."

What does this statement of intent have to do with "about me"? I've been a publisher of metaphysical books for a half century, and a student of metaphysical subjects for three quarters of a century. But, more pertinent to this, just like Ben Franklin I've never seen something that

I didn't think could be improved. That's my nature. And even though I had a hand in this book forty years ago, I know we can make it better and that as such it is an outstanding book fulfilling a mission of great purpose.

I was born September 10, 1930, in St. Paul, Minnesota, to a relatively prosperous family making their money through the pharmaceutical company founded by my paternal grandfather. My grandfather, a pharmacist, was a Theosophist, and at one time served as a vice president of the American group. (I "consumed" the occult books in his library!)

My mom was a Roman Catholic and a very good mother to four kids—my two older sisters, myself, and my younger brother. Dad was a naturist, a vegetarian, and a horticulturist. He was a "health nut" in more ways than one, for he was devoted to growing many varieties of nut trees, hybridizing them for greater productivity and resistance to disease and environmental stress. He even sent a man to the Carpathian Mountains of eastern Europe to bring back particular black walnuts he introduced to American soil. We ate lots of nuts.

I attended a private boys school, and then graduated from Babson College in 1951 with a bachelor's degree in business administration. I worked in the family business and in other companies as well, but my passion remained the study of "occult" subjects. I was a mail-order student of the Rosicrucian AMORC and of Dion Fortune's Society of the Inner Light and Alice Bailey's Arcane School. I studied astrology, Kabbalah, magick, and Wicca.

I was also a civil rights and a civil liberties activist in the 1950s and '60s, marching and organizing legislative efforts to bring about fair employment and housing practices.

After buying Llewellyn Publications, I was also leader of a small Wiccan coven and an officer in Aurum Solis. My studies and practice continued but I was also influenced by the authors I met in the course of our publishing work.

In my publishing work I've done everything from sweeping the floor to packing books, to editing and typesetting, to writing advertising copy, to selling to our retailers and wholesalers, to working conventions and conferences, and to practicing magic and astrology.

I have a most wonderful wife Sandra and a wonderful son Gabe—both of whom are now the backbone of Llewellyn as I take a less active management role and switch to what I always wanted to do: writing esoteric and self-help books. Having had a near sixty-year span as a business executive, and determined to live to age 120, I hope to have a forty-year career as a writer.

I hope you enjoy and benefit from this book.

Carl Llewellyn Weschcke

March 21, 2009

Definitions and Discussion Points

A∴A∴ (Argenteum Astrum, or Order of the Silver Star). A magical order founded in 1907 by Crowley after leaving the Golden Dawn. It was reputed to reflect Crowley's bisexuality. See the website www.ordoaa.org/ for information and essential instructions for aspirants of the A∴A∴.

Arcane School. An occult organization, founded in 1923 by Theosophist Alice A. Bailey and her husband, Foster Bailey, designed to bring in the New Age by the Great White Brotherhood, the spiritual hierarchy of masters who are believed to guide human destiny.

Over the next years Bailey dictated a series of books that laid out a program for bringing in the New Age. In addition, there is a correspondence course: International Headquarters, 113 University Place, 11th Floor, Box 722, Cooper Station, New York, NY 10276. More information can be found at their website www.lucistrust.org/en/arcane_school.

Llewellyn. Since 1901, Llewellyn has lead New Age publishing with titles that inform, educate, and inspire readers. We are committed to providing books and tools for exploring new worlds of mind and spirit, thereby aiding in the quests for expanded human potential and spiritual consciousness. Some of the topics we are best known for include alternative health and healing, astrology, earth-based religions, shamanism, Gnostic Christianity, and Kabbalah. We also just announced a line of mystery novels. Llewellyn is over 100 years old, employs over 100 people, and the Weschcke family has owned it since 1960. Find us at www.llewellyn.com.

O∴T∴A∴ (Ordo Templi Astartes) This Order was founded in 1970 by Carroll (Poke) Runyon (Frater Thabion) following a near-death experience and mystic vision. From their own description, the "O∴T∴A∴ is now America's oldest continually operating Ritual Magick Lodge. We are first and foremost a working lodge. Our emphasis is on doing magick—and by that we mean good old fashioned wizardry: summoning spirits to visible appearance in the Dark Mirror and bringing down gods, goddesses, and angels to illuminate our crystal orb so that we can communicate with them. We use powerful hypnotic and yoga techniques that we have developed and perfected in over a quarter century of practice. The O∴T∴A∴ is the oldest continually practicing ritual lodge in the U.S. We are the recognized leaders in the art of evocation (conjuration to visible appearance in the Dark Mirror) and our Pathworking System combines the best aspects of Eastern technique with Western symbolism. Classes are offered on these unique techniques, as well as on the history of the origin of our Hermetic Tradition, at our Rivendell Lodge in Silverado, California. For more information, please contact Frater Thabion, Archimage at: Kingsword@aol.com."

O∴T∴O∴ (Ordo Templi Orientis—The "Order of the Temple of the East") The O∴T∴O∴ was, or is (depending on how you look at it), a magickal order founded by Karl Kellner (1851–1905) in 1890. Upon Kellner's passing in 1905, the leadership passed to Theodore Reuss (1855–1923) and then to Aleister Crowley in 1922. Currently there are (or were) two O∴T∴O∴ organizations: one in England headed by Kenneth Grant, and the other headed by successors to Grady McMurtry.

The distinguishing characteristic of O∴T∴O∴ rituals is their overt intention to arouse and direct sexual energy. Kellner claimed to have been given secrets of a sexual yoga during travels in the Middle East and India, and he believed that the Knights Templar had this same knowledge.

Per their website, the "O∴T∴O∴ is dedicated to the high purpose of securing the Liberty of the Individual and his or her advancement in Light, Wisdom, Understanding, Knowledge, and Power through Beauty, Courage, and Wit, on the Foundation of Universal Brotherhood. U.S. Grand Lodge is the governing body of O∴T∴O∴ in the United States. It is the most populous and active branch of O∴T∴O∴, with 44 local bodies in 26 states as of March 2009. If you are interested in becoming a member of Ordo Templi Orientis, see the membership page for more information. To find an O∴T∴O∴ body near you, consult our list of local bodies. Our FAQ answers many common questions about O∴T∴O∴ and Thelema." Visit their website at www.oto-usa.org.

Parrott, Wanda Sue. Founder of the Amy Kitchener's Angels Without Wings Foundation, Wanda was born in 1935 in Kansas City, Missouri, but was raised and educated in southern California. She returned to Missouri in 1988 where she has been president of Springfield Writers' Guild, honorary life member of Missouri State Poetry Society, and founder of Springfield Writers Workshop, which has been meeting in Springfield-Greene County Library since 1992.

She was an investigative reporter with the *Los Angeles Herald-Examiner*, syndicated feature writer with *Ozarks Senior Living* newspapers, and holds many awards for poetry and short fiction, as well as newspaper columns and features. She won several "Best Feature" awards in the Hearst Corporation's chain of newspapers. In 2002 she was honored recipient of the Alumnus of the Year Award from her alma mater, Citrus College in Glendora, California, where she served as president of the Associated Women Students in 1953–1954. In 2004 her science-fiction story "Power Lunches" won first place in the Writer's Challenge Literary Association's transcendental tales contest. She won the 2007 Mistress of Mayhem Award from Sleuths Ink Mystery Writers for her short story "Elfinetta's ETs."

She has published under eighteen pen names, including Prairie Flower and Edgar Allan Philpott. As Diogenes Rosenberg, she invented the Pissonnet in 1997; the world's shortest sonnet form is now in public domain and she has admitted being its inventor. She is co-founder and sponsor of the National Annual Senior Poets Laureate Poetry Competition for American poets age fifty and older, now in its seventeenth year. Visit her website: http://www.amykitchenerfdn .org.

Rosicrucian (AMORC) Order. The AMORC has been operating since 1915, and has affiliated lodges and chapters all over the world. The Rosicrucian system is unique—it provides a foundation that ties to-gether all of the different aspects of metaphysical study, and demonstrates their interconnectedness. Contact them at http://www .rosicrucian.org for more information.

Rosicrucian Fellowship. Founded by Max Heindel with its main teach-ing presented his book *The Rosicrucian Cosmo-Conception*, the Rosi-crucian Fellowship according to their website is a "Christian Mystic Philosophy presents deep insights into the Christian Mysteries and establishes a meeting ground for Art, Religion, and Science. Max Heindel was selected by the Elder Brothers of the Rose Cross to pub-licly give out the Western Wisdom Teachings in order to help prepare mankind for the coming age of Universal Brotherhood, the Age of Aquarius." Read more from their website at http://www.rosicrucian .com.

Society of the Inner Light. A Mystery School within the Western Esoteric Tradition founded by Dion Fortune. The Society accepts students for both a Supervised Study Course and an Unsupervised Study Course. More information is available through their website at http://www.innerlight.org.uk.

Theosophical Society. The Theosophical Society was founded in New York City in 1875 by H. P. Blavatsky, Henry Steel Olcott, William Quan Judge, and others. Its initial objective was the investigation, study and explanation of mediumistic phenomena. After a few years Olcott and Blavatsky moved to India and established the International Headquarters at Adyar, Madras (Chennai). There, they also became interested in studying Eastern religions, and these were included in the Society's agenda.

The Theosophical Society in America is a branch of the world-wide organization dedicated to promoting the unity of all humanity. To achieve this end, the Society promotes the study of science, religion, and philosophy to better comprehend ourselves and our relationships as parts of the universe. The Society stands for complete freedom of individual search and belief, and has lodges in most cities. Look for more information at their website at http://www.theosophical.org.

The G∴B∴G∴, Magick, and Lou Culling
by Carl Llewellyn Weschcke

The book *The Complete Magick Curriculum of the G∴B∴G∴* by Louis T. Culling was first published by Llewellyn Publications in 1969.

Lou Culling was one of my favorite people and I was very saddened by his death in 1973. We first met when Llewellyn Publications purchased a small New York publisher, Life Resources Institute, who had published a popular I Ching kit-product that Lou had designed and written.

I wrote Lou with regard to furthering Llewellyn's business interests, and he responded with a proposal for this book—which for my convenience we'll just refer to as "the G∴B∴G∴"

What the G∴B∴G∴ promised was a "Shortcut to Initiation." (What Occult student would not be intrigued by such a promise!) I asked for the manuscript and we published it in a nice hardcover edition. In fact, I edited it, designed it, typeset it, and did the artwork for the dust jacket myself. And now I am editing and adding a lot of new material for the second edition.

We met after the book's publication when he traveled to Minneapolis to participate in the "Gnosticons" that Llewellyn used to sponsor.

We met again when I visited him in his Los Angeles home with Marsha Wright, who was editing his second book, *The Manual of Sex Magick*. Even though he passed away shortly after this, he was then wonderfully alive, filled with radiant vitality, and charged with joy and enthusiasm.

As I write these words, I can see his puckish grin and sparkling eyes, and feel his approval for this project.

Lou followed the book on Sex Magick with *The Pristine Yi King* and then a short booklet titled *Occult Renaissance 1972–2008—The Great Prophecy for the Golden Age of Occultism* in which he predicted not merely the growth in occult interest but what we now more commonly refer to as the New Age. Using my magical-name Gnosticus, I contributed a short section relating to Wicca in relation to this theme and my concern for the coming global crisis. In addition, he sent me several partial manuscripts, which I hope to complete using the voluminous files of our correspondence as a resource.

What does the 'G∴B∴G∴' stand for? The Great Brotherhood of God.

The promise of the Order was "A Shortcut to Initiation." That was the headline of a 1931 announcement appearing over a Chicago box office number. The founder of the G∴B∴G∴ was C. F. Russell whose magical name was Frater Genesthai. Culling describes Russell "as a teacher in Practicing Magick, was, without question, the greatest genius of this century, or of several past centuries that I have been able to trace." Culling also said this was the man "who had a tiff with Crowley at the Abbey in Cefalu, Italy, about giving up his room" and later Russell "went up on 'The Rock' for a magical retirement and had been there sixty hours without food or water."

Unless you are both interested and a good historian in regard to the world of Crowley, this information won't mean much to you, and perhaps it really doesn't mean anything other than to tell you that Russell was a magician who studied with Crowley and was intimate enough to be part of Crowley's inner circle.

Following this event, Crowley gave Russell his blessing to found his own Order to be based on these three points:

Liber Legis. Crowley's "Book of the Law."

Thelema

The Aeon of Horus

Reading that 1931 announcement, Louis T. Culling wrote of his interest, being the first to have responded. He was required to pay a fee of $5.00 and to secure at least eight "loyal and active" members to form a "Neighborhood Lodge." We have only limited information about the full size of the Order. In San Diego, there were twenty-five members, in Los Angeles seventy-five, in San Francisco fifty, and in Denver one hundred twenty-five. Culling writes that there were other local lodges in all the large cities. (Note to readers: We at Llewellyn would really appreciate hearing from any of those members!)

Even putting aside the seeming masculine emphasis, isn't "The Great Brotherhood of God" a rather extreme claim? The term "brotherhood" is usually defined as an organization of men of mostly equal status united for a common purpose. As a "Brotherhood of God" we seem to have a statement of equality with God.

But the G∴B∴G∴ was not an exclusively male organization; it had both men and women in equal status. (However, see "Choronzon Club" in the Definitions section following this chapter regarding a dissident Chicago group.)

In this second and expanded edition of the book, we will first answer a number of your likely questions about the preceding history of occult orders including the Hermetic Order of the Golden Dawn and Crowley's own A∴A∴ and then the O∴T∴O∴. We will then answer your questions about *Liber Legis,* Thelema, and the Aeon of Horus, and then on to those in relation to Initiation and what a "Shortcut" can mean.

The G∴B∴G∴ closed its doors to new members in 1936, and then ceased entirely in 1938. In 1936 Russell, as Head of the Order, wrote to Lou Culling:

> *The closing of the doors of the G∴B∴G∴ does not mean that the Great Work must be lost to the ken of man. I appoint you to reveal the entire curriculum of our Magick Order. This is not to be before the year 1956, and furthermore, only when you are ready to assume the responsibility.*

Why was the Order closed? At present, we can't provide a conclusive answer to the question but apparently the closing was planned at the time of its beginning. Culling writes, "As early as 1932, I received official notice that the doors would be closed to new members after 1936, after which the existing members would continue operations until the final closing period of 1938." Culling also noted in an interview I transcribed in 1971 that "Russell's prediction was that after the G.·.B.·.G.·. closed its doors, that all occult orders were losing their dispensation [amount to nothing] and there would not be another legitimate order of any kind with any real dispensation until the year 1972."

Culling continues: "In 1956, after experimenting with a few small groups, I decided that I was not yet ready to 'take on the responsibility.' So it is now after thirty years that the time has come to assume the responsibility. In preparing this book for publication, I owe much to the help of my collaborator, Soror.·. Sophia, Katherine Peacock.

"The significant question is: *What is so great and valuable about the Magick Workings of the Order.*

"The G.·.B.·.G.·. opened its doors with the short announcement in the then quite respectable magazine, *The Occult Digest* as follows: A Short-cut to Initiation. Write to Box Number ____ Chicago, Ill.

"But there are self-stated 'Initiates' in the many self-styled 'Occult Orders' who bleat the cliché that there are no shortcuts to occult development. In actual fact, *this is the same as saying that there is no short-cut to attainment in any and all of Man's endeavors.*

"The first requirement for a 'short-cut' is an excellent instructor or teacher. Well then, Frater Genesthai, C. F. Russell, as a teacher in Practicing Magick, was, without question, the greatest genius of this [twentieth] century, or of several past centuries that I have been able to trace.

"The 'Neighborhood Primate' was the only one who received official documents from headquarters, and had other special duties. For this reason, the ubiquitous pronoun 'I' appears in this book, but this is not to overlook the great help and personal contributions of Soror Sophia. It is therefore fitting that she also contributes her word in this foreword."

Frater .·. Aequila—Louis T. Culling

In contradistinction to the practices of the Far East, the G∴B∴G∴ was the repository of Western Magick—apparently the last one to-date that had a real dispensation. Therefore it seems exigent to give a brief history of the relatively recent development of Western Magick.

True, as far back as the Holy Crusades, the Order of Templars had fraternized with the enemy Arabians, and many of the Templars had been initiated in Esoteric Sufi Magick. However, all that we know of these Mysteries is that the Rubiyat is a heavily disguised document of the original Sufi Magick of Eros—the "Ecstatic School."

Then also it is impossible to trace any continuous history of the Tarot, or of Alchemy, the Qabalah, and the Tree of Life even though we can recognize a very evident continuum from century to century. It is better to bypass these obscure histories and start with definite known data.

Our history begins with the founding of the Hermetic Order of the Golden Dawn in 1887. We can do no better than to quote the eminent member and authority of the Golden Dawn, Israel Regardie, who wrote in 1937:

> *There can be little or no doubt the Golden Dawn is, (or rather was until recently) the sole depository of western magickal knowledge, the only Occult Magickal Order of any real worth that the West in our time has known. A great many other occult organizations owe what little magickal knowledge is theirs to leakages from that Order and from its renegade members.*

Aleister Crowley had been a member of the Golden Dawn and, when after a great internal upheaval the doors of the Order were closed, he founded the A∴A∴ in which the magick workings were basically derived from the Golden Dawn. Then C. F. Russell, who had been a prize disciple under Crowley, was given sanction to found an independent order based on the fundamental principles of the A∴A∴. That is the known outer world lineage of the G∴B∴G∴.

Despite the mind-bewildering amount of Western Magick material of the Golden Dawn and the A∴A∴, there was one great lack. A real genius as a teacher was needed to sift out the material that would be both necessary and most efficient to formulate a system and curriculum leading directly to balanced initiation. This genius was C. F. Russell, the founder of the G∴B∴G∴.

The entire curriculum outlined in this book can be followed and practiced by a single individual as well as in group workings. However, in our experience in the Order, there are greater advantages and added stimuli in group working. I suggest therefore that the serious student attempt to form a small group—even just three persons would be sufficient. It is not necessary that one should have been an occult student. Some of our best members had not even heard the word occultism. In fact, know-it-all students of the occult are generally the worst in actual practice.

Soror∴ Sophia—Katherine Peacock.

What the G∴B∴G∴ claimed to have accomplished was to reduce all the extensive magickal material derived through the Golden Dawn and Aleister Crowley to an efficient and essential curriculum of personal or group study and practice as a true "Shortcut to Initiation."

The purpose of all magickal study is this Initiation, which culminates in the attainment of the Knowledge and Conversation of one's Holy Guardian Angel—one's true Inner, or Higher, Self. While Culling claimed that the practice of this curriculum would also lead to the attainment of magickal powers, these are considered here only as aids in the Great Work, described in psychological terms as "the integration of the subconscious with the conscious personality," and ultimately union with the Highest Self.

It is this that we are born to accomplish for this is the path to becoming a Whole Person, and this is the purpose of life—to become more than we are.

The techniques taught in this curriculum include:

- Dream Recall and Interpretation
- Functioning in the Borderland
- Finding one's true Magickal Identity
- The Retirement Ritual

- The Invocation of Thoth
- Ritual Divination
- "Imprinting" the I Ching on the body
- The three degrees of Sex Magick
- "Thelema" and the Magickal Will
- Invocation of Human Quality
- The Rite of Transubstantiation
- Conversations with a god
- Magickal Offspring—the "Familiar"
- The Great Lunar Trances

Information is also given showing the construction of a ritual, the Tree of Life correspondences, the correct order of the Tarot, the use of the Magickal Imagination, the Calypso Moon Language, the Qabalah of Numbers, and more. Complete rituals for group as well as individual performance are included, along with the Oracular Meanings of the I Ching Hexagrams.

Commentary

My purpose in writing a commentary following each chapter is to do my best in simplifying the instruction given in the chapter. Since there's not much "instruction" given in a foreword, there's not much to say here in my commentary.

I can say that working on this book again is something of a "work of love." I had been studying Magick, Wicca, and Kabbalah for nearly thirty years, and I've been looking at my copy of the first edition ever since it went out of print—after the author's death—and wishing to bring it back into print. However, I knew the book needed updating and some revision, and Lou Culling wasn't available anymore.

In 2008 I started co-authoring a series of books with Dr. Joe Slate, and one morning I woke with a strong psychic message: "Co-author a new edition of the G∴B∴G∴ with Lou Culling." Well, Lou was gone, but that message had authority to it. Maybe Lou would come back in spirit to work with me.

Well, I am writing this after finishing the entire project. No, Lou didn't show in some kind of visible spirit form, nor did he start dictating channeled messages. Nevertheless, just as with the certainty of that first morning "message," I felt that same certainty as I progressed through the book, except at a few points. I would skip over them until I felt the urge to go back and then I would easily move through those points.

I make no claim for spiritual authority speaking through this book, but I believe this book will be right for its intended audience—people who have the self-discipline and self-determination, and who are ready to undertake this "Shortcut to Initiation."

It's not an easy program. In "Eastern" terms, it involves the acceleration of karmic workout so that you can accomplish in one lifetime what otherwise would be many. And it's not that Initiation will bring you some kind of posh glorification and a new job title. It is a push up the evolutionary ladder, but that means more work, more opportunity to function in a greater role of "co-creatorship." It's like becoming the captain of a ship: you do get a new uniform and a hat with more gold braid, but the captain now works harder and has more to worry about than does the common sailor. The difference, though, is you won't go down with the ship if there's a failure, and with each victory—for every person who goes through this Initiation—all of humanity benefits. We all get an evolutionary nudge for this work is cumulative and the results flow through the network connecting us into unity.

So, I, and billions of others, owe you our gratitude for the effort you are now making.

Thank you very much, indeed,

Carl Llewellyn Weschcke,
and I think I can add,
Frater ∴ Aequila—Louis T. Culling

Study and Discussion Points

∴ Many readers may also wonder what the triangle of three dots (∴) used in the title and elsewhere throughout the text signify. This usage derives from the very old Masonic connections of the early Occult orders. The meaning attached to it varies according to the way in which it is used. Thus, at one time, it will mean "Honorable Initiate," at another time it means "sacred" or "Illuminated." The symbol always signifies something "holy" or that an esoteric meaning is involved.

A∴A∴ (Argenteum Astrum, or Order of the Silver Star) A magical order founded in 1907 by Crowley after leaving the Golden Dawn. It was reputed to reflect Crowley's bisexuality.

Abracadabra. The spelling of the word was changed by Aleister Crowley to "Abrahadabra" to place the name *Had,* the second person of Crowley's Thelemite trinity, at the center. Abracadabra is traditional outside the Thelemite community.

Aeon of Horus. Following the channeling of *Liber Legis*—The Book of the Law—(see below) in 1904, Crowley believed he was to lead a new age, the Aeon of Horus, replacing the older matriarchal Aeon of Isis and the patriarchal Aeon of Osiris. The Aeon of Horus is based on the magical union of male and female polarities, and replaces all repressive religious traditions. According to Kenneth Grant, the Aeon of Horus will be followed by that of Maat, the Egyptian goddess of truth and justice.

Brotherhood. While, technically, this word defines an organization of men, the G∴B∴G∴ and many other organizations (some with masculine sounding names) admitted women on an equal basis with men.

"Of God." A "Brotherhood of God" becomes an association of men and women with God. Perhaps this is not a claim to equality with God, but when we look to Biblical texts we see that "God created man in His own image, in the image of God created He him, male and female created He them" (Genesis 1:27). Elsewhere we read that Jesus—equated with God—promises that men will be able to perform miracles just He does. Does this make us equal to God? Perhaps, for we are all part of one creation, and quantum theory demonstrates that the process of creation is continuous and that with will and intention we can bring about change.

Choronzon. Choronzon is a "demon" within the Enochian writings of Dr. John Dee, likewise within Crowley's system where Choronzon is "the Dweller in the Abyss," believed to be the obstacle between the adept and enlightenment. If met with proper preparation by the magician, his function is to destroy the ego, allowing the magician to cross the Abyss.

The Choronzon Club, or C∴C∴, appears to have been a magical group active in Chicago as early as 1931 and at least as recently as 1979. Exactly what it was or is is confusing and probably of no pertinence to our study here. According to the occult scholar P. R. Koenig, in 1933 a small group of homosexual men split off from Russell's original group in order to practice Crowley's XI°. It was led in recent history by Michael P. Bretiaux teaching Haitian Voodoo and O∴T∴O∴ magick.

Unfortunately, the study of Western magickal philosophy is often obscured by the number of "secret orders" cast on Masonic models that claim to teach true magick. At least in some instances these are successful business operations and in some other cases provide opportunities to indulge the vanities of members who adore dressing in expensive robes and addressing each other by their secret names. Most of their magickal teachings of value were derived from the serious work of the Hermetic Order of the Golden Dawn and the Aurum Solis. These teachings were long ago made available in book form. Experience demonstrates that the study and practice of magick is as suitable to the solitary person as to group membership.

Crowley, Aleister. (1875–1947) One of the most controversial figures in recent Western occultism. He inherited a considerable fortune but died a pauper. He had great intellectual genius and wasted a lot on shocking the world as he knew it with occasional bizarre antics and lifestyle. He was trained in the Hermetic Order of the Golden Dawn and later formed his own Order of the Silver Star and then took over the O∴T∴O∴ (Ordo Templi Orientis). He was a prolific and capable writer of magic technology and is best known for his transcription of the *Book of the Law* received from a spirit named Aiwass proclaiming Crowley as the Beast 666 in the Book of Revelation and announcing a New Aeon of terror and advancement for the world. His magickal books and his Thoth Tarot Deck are worth studying.

Gnosticon. These gatherings were originally called "The Gnostic-Aquarian Festival of Astrology, Magic and Witchcraft." But the name changed at the suggestion of Isaac Bonewits who moved to St. Paul to serve as editor of our house publication, *Gnostica News,* later to become *Gnostica* magazine. Both gatherings were named after the metaphysical bookstore we had opened just off the Minneapolis downtown district, a block away from the large Basilica Catholic cathedral. These festivals drew people from all over the United States, Great Britain, Canada, and Australia. They were the first of what later became psychic fairs and then conferences serving various interests of the larger New Age community around the world. Llewellyn discontinued the Gnosticons in 1976. They were a cash drain on our small publishing firm that we could no longer afford.

Initiation. The word has been given a variety of definitions over the years—everything from the pledging and hazing of college (and even high-school) students into fraternities and sororities to the admissions trials of secret societies, entry into occult and Masonic lodges and their grade or degrees, and to the more serious dramatic and transformative rituals of Wiccan and other esoteric groups. In some cases, the initiation rituals are truly effective in raising the consciousness of the "candidate," whereas in other cases the initiation is more a certification of the levels of study and practice the student has mastered.

In the true Occult (and psychological) sense, an Initiation is more an inner experience than an outer one—even though a dramatic ritual may induce an inner transformation and flowering of the psychic potentials and powers of the person. Despite the promises of various teachers, gurus, priests, and adepts, it is less something done to the person and more something that happens "when the student is ready."

Initiation has been called a "tearing away of the veil" so that the new initiate now sees with new eyes, and perceives a world of greater complexity—one of added dimensions, forces, and living beings. Progressive initiations mark further growth and development as the person becomes more of the Whole Person each is intended to be. The potential is there from birth and before, and can be realized through knowledge, experience, and growth practices.

Kabbalah. There are various alternative spelling of this word: *Qabala* and *Qabalistic.* The most common is "Kabbalah" and "Kabalistic." Another is "Kabala," and then "Cabala," and even "Cabalistic." All are transliterations of the Hebrew word "QBLH" meaning "an unwritten tradition transmitted orally from teacher to student." "Kabbalah" and "Kabala" generally refer to the original Jewish version, "Cabala" refers the Christian version, and "Qabala" and "Qabalah" for the magical or Hermetic version.

The Kabbalah—no matter how spelled—is probably the most complete "preview" of the world as perceived and experienced through spiritual vision that we have. It is a systematic organization of spiritual reality into a manageable formula for human study along with a methodology of "correspondences" to organize all of human knowledge. It is a treasure trove for practicing magicians and the most expert self-study program of progressive mediation the world has ever seen.

Liber Al vel Legis. Crowley's "Book of the Law," channeled to Crowley by an entity known as Aiwaz, and considered the holy book of the Aeon of Horus and the foundation of Crowley's spiritual tradition, Thelema.

Magickal Name. It is common practice with magical orders as well as Wiccan, neo-Pagan, and other "secret" groups that members will adopt a magickal name or motto for use within the group. In many magical groups, the name is in Greek or Latin, whereas in others it may be a name derived from mythology, folklore, Sanskrit, various

African languages, etc. The purpose is both secretive and a declaration about one's personal goals or sense of inner identity. The meaning of C. F. Russell's Hebrew name, Genesthai, is somewhat confusing in the absence of a statement from him. His Magickal Name is generally interpreted to mean "To cause to be" or "To become," or even "To become again." From a purely magical perspective, I suggest that it is "To become" as a statement of intent to be transformed.

Magick. Readers familiar with the writings of Aleister Crowley will recognize the somewhat unusual spelling of the word "magick." Crowley did this to distinguish Occult "Magick" from the "magic" of legerdemain, and also to separate the new Occult Magick from that of the old, which was often sadly loaded with useless junk! It may also be seen that the Qabalistic value of "Magick" comes to 83, and $8 + 3 = 11$. From Crowley's *Liber Legis*: "My number is 11 as all their numbers who are of us." The number 11 stands for the Great Work accomplished—ABRACADABRA.

O∴T∴O∴ (Ordo Templi Orientis—The "Order of the Temple of the East") The O∴T∴O∴ was or is (depending on how you look at it) a magickal order founded by Karl Kellner (1851–1905) in 1890. Upon Kellner's passing in 1905, the leadership passed to Theodore Reuss (1855–1923) and then to Aleister Crowley in 1922.

Currently there are (or were) two O∴T∴O∴ organizations:

1. One in England headed by Kenneth Grant
2. One headed by successors to Grady McMurtry

The distinguishing characteristic of O∴T∴O∴ rituals is their overt intention to arouse and direct sexual energy. Kellner claimed to have been given secrets of a sexual yoga during travels in the Middle East and India, and he believed that the Knights Templar had this same knowledge.

Puckish. When I used this word when describing Culling to my wife, she asked what it meant. When I explained that "Puckish" means "mischievous in a playful way," she wanted to know why I just didn't say he had a mischievous grin! Well, it really isn't the same thing. The word is Old English, and comes from Puck, which is the name of a mischievous or "naughty" spirit in Old English folklore. I was inspired to say that Culling had a puckish grin because there was so often a secondary level to the words he himself used.

I have to interpret his "puckish grin" for myself as implying that my vision of him suggesting that I co-author a new edition of this book with him as a challenge to do more than merely re-package the old book.

Regardie, Dr. Francis Israel. (1907–1985) A widely respected authority on magick and Kabbalah, once personal secretary to Aleister Crowley and member of the Golden Dawn. His *The Golden Dawn* is a principal resource of Western Magick. His *Tree of Life, The Middle Pillar,* and *A Garden of Pomegranates* are considered modern classics.

Sufi Magick of Eros. The "Ecstatic School." Sufi Mysticism and Sex Magick, with ecstatic dancing and other shamanic practices.

Templars. The Order of the Temple of Jerusalem founded in 1118 to protect pilgrims traveling to the Holy Land. Originally poor, the Order became rich with gifts from King Alfonso of Aragon. Folklore claims their wealth was derived from alchemy, from the practice of the magic of "attraction," and the discovery of King Solomon's Treasure. With their wealth, the Order grew to 30,000 members, a very powerful force. King Phillip IV of France was jealous and instigated the accusation of heresy in which they were accused of denying Christ, of worshipping the devil, and of engaging in "unnatural sex acts." Confessions were extracted by torture and many Templars were burned to death. An investigation by Pope Clement V found no evidence of heresy. Their real crime may have been their interest in Gnosticism and the esoteric traditions of Manicheism. In addition, some claim that the Templars were involved in practices of sex magick and Sufi mysticism.

Thelema. ("Will," in Greek) This is one's True Will, which can be discovered through the sincere practice of Magick. Crowley constructed this into his axiom: "Do what thou wilt shall be the whole of the law."

Western Magick. Magick as practiced in the Western Hemisphere. In this now global civilization, is there a distinction between Eastern and Western magick? Yes, but it is less a distinction than so sincerely proclaimed when it was assumed that the Eastern mind was different than the Western. We can understand that various esoteric methods have a cultural history without saying that yoga is only for people born in India just as we've learned that computer science is not the sole province of Americans. Western Magick has a distinctive system of knowledge and application, just as does Indian Tantra and Chinese Alchemy, but anyone can learn and apply these techniques without limitation.

Western Magick is largely founded on the Kabbalah and today includes Tarot and Ritual Magick. At the same time, there are differences in different traditions as to the understanding of various correspondences and symbols. At the practical levels, one system is not necessarily enriched by another. Learn the basic correspondences and symbols of the system you practice.

The Order of the Great Brotherhood of God:

Its Origins and Beginning

In the first edition of this book there was a color reproduction of a painting done by Aleister Crowley circa 1912 that depicts "the demise of man being ruled externally by patriarchal regimentation and the coming of the 'New Aeon of Horus' when Every Person is a Star moving by his own inner light and will. It therefore also pictures the joyous enlightenment and freedom of the initiate as he surmounts the 'restrictive self' and lives by his own Light and Individuality."

We are challenged to understand the meaning of this painting simply from this description. Crowley says that the New Aeon, or New Age, will bring to an end the restrictive external patriarchal regimentation and will bring the promise that "Every Person is a Star moving by his own inner light and will."

Crowley notoriously proclaimed himself as the world's greatest poet, and no doubt also its greatest artist as well as the sole prophet of this New Aeon. It is not only copyright concerns that cautioned us from reproducing this painting; it is more the doubt that it introduces sufficient value to justify the higher price color plates would require for this book. It is Crowley's magical philosophy that is of importance to us, not his poetry, his art, or his notorious lifestyle.

Culling also tells us that the painting "pictures the joyous enlightenment and freedom of the *initiate* as he surmounts the 'restrictive self' and lives by his own Light and Individuality." It is the *initiate* who becomes a Star moving by his inner Light and Will. In other words, it is not merely freedom from external regimentation but inner spiritual growth that culminates in movement by one's own Light and Will that is the goal of our magickal work.

Crowley tells us that this new age brings us the freedom and the *impetus*—a "call" and urging to step ahead of the external regimentation. We, individually, have to make the effort while the energies of the age make it possible to succeed. Magick is no longer for the few, the elite priesthood of the secret lodge, but for everybody who makes the effort. Magick is the technology for self-transformation and self-empowerment. Every Man and every woman can become a Star by employing the esoteric technology now available to everyone.

Culling writes: "It is my conviction that the founder of the G.˙.B.˙.G.˙. was the greatest and most efficient teacher of this [the twentieth] Century in that field of occultism known as 'Magick'. All members have concurred in this. I make no statement as to the height of his Initiation; only that he was the greatest and most efficient teacher, and upon this alone it is sufficient to postulate he had a dispensation.

"Now be it known that being the greatest teacher does not mean a great pedagogue, per se. The head of this Order knew what to teach to get the best and most rapid results, how to teach it, and how to get the best response from the neophytes. All of this is included in this exposition of The Complete Magick Curriculum of the Secret Order G.˙.B.˙.G.˙..

"It is a mistake to evaluate one's personality against his ability and attainments, but it cannot be overlooked that some identification of a person is demanded, so here is a brief statement about the head and founder of this Order.

"In the outer world his name was C. F. Russell; his magickal name was *Frater Genesthai*. Some further identification is to be had from the book *The Great Beast* by John Symonds. Russell was the man who had a tiff with Crowley at the Abbey in Cefalu, Italy, about giving up his room. Russell went up on 'The Rock' for a magical retirement and had been there sixty hours without food or water. Jane Wolf (called Elizabeth Fox in Symond's book) took food and water to Russell and brought him down.

"Jane Wolf, whom I knew for years, told me that Crowley recognized the attainment of Russell and had given Russell his blessing for him to found his own Order—naturally based on these three points: (1) Liber Legis, (2) Thelema, (3) The Aeon of Horus.

"The foregoing is given more for the purpose of providing an outline of the lineal descent and character of the Order.

"In this, we begin with the Hermetic Order of the Golden Dawn founded in England in 1887. This was the one and only great Order with a dispensation for the repository and promulgation of Western Magick. The Order of the Golden Dawn had been rocked by inner dissension about the same time that Crowley founded his Order A∴A∴. Crowley had been a high initiate in the Golden Dawn, and Russell had been a member of it also.

"The (original) Hermetic Order of the Golden Dawn is long since closed. Crowley's A∴A∴ and O∴T∴O∴ are now closed. It is not within the scope of this book to venture theories as to how and why these orders die a natural death. Since the beginning of history occult schools have arisen, flourished and then disappeared from objective existence. Then in other times, in other places, other schools come to objective existence. Nations also rise, flourish and decay. So it is with all living forms."

(I have to interject that at this time, forty years after Culling wrote the above material, there are active Golden Dawn groups, and that the A∴A∴ and O∴T∴O∴ also are active and can be contacted at their websites found on Google. In addition, the O∴T∴A∴, the Ordo Temple Astarte, is also active. The "Occult Renaissance" that Culling predicted has happened! CLW)

"The G∴B∴G∴ is now also closed, since 1937. This was a most esoteric Order, with binding oaths of secrecy. It is only because of the time elapsed since the demise of the Order that the entire workings can be revealed. The Order was founded in 1931. Russell told me that he would 'close the doors' in 1936, and he did. Activity continued in several groups, however, until as late as 1938.

"In the year 1931 this announcement appeared in The Occult Digest:

A Short-cut to Initiation
The Choronzon Club
Box ____ Chicago, Ill.

"Being one of the first to answer, a notice was received that if I wanted to receive full attention and benefit from Headquarters, there should be at least eight 'loyal and active' members to form a 'Neighborhood Lodge.' My neighborhood was San Diego City and County in California.

"Lest one think that this was a method for getting easy money and members, it should be stated that the fee for joining was only $5.00, and that if a member brought in a new member he was allowed to keep half the $5.00. Furthermore, there were no dues, and no solicitation for donations. Thus at the very outset the G∴B∴G∴ was unique among occult orders.

"The structure of the Order was a hierarchy. When member A took member B into the Order, and B in turn secured member C, then it was B's responsibility to instruct C, and it was A's responsibility to instruct B and also to supervise his entire hierarchy chain. The importance and efficiency of this system should be obvious. Also it should be stated that there is only one thing which qualifies me to set down the entire curriculum of the Order, and that is that I was the 'Neighborhood Primate' (N.P.) for the San Diego 'neighborhood.' The N.P. was the only member that was in communication with Headquarters; furthermore, he was the only one who received the official documents. The very good reason for this will also be explained.

"There are those who would want to know about the extent of the membership of the Order. First, it should be stated that the curriculum was very demanding on the member's interest, effort and time, and this naturally led to dropouts. Therefore, we limited the word 'member' to those who proved to be loyal and active members. In San Diego the membership averaged 25. In Los Angeles there were three lodges, total average membership of 75. In San Francisco, average of 50. In Denver the average was 125. Of the membership in other localities, I cannot give any idea."

Commentary

Therein we see all the limitations of a closed system. Unless you lived in the Primate's Neighborhood, you are just out of luck as far as spiritual growth and development is concerned! Is that at all sensible?

Look at the key word in all of the above: Instruction. Instruction is information (knowledge) organized and structured to enable the student to gain wisdom through understanding and practice of certain exercises (or rituals).

"In the Beginning was the Word." The beginning of anything starts with the Word, with information and instruction. The beginning of your journey, like the journey of the Tarot's Fool, begins with the first step—only you can proceed knowingly with the aid of this Curriculum. Then yours is not a "Fool's Journey," but one of purpose with the goal of Enlightenment and Empowerment.

The Program of Modern Occultism

Aleister Crowley founded the magickal order A∴A∴ (Latin: *Argenteum Astrum*—"Silver Star") in 1907 after leaving the Golden Dawn. Its Holy Book is the *Book of the Law* and its motto is "The method of science, the aim of religion." The magick workings were basically derived from the Golden Dawn. Then C. F. Russell was given sanction to found an independent order based on the fundamental principles of the A∴A∴ That is the known outer world lineage of G∴B∴G∴

Culling wrote that Russell's genius was that he "knew what to teach to get the best and most rapid results, how to teach it, and how to get the best response from the neophytes. All of this is included in this exposition of *The Complete Magick Curriculum of the Secret Order G∴B∴G∴*" Therefore, we have to presume that everything needed is here in this book and that you do not need to find a teacher with special dispensation to initiate you into a higher state of consciousness. All you have to do is study and work, the same as if guided by a one-on-one teacher, but with the book as your guide.

"When the student is ready, the teacher will appear." That has always been the promise to those seeking esoteric knowledge and who are ready to undertake the Great Work. Now, the teacher has come to you. Now the Magickal Curriculum is here. Now, in this New Aeon, you are your own best teacher. But, as a self-taught student, you have to assume the obligations of a teacher and provide to yourself both discipline and organization. Using this curriculum gives you a basis for both.

Today, while there are organizations derived from the original Golden Dawn and the O∴T∴O∴, and there are other orders such as Aurum Solis that proclaim themselves as powerful initiatic orders, their greatest contribution has been the release of their teachings to the public in book form. As Culling prophesied, this was the "golden age of occultism."

These old and new initiatic orders are hierarchies, run by the few supposedly for the benefit of the many. There was (and is) a belief in "dispensation" defined as a divine transmission of power from one initiate to another. This is the logic of the priest as intermediary between man and God. But, where did that power first come from? Can't any of us go directly to the source? Isn't that source still available to all who ask and seek?

This is the program of modern occultism, based on the transmission not of power but of knowledge through which the individual person attains self-initiation, defined as self-transformation leading to self-empowerment.

What is this "esoteric technology" of Self-Transformation leading to Self-Empowerment that we call Western Magick? "Every man and every woman is a Star." Within each of us there is Divinity. Within each of us there is the power to awaken that Divinity. And today we have the knowledge to do so. That's what we will learn in this book.

Yes, the initiatic orders are worthy, and their hierarchical method of teaching is valid as a system, but as a system is creates a chain of dependencies that can be abused. When the system is supplemented with an open curriculum of knowledge, and the student is given full and public access to that knowledge, and charged with the self-responsibility for its employment, then we may have a program fitting for the New Age, or the New Aeon.

What of this New Era?

On December 9, 1971, Louis T. Culling wrote

> *"I hereby grant all rights to my small book which is the prophecy of the Golden Era of Occultism to being at the Spring Equinox 1972—including the right to copyright same under your name, Carl Weschcke."*

The actual title was "Occult Renaissance 1972–2008—The great prophecy for the golden age of occultism," and at Lou's request I added a short epilogue, "Occult Reformation." Yes, there certainly was an Occult Renaissance from 1972 through 2008, which leaves the question of, what happens after 2008? In that short epilogue I wrote:

The Aquarian Age demands that Knowledge be applied to Man's Spiritual Needs, and that schools as "places of knowledge," become the temples (not that temples become schools!).

There is no real secrecy in the Age of Aquarius—no magical secrets that only the initiate can attain, the Knowledge is coming out into the open to provide the opportunity to everyone who can to "walk with the Gods." The World of the Mind is the new dimension for exploration—it is Inner Space through which we travel now. Our scientific and technological thrust must direct itself to saving the planet and opening the inner doors of consciousness as well.

There are today opportunities for people to come together in learning Occult Knowledge, to come together in research and the sharing of discovery, to come together in participation in the revival of the Nature Religion, to come together to learn how it is that Man and Woman can liberate each other.

The new Aeon of Horus, the demands of world crisis, requires us to make of our spiritual knowledge a living and growing knowledge, not a static faith. That is why we make our celebrations renewals, conventions of discovery and teaching as well as festivals. We can take joy in the responsibility that the Age thrusts upon us, for with it is the opportunity for a tremendous leap forward in spiritual evolution.

Man is balanced upon a precipice—but he has the opportunity to ascend to the Gods if he chooses not to fall. He must, like Icarus, make his own wings if he is to fly—but he must turn to the guidance of proven Occult Knowledge and Technic if, unlike Icarus, his wings are to carry him through to his victory.

What happens after 2008?

The Occult Renaissance in Culling's prophecy ended in 2008. It means an end to occultism as secret knowledge. The world "occult" simply means "hidden," and that's over with. Knowledge is no longer hidden away in underground libraries and secret orders. It's available to anyone looking for it, and the great secret is that the way it works is self-transformative.

Stop looking for hidden treasures and waiting for the hidden master to appear! Get busy and apply the principles that are readily available in books and weekend courses. Apply the Knowledge and then you are your own master and teacher. Yours is the Way, and it's not the One Way. All Paths lead to the Center and it's up to you to start walking.

And you will discover that the road need not be long and arduous. This book shows you the "Shortcut to Initiation."

Study and Discussion Points

Aurum Solis. (*Gold of the Sun*) A magical order founded in England in 1897 by George Stanton and Charles Kingold, which claims descent from the Ogdoadic Tradition of the Western Mystery Tradition. It is best known through the published works of two of its leaders, Melita Denning and Osborne Phillips, pseudonyms of Vivian Godfrey and Leon Barcynski. Together, they authored many books on magical practice, such as *Astral Projection*, *Creative Visualization*, and *The Magical Philosophy*.

Choronzon. Choronzon is a "demon" within the Enochian writings of Dr. John Dee, likewise within Crowley's system where Choronzon is "the Dweller in the Abyss," believed to be the obstacle between the adept and enlightenment. If met with proper preparation by the magician, his function is to destroy the ego, allowing the magician to cross the Abyss.

Choronzon Club, or C.·.C.·., appears to have been a magical group active in Chicago as early as 1931 and at least as recently as 1979. Exactly what it was or is remains confusing and probably of no pertinence to our study here. According to the occult scholar, P. R. Koenig, in 1933 a small group of homosexual men split off from Russell's original group in order to practice Crowley's XI°. It was led in recent history by Michael P. Bretiaux teaching Haitian Voodoo and O.·.T.·.O.·. magick.

Unfortunately, the study of Western magickal philosophy is often obscured by the number of "secret orders" cast on Masonic models that claim to teach true magick. At least in some instances these are successful business operations and in some other cases provide opportunities to indulge the vanities of members who adore dressing in expensive robes and addressing each other by their secret names. Most of their magickal teachings of value were derived from the serious work of the Hermetic Order of the Golden Dawn and the Aurum Solis. These teachings were long ago made available in book form. Experience demonstrates that the study and practice of magick is as suitable to the solitary person as to group membership.

Dispensation. A special empowerment to dispense and manage religious or spiritual instruction and practice. Within Christianity, it is the official granting of a license to organize a church. It is also a special time period designated by God for certain things to happen. For Esotericism, it is believed to be both a time period and a "licensing" to a particular group or groups to establish themselves and their message seemingly granted by spiritual "higher-ups."

There are those of us who believe that we live in a special time when dispensation is universal for all who will open their mind and spirit to the influx of higher consciousness happening now. We are approaching a turning point when the "world as we know it" will end and a new world order will begin to replace the old. Few things happen overnight, but time is critical and changes will be rapid as global conditions require new world organizations and new worldwide solutions to problems arising from the past.

Hierarchy. Nearly every kind of group is formally organized in ranks of power, authority, and seniority. Whether in government, business, social club, military group, non-profit organization, church, or religious order, a hierarchical structure has generally proved to be more effective in accomplishing the group mission than an unstructured democracy.

What is important, however, to the health of any organization, is the basis of the ranking. In an esoteric group it should be by knowledge and expertise, and demonstrated merit in any degree or level of initiation. Nothing is worse than authority without demonstrated merit.

It is both unfortunate and passé that some esoteric groups, like the Catholic Church and some Masonic lodges, devote so much of their resources to the embellishments of office instead of effective teaching or service. A simple badge of office should normally be sufficient. Within a ritual drama, symbolic costuming may be important just as are other elements of ritual.

New Aeon of Horus. A specific era of time according to Crowley. Is this the same as "the New Age" or "the Age of Aquarius"? Perhaps yes, perhaps no. Sincere followers of Crowley would likely say there's no connection. Astrologers are just as likely to say that the zodiacal entry into Aquarius has little connection to either, while maintaining that Aquarius does embody much that is claimed for the New Age and for the New Aeon.

My own inclination is to believe they are all manifestations of the same thing—that we are indeed in a "new age" opening up opportunities for growth and development of the Whole Person. Maybe the astronomical/astrological precession triggers a more "Aquarian perception" in all of us, leaving behind what has been claimed as repressive in the Age of Pisces. And maybe this is the same as the New Aeon. Why not?

I believe we are in a new "era" (to substitute those three loaded concepts with a neutral word for purposes of discussion) in which there has been a shift of energies allowing more people to open up to new ideas and to respond to new ideas. And, yes, it is likely that the transition from Piscean to Aquarian energies facilitates this. Again: Why not?

Regardless, any study of history will demonstrate that we have more intellectual freedom and opportunity today than in any previous era we know anything about. Myth may claim that in some ancient past, perhaps in some Atlantean civilization, we had a similar situation that led to abuse of knowledge by the few to the detriment of all.

Myth always contains some kind of truth, and perhaps this warns us of needs for awareness of potential hazards as more people are enabled to develop their psychic powers and to more easily gain deeper understanding of the human psyche and of quantum theory.

With greater power there is always danger to and from those who are not ready for it. When I was a five-year-old boy eager to imitate what I saw adults doing, I found a sharp hatchet and some wood I thought needed trimming. The net result was that I cut off the last joint of my left index finger. One adult grabbed the cut-off part and held it tightly against the stub while another adult drove seven miles to the nearest hospital where it was stitched on. Against medical expectations, it did work. It took a long time—for two years I wore a bandage as the wound continued to fester and bleed sometimes smelly greenish fluids. (This was long before the age of antibiotics.) For the next dozen years it was sensitive to cold and any kind of bump. Still, I played all the necessary sports that are part of the curriculum of growing up, and today I have a nearly normal but slightly crooked finger. Perhaps I learned a lesson.

Pedagogue. A pedagogue is a teacher who is particularly pedantic or dogmatic in their approach, overly concerned with "correctness" and even the minutest details. This is the teacher who follows the official curriculum without discussion, who demands memorization of details so that they can be repeated back by the student without error.

Culling is making the point that a good teacher involves the student, often with discussion and even debate, sometimes with dramatic presentations and even getting the students into the act.

That's why I am providing these "Study and Discussion Points." If you didn't know what a pedagogue was, you could have looked it up. But by giving you my definition and my opinions, I am hoping to enliven your reading even if you are working alone. And, if you are working with a small group, well here's an opportunity to discuss things.

Russell, C. F. Cecil Frederick Russell (1897–1987). Russell wrote in 1922: "Magick is aptly defined as the science and art of doing one's Will—achieving one's purpose, fulfilling the Law of THELEMA. Thus theoretical magick is the art of perfecting mental processes, and practical magick the art of perfecting volitional processes. These definitions are hardly conclusive, but they are scholarly enough for practical purposes, I think. I think that every member should be drilled in ceremonial magick until he subconsciously acquires the attitude of doing the right thing at the right moment with omnipotence at his command and eternity at his disposal. The ideas that dissolve the sin complex, viz that nothing really matters, that it is impossible to make a mistake, etc, cannot be rooted in the organism by any other method."

Russell was a member of the A.˙.A.˙. and O.˙.T.˙.O.˙. (Fr. Genesthai) and was secretary to Aleister Crowley during the (in)famous 1920s Cefalu period. Some speculation suggests that Russell's experiences on "the Rock" during this period at Thelema Abbey subsequently led to his establishment of the Gnostic Body of God (G.˙.B.˙.G.˙.) and his personal magickal explorations into the fields of mathematics and logic. More can be found at the website http://cfrussell.homestead .com.

chapter one

The Ultimate Aim of Magick:

The Knowledge and Conversation
of One's Holy Guardian Angel

"A Shortcut to Initiation!" The know-it-all says, "There is no shortcut." This is tantamount to saying that the best material, the best methods, the best technique, the best direction, and the best time-savers cannot bring quicker and better results than the worst—in ANYTHING.

The G∴B∴G∴ demanded regularity in the work, day in and day out, not missing a single day. Let this be the first and most valuable lesson to anyone—REGULARITY. Thirty minutes daily until one has put in twenty hours brings more accomplishment than fifty hours of desultory practice, at least in Initiatory Magick.

The First Official Document

We recognize no less than the ultimate aim in Magick, which is to attain to the Knowledge and Conversation of one's Holy Guardian Angel (abbreviated in our literature as K & C of H G A). Albeit one may attain to actual UNION with the H G A if they are so blessed. The H G A, though really nameless, has been called the Higher Self, the Augoeides, the All-Knower, the Divine Genius, the True Ruler, Adonai, the Indwelling Spirit, etc. Carl Jung calls it his Daemon (not demon!).

You will be given work which leads to the attainment of Magickal Powers, but these powers are never to be regarded as ends in themselves.

They are aids to you in the Great Work (abbreviated as G.W.), which is the attainment of the K & C of H.∴G.∴A.∴.

All official documents are sent only to the N.P. He or any other Immediate Superior allows the Immediate Inferior to read them only in the presence of the I.S. The I.I. is not allowed to make copies of these documents. Definitely we do not give out copies of documents for members to casually read and then file away. The member receives the communication of a document because he is NOW ready for it, and he must NOW thoroughly digest it and proceed with his work, NOW! The I.S. should and must explain everything in the document until satisfied that the I.I. has mastered the contents and is ready to proceed.

Being groomed for the responsibility of N.P., I received the following letter from Headquarters:

The documents from Headquarters give the practices and workings demanded from each member. We do not give explanations of WHAT, and HOW, any given work is supposed to accomplish. In the first place, this would be a demand upon our time at headquarters. In the second place, we are not interested in passing our material which serves only to titillate the intellect. In the third place, to tell the member just what results he may expect and how and why it works, serves too often to defeat its own purpose. If a member cannot and will not begin at once to follow out the various practices given to him, then he is not a loyal working member. It will be HE who squeezes himself out of the Order—not the Order. It is very important that the N.P. and the I.S. see to it that this is understood well, and willingly accepted.

In the following chapter is given the first two practices that were undertaken by the beginner in his quest.

Note—the author of this book holds firmly to the points in the above letter. However, I shall frequently give various results of practices of members of the Order, actual empirical experiences—without contrived theories.

Commentary

The Goal of High Magick is "Initiation"

Here we re-affirm that the goal of the rituals and training in this book is none other than the attainment of Knowledge and Conversation with your personal Holy Guardian Angel. It's the "initiation" that marks your transition from a mostly unconscious human being to a mostly conscious Whole Person.

There are many Paths to the Center (becoming Whole), but this Magickal Operation has the advantages of being designed just for that purpose. Even the solitary Magick of Abramelin the Mage required six months for accomplishment of the Knowledge and Conversation of the Holy Guardian Angel. The G∴B∴G∴ program offers help in accomplishing it even faster.

The G∴B∴G∴ was neither a "social" club nor a traditional magical order in which other magical operations and celebrations might be practiced. The "Shortcut to Initiation" is the substance of the G∴B∴G∴'s work. Nevertheless, it will become clear that each group met often and regularly, repeating the ritual again and again without loss of pertinence and interest.

Why? Because the program speaks to the soul of the aspirant. The Higher Self is gathering the strands of self-discovery as the Lower and Middle Selves work their way through daily life, weaving those strands into thicker skeins to become the Rainbow Bridge of conscious integration made possible through life-experience.

It is valuable to see the hierarchical system at work exactly as is traditional in most initiatic orders. The relationship of Immediate Superior to Immediate Inferior can continue ad infinitum in an endless chain, but like any other such chain of communication we can assume the message would get distorted if extended too far. Before that, certainly one lodge would split into two.

Even without the benefit of a group, the G∴B∴G∴ program can be followed by the solitary student with advantage. The student must do for herself what an Immediate Superior would expect of her, and as her own Immediate Inferior she needs to self-consciously adhere to the program and monitor her progress. Even working alone, the student is part of an invisible lodge of fellows making the same journey to Wholeness.

For some, it may even take on a kind of subjective reality where they may discover their brothers and sisters in a kind of astral lodge. Even so, your goal ever remains single: the Knowledge and Conversation of your Holy Guardian Angel.

Note that it is both Knowledge and Conversation—the goal is two-way Communication but the realization of Union and Self-Knowledge is instantaneous.

Study and Discussion Points

Daemon. Not a "demon," but a mythical being, part-human and part-god, serving as an intermediary between God and humanity. Hence, an inspiring intelligence similar to if not identical to the Holy Guardian Angel.

Note the role of "an intermediary between God and humanity." Once attainment of the Knowledge and Conversation of the Holy Guardian Angel is achieved, the Great Work takes on added dimension. The role of a Co-Creator expands in service to all humanity, and to all life and consciousness of our planet as a whole.

The path to glory is endless to our still limited vision just as Love knows no bounds.

Great Work. This is the object of your incarnation and the meaning of your life. The Great Work is the program of growth to become all that you can be—which is the realization that you are a "god in the making." Within your being there is the seed of Divinity, and your job is to grow that into the Whole Person that is a "Son of God." It is a process that has continued from "the Beginning" and may have no ending but it is your purpose in life. It is that which gives meaning to your being.

Yes, the book contains the original instructions regarding the relationship between teacher and student, superior and inferior, that you are to internalize. In this new age, you are both teacher and student and you must accept responsibility for your own destiny. Time is of the essence! Older methods give way to new ones because the entire process of growth and self-development has to be accelerated. Humanity has created a time bomb that's ticking away, and only our own higher consciousness can save us from self-destruction. But for now—have faith and do the Great Work for it is all part of a Great Plan.

Higher Self. Even though the Higher Self is also known here as the Holy Guardian Angel, there is value in using a more easily comprehended psychological term. Words are words and there are often many names for the same thing. But each gives a particular shape or color or tone to the thing named to expand our understanding comprehension when we are relating to larger concepts.

Knowledge and Conversation... This is an important concept for you are to recognize in your Holy Guardian Angel your own teacher with whom you, the present personality or (small *s*) self must actually converse, recognizing the HGA as your (big *S*) Self.

...Of One's Holy Guardian Angel. Yes, this is the Big *S* Self, the Higher Self, the Augoeides, the All-Knower, the Divine Genius, the True Ruler, Adonai, the Indwelling Spirit, your Daemon (not demon!), your Spirit Guide. It's the BIG SHOT, the God Father, of your personal family of psychological parts you will integrate.

This conversation between personality and Higher Self is an art as well as an "act of faith" that you must believe in. There are practices that will establish the reality of this Indwelling Spirit as well as that of your communications. For the moment, accept as fact that you are a "fractured" being of subconscious and conscious-mind and of higher-consciousness, which will eventually unite in a Whole Person as you become more than you are.

Regularity. The rule of Regularity is not unique to Magick, but is the proven key to every program for the attainment of knowledge and skill. It is necessary because every practice builds upon the previous one. You are building skills the same way that you build muscles— by practice and use. Any system of knowledge is accumulative, and regularity of study is like laying bricks to build a building—it is a continuous process, and if stopped the lower layers are exposed to weather and loss. Set up a schedule for what can be done within your other obligations, and stick to it. If you are interrupted for any reason, review the work you've done from the beginning.

While it is not mentioned here, regularity of practice is reinforced through the use of a daily Journal—whether called a "Magical Diary" or "Book of Shadows" or "Dream Book" or some other name of your choice. It is here that you should record not only your magical study and practice, but also your insights and record your dreams. And note things that happen in daily life that are obviously related to the inner work. As you progress there will be increased continuity "between the worlds."

One of the key teachings of the G∴B∴G∴ was to "regard every event whatsoever as a particular dealing between myself and my daemon." This is, of course, a factual impossibility, but Lou went on to explain it with an example. If you are driving down the highway, and something calls your attention to the mileage on your odometer, then that is an "event" by which your Higher Self is sending you an important message. In this example, the mileage is a number to be interpreted through numerology. And this event and your interpretation should be recorded in your diary.

Shortcut… A shortcut obviously contrasts with the longer route. Often a shortcut is a rougher road; one with particular hazards and without some common comforts and resources, and sometimes it doesn't even show up on the official map. But there are reasons to take the shortcut: it is more efficient, often both shorter and faster, and sometimes more adventurous. You learn faster, you experience more deeply, you grow and use your own resources, becoming stronger all the time.

A shortcut may go through dangerous territory, and sometimes it may leave the paved road completely and take you cross-country through which you have to make your own trail. There may be no rest areas or food stops or gas stations—so you have to plan ahead and be able to take some risks. There's no guide to lead you. You are on your own!

But, ultimately, you are always "on your own." The work can't be done for you—so whether you take the "high road" or the "low road," the better mapped route or the shortcut cross country—you are the one! You will learn more because you are your own guide, your own resource. Instead of a teacher watching over you, you have only your own Higher Self who will respond to your need!

… To Initiation. "Initiation" is one of those ambiguous words that are used variously. In esoteric practice, it sometimes seems to mark one's "graduation" for the completion of under-graduate studies. But "to initiate" also means "to start a process."

In our magickal curriculum it means both. The goal is to make you a Whole Person so that you can become a Greater Being. Like the good Boy Scout, the Initiate is prepared because of the work he has completed. The Initiate is ready for the Great Adventure leading to God.

Technic. "Technic" is not another word for "technique." It means rather "the applied science of this field of knowledge." It is not theoretical science, but science applied to obtain specific and practical ends. I prefer to think of Technic as technology applied with scientific understanding.

chapter two

The Borderland Consciousness:
Dream Recall and Magickal Identity

The first practices undertaken by the neophyte occupy approximately two months' time, and really start the process of Integration at the beginning!

The First Practice Directive

Get a blank book and label it "Dream Book." Begin at once to record your dreams every morning—each and every morning—without skipping. Write down in all possible detail the dreams you recall. Seemingly insignificant details may be very relevant clues. However, one does not make any attempt to interpret the meaning of the dreams at the time of recording them. Why record the dreams? Most dreams are soon forgotten, and it is in the light of the passage of time that one can see the significance of one's dreams.

Upon reading a dream of two months past, one can often decipher the code and symbols of the dream. Indeed, in some cases, one does not get the message until a year or more later. Furthermore, within a few weeks of working in the Order Curriculum, many dreams have significance in terms of the conditions and progress in the magickal work and may serve as a valuable hint to the working neophyte—and to the Immediate Superior.

If the foregoing was solely for the purpose of capturing and recording dreams, one might well say, "This seems to be too much work and trouble for this end." Therefore, this is one case where I feel I should not maintain the rule of not explaining the hows and whys of a prescribed magical practice.

When one is 100 percent asleep, one does not dream—at least dreams as we know them. When dreaming, we are in a partial state of waking consciousness. Be it 85 percent asleep and 15 percent waking (to hazard a percentage), this is a unique state of mind. In a private manuscript issued by "Ida C." called *Heavenly Bridegrooms,* she has called it the "Borderland." Again to hazard a percentage, even 15 percent sleeping state and 85 percent waking state is of the Borderland. The substance of the manuscript by Ida C. is given later in this book as a very potent magick practice.

So, the dream state is the Borderland consciousness state. The importance of the ability to function in a quasi borderland-state may well be more than half of the Technic of Magick. It is involved in making the IMAGINATION to be SUBJECTIVELY REAL. Without this, a large part of Magick is a futile thing. Further, the ability to get the message of symbols, the intuition, a certain sense of awareness, all of which are magickal "tools," have some connection or relation with what is here called the Borderland consciousness, and it is even involved in those important essentials called aspiration and inspiration.

"But," someone says, "everybody dreams. What is so important about this dream business?" At this point, the plaint seems to have some validity—but there is more to be explained.

Certainly we all dream, but only a few dreams are recaptured unless one has mastered this practice of recalling them.

The Technic of dream recall is very simple, but strangely enough it is not well known. Upon awaking, it is important that one not even stretch the body or do any other thing that "shakes the sleep out" of the eyes. Just lie in bed supine and relaxed, waiting to see if a dream comes to mind. Do not think too intensely lest it bring you closer to a full waking state. If nothing comes to mind, do not give up. Resort to the mnemonic system. Ask yourself, "Was my dream in a familiar place? Strange place?

Weird place? About animals or insects? Familiar people or strangers, or relatives? Going someplace?" etc. The entire modus operandi here given is so efficient that a person who has been recalling only a few dreams in a month, within a week is recalling at least one dream every morning.

As efficient as this method is, I have seen it in print in only one book, which is published in Spain under the title *Secretos de los Suenos*. This book, however, fails to mention the thing of utmost importance—regularity. To miss one morning is to fall back two steps of the three steps advanced the previous morning.

Within two months of regular dream capture practice, one begins to remember so many dreams each morning that it would be impractical to record them. One may then cease the recording but not the practice of recalling the dreams.

The subject of dream recall practice is closed with a statement of the empirical observations of scores of G∴B∴G∴ members. For the accomplishment of the aforementioned aims and results, other methods require three or four times as much time and effort to get equal results.

After two weeks of dream recall practice, the neophyte member received the second practice directive, as follows:

> *Every man and every woman is a Star*—at least potentially. We assume that your one excuse for existing as an Individual is that you are unique from all other Individuals. Each Star is in its own unique orbit under its own self-direction, albeit there is some inter-relationship among the totality of Stars.
>
> The Great Work is to attain the "K & C of the HGA" (the "Knowledge and Conversation of the Higher Guardian Angel")—and even, ultimately, that Union when "Countenance beholds Countenance." The Higher Guardian Angel (HGA), or your Daemon, is the arbiter or your unique true identity. Obviously it is consistent with the Great Work that you aspire to discover more and more of your true Magickal Identity.
>
> Get another blank book and name it "Magickal Identity." On each and every evening (until notified to discontinue), concentrate on what you want to be—not what you want to do. This is

not easy to do. You may find it difficult to make an entry in your book that is different from the entry of the previous day, and yet the previous entry seems to you to be inane or superficial. Concentration is necessary; perhaps no less than ten minutes.

This Identity exercise is carried on for only two weeks. The Immediate Superior examines the record of the Immediate Inferior on only the seventh and fourteenth entries. The Immediate Superior does not criticize the record; he makes some corrections that were invariably called for. Here follows a sample record, and the corrections:

"I want to be a great singer. (1) I want to sing before thousands of people. (2) In order that I can give inspiration to them."

Correction by Immediate Superior: "you were instructed to write only what you want to be, but under (1) you have written what you want to DO. You have gone even farther astray under (2) where you write your reasons for wanting to "do" what you list under (1). It is a very necessary lesson in Magick that you learn instructions PRECISELY and EXACTLY, and that you carry the instructions out in the identical way."

Note that there has been no explanation as to what this two weeks' practice accomplishes, and how it is done. Any psychologist worth his salt can clearly see how these explanations weaken or even completely defeat the purpose. In due time, the member sees the light—if he or she sincerely and diligently follows the directive. What more can be asked?

For centuries, it has been a tradition to "Know Yourself," and this does not refer to the outer personality.

Throughout the total Curriculum of Magick operations it is almost essential to know something of who you are, where you are going, and what is the hidden purpose of your going in your own individual unique orbit.

Understand well, if you dig deep enough into your "Magickal Identity" you have then obtained to some small degree of the K & C of the HGA.

Recapitulative Reminders of Chapter Two

Practice of dream recall is an easy yet most efficient method of enhancing the "borderland state" in all magickal operations such as the magickal imagination, inspiration and aspiration, and the awareness.

The importance of continued regularity, whether hourly, daily or weekly, should be realized and followed.

The "Magickal Identity" record is the first step in coming to the knowledge of one's True Identity, and is a drill in self-honesty. "Veil not your vices in virtuous words."

Commentary

Dreams: The Doorway to the Subconscious

We start at the beginning. Dreams are the doorway to the Subconscious Mind, which is the repository not only of personal forgotten and repressed memories but of part of the legacy of common knowledge shared by all humanity.

Recording, and then later exploring and interpreting your dreams, is the foundation for a disciplined awakening of the Unconscious.

In this process, we uncover childish conditioning and memories that are still functioning, and from our adult perspective we will "clean house."

We don't need those childish fears of the boogeyman in the closet. We don't need the childish dependence on Mom or the childish values that served us well in growing up. We don't want adolescent emotions of fear or arrogance, of bullying or trembling, of envy and jealousy, and the hormonal exaggerations that distort our formative relationships.

We don't need them, but as long as they are there they still hurt us. They lurk, like a shark swimming in dark waters, ready to snap a bite of meat—your meat. Fears require fresh energy; you are their source. Your unconscious fears and childhood fantasies draw upon your energy like a psychic vampire, leaving you fatigued and even suffering lower immunity.

Through our honest explorations of dream symbols and relationships we progress toward clear vision and free up energies previously stressing mind and body.

When we start the work of daily exploring "What we want to be" we are finding our magickal identity in the purpose of this life.

Study and Discussion Points

Borderland consciousness. I will quote Culling for emphasis: "the dream state is the Borderland consciousness state. The importance of the *ability to function in a quasi borderland-state may well be more than half of the Technic of Magick.* It is involved in making the IMAGINA-TION to be SUBJECTIVELY REAL. Without this, a large part of Magick is a futile thing."

He describes the Borderland Consciousness as approximately 15 percent awake and 85 percent asleep. Regardless of the actual percentage, these states are also called the hypnagogic and hypnopompic states of being awake and falling asleep and being asleep and waking up. It is during this state of consciousness when we are most receptive to images, symbols, impressions, sounds, ideas, and feelings. It is also a state very receptive to intuition.

Carry the instructions out in the identical way. When you are a beginner, you need to follow instructions exactly. And even if you already consider yourself a magician, you are here following a new curriculum so it is again essential to follow the instructions, and when repeating to do so in exactly the same way. It's like a scientific experiment: the procedure needs to be repeated in the identical way for results to be comparable. Once you have mastered the particular curriculum, then it is the time to experiment and try modifications.

Dream Book, Dream Journal. Record the elements of a dream immediately upon awakening (see Dream Recall below), but do not stop to interpret them. Later, you will also record your interpretation, and start a "dictionary" of the symbols and other elements that seem meaningful to you, and what they seem to mean.

Dream Interpretation. An important factor in the process of integration is the more complete utilization of lines of communication between levels of consciousness. While commercial "dream dictionaries" rarely have much value, one that you compile yourself will become immensely helpful. Through the regular use of a Dream Journal, you become familiar with your own symbol meanings and can explore each further for more insight. When you actually pay attention to your dreams, they start to pay attention to you and can deliver information and even guidance of immediate application.

Dream Recall. The most important part of the process is to tell yourself to remember your dreams just before falling asleep and that you will wake up from those dreams and immediately record the details you can remember. At this time, no effort is made to interpret the dream. Dream interpretation can wait for a day or more. If there is no immediate recall, then assume you did dream and just don't remember it. Lie there and ask yourself questions about the un-remembered dream—what was it about, were there people, what was the time period of the dream, were there messages in the dreams, etc. If no dreams are recalled, ask one more question: Why can't I remember? Record that answer.

Your recall, recording, and interpretation of dreams is part of an overall process of building lines of communication between the conscious mind and the subconscious, and ultimately with the super consciousness. Part of the process of dream recall and developing your own personal dream is to bring order to the chaos of forgotten memories and childish experiences. (Don't presume that your dream dictionary is universal! It is your dream dictionary, and no one else's.) As you do so, you are also engaging in the "housecleaning" necessary before total integration is attempted.

Every man and every woman is a Star. This is from Crowley, and is one of the most important as well as poetic things he ever wrote. There is a dual meaning here: (1) that every one of us is Divine at our core, and that our destiny is to make our Whole Person Divine; (2) that we are all evolving towards roles of greater responsibility. Some have interpreted this to mean that as we become greater we can actually become "stars" in the astronomical sense for every planet, every star (sun), every solar system, every galaxy is a living system similar to a person only on a macroscale.

Whether we really can evolve into a star or an entire galaxy I don't know, but I believe in the analogy for all is consciousness and our source is universal.

Great Work. This is the path of self-directed spiritual growth and de-velopment that is the life work of each and every person. This Great Work has been the subject of study and organization so that it may be accomplished faster using different techniques and procedures. In the G∴B∴G∴ the goal is to attain to the Knowledge and Conversa-tion of your Holy Guardian Angel. Another way of expressing this is as Integration of the Personality with the Higher Self, and this also calls for work upon the sub-conscious mind.

Heavenly Bridegrooms. The author was Ida Craddock. The book is currently listed as out-of-print but was reprinted in 1982 by AMS Press. Used copies may be available. As of this writing, the whole book is available for reading online at http://www.idacraddock.org/bridegrooms.html.

I.S. Immediate Superior. This is your teacher. But, remember, it is not only more likely that you are a solitary rather than a member of a study group, but we have established that you are your own best teacher so long as you follow the outlined disciplines of study and of recording dreams and your magickal work. The G∴B∴G∴ cur-riculum is complete.

Inspiration. Usually a sequence of ideas suggesting particular actions, originating at the psychic level. As you learn to "listen" to your Higher Self, true inspirations will become more easily recognized as such.

Integration. Integration is more than a bringing together: it is the unit-ing of parts into a new whole. It is used to describe the goal of psy-chological development in Jungian Psychology culminating in the person actually becoming the Higher Self rather than the personality.

It is a difficult concept because it is a change of identity from the "I" of the personality into a new "I" that incorporated the transformed elements of the old personality into new Whole Person centered on the Higher Self.

"Who am I?" requires a new answer.

Intuition. Intuition is a different kind of knowing usually experienced as a blinding flash of insight answering a question or solving a problem originating at the Soul level of consciousness.

Know Yourself. The process of self-discovery, of self-knowledge, of self-understanding is endless until such time as we become one with the Highest Self. But the process of self-knowledge is the process of becoming more than you are.

Magickal Identity. The instruction is to get another blank book and name it "Magickal Identity." Every evening, perhaps during your daily review, you are to concentrate on what you want to be—not what you want to do. You are discovering who you really are, the person you are coming to be.

Making the IMAGINATION to be SUBJECTIVELY REAL. Imagination is the making of images, and magick is accomplished by making images and their movement real. Some of that reality comes in the process of charging those images with energy, but more comes by the acceptance of their reality on the astral plane. As images are charged in the astral world, they can be drawn into the physical world, or to have an effect on the physical plane.

Neophyte. The word means "beginner," of course, but it also has other meaning: novice, which suggests a certain naiveté, even a person who has unwittingly "bitten off more than he can chew." Both "neophyte" and "novice" are terms applied to a recent religious convert or a new resident to a religious community who has not yet fully committed to the community by taking religious vows usually involving chastity, devotion, isolation from the outside world, etc.

Personally, I think it is an inappropriate word to apply in a magickal situation as it also suggests that the interest is emotional rather than intelligent. Magick, first of all, does require intelligence. Emotion is recognized as the engine of energy that can be directed into a magickal operation, but not as the basis for the understanding an application of magickal principles.

Oaths. Oaths are common in magickal work. If you are a member of an active coven or lodge you may be expected to swear to secrecy of the group name and the names—magick and mundane—of the members, you may be required not to reveal the teachings of the group, and in particular the names of the gods evoked in group work.

There are two primary reasons for such Magickal Oaths: (1) to establish a feeling of respect for magick itself, and (2) to protect the members' identities. When you take an oath, you do so because of the perceived value and importance of those identities, and the wishes of the people involved.

A third reason for secrecy is to isolate and contain the energies involved with magickal work, including the particular egregor, or thought form that is the magickal identity of the particular group or even of the individual.

Oaths are best chosen and understood as important to the project and not as part of the pageantry of the group. Think of your Magickal Oath, and of secrecy itself as an internalizing. Your own magickal name takes on a greater psychological and spiritual importance by being held secret, and the oath feeds energy to the process.

Process. It is important to understand all the practices of magick, and especially those involving self-transformation, as parts of a process and not merely as single and isolated actions. Dream Recall has value in itself, but here it is presented as part of the process leading to psychological integration itself as part of the process that is a "shortcut to initiation."

Regularity. The need for and value of regular and consistent practice will be emphasized again and again. It is regularity and recording that are the foundations of process; these are the practices that are compared to gardening, for the consistency of these basic practices are what nurture the transformation of personality into the Higher Self.

"Too much work." Culling takes the opportunity to explain the hows and whys of the magickal practice, but there is another point that should be made: If it's "too much work," then you are not valuing the Work itself, and unless you value it you might as well quit all magickal and psycho-spiritual work. On the other hand, as you progress in the Work, it will become less and less "work" and more and more "enjoyment" and hence the source of meaning in your life.

True Identity. Your True Identity is your Magickal Identity, your True Self. We use different words to describe the same thing in order to "fill in" and expand our understanding, and to provide a vocabulary for different occasions and different audiences.

chapter three
_____

The Magickal Oaths:

Putting Meaning into Daily Life

Within two months (or less) of active membership, the neophyte received two directives, as follows:

1. I swear to tell myself the truth.

2. I swear to regard every event (or condition) as a particular dealing between myself and the Holy Guardian Angel.

First we should note that these "oaths" are in no sense related to New Thought "Affirmations." In the first oath, an affirmation would be "I am Truth," which is not only a lie but also does not lead to that awareness and self-examination, and a concomitant *qui vive,* which is the purpose of this Magickal Oath. (If a person is "Truth," then he has attained to the Crown and is way beyond "the Knowledge & Conversation of the Holy Guardian Angel"!)

For an exemplar of the Oath of Truth, let us take the Magickal Identity entry given in the second chapter. In that entry was: "I want to be a great singer so that I can inspire thousands of people." After having practiced the Oath of Truth for a few days, the neophyte said: "It now comes to me much more forcibly about trying to kid myself... veiling one's vices in virtuous words. Actually the desire was to have the applause of the multitudes and for the money in it."

It should go without saying that this oath is not something to repeat once daily. Indeed, it need not ever be spoken aloud; it is an attitude of awareness that should persist continually throughout the day. Yet the beauty and economy of this oath is that it does not require one single minute of one's time. One lives it!

Nor does Oath Number II require any added expenditure of time.

I swear to regard every event or condition as a particular dealing between myself and the Holy Guardian Angel.

Naturally, "every event" means what is within the sphere of one's personal experience; it does not apply to the rise of the price of prunes in Zanzibar! Even within the sphere of personal awareness, "every event" is to be regarded as a latent potentiality of the particular dealing. To regard, or rather to believe, that everything which a person sees, feels, or hears is an omen or message is a psychopathic condition.

In one way of looking at it, every event is a "particular dealing," but in the sense intended that most of the events are of small import. Even from a practical standpoint, one does not regard every event to be of major significance. The main point is that one must maintain a sense of keen awareness. When this is done, the way is open for one's intuition or inspiration to inform one on any possible oracular import. Have no doubt about it, if one has assiduously and regularly carried out the practices so far given, then one can get much symbology and "conversation" concerning his or her Great Work in the many things that touch his or her life. As he progresses, both the events and their messages are greatly increased—those that are of value.

Under this oath, the budding magician stands between two extremes. On the one side is the near-psychopath who regards everything that touches the eye and ear as a particular secret personal message. On the other side is the impervious one who sees no soul message in anything. Here, the neophyte stands in the middle ground, with open eye and ear to heed anything that may be relevant to his Great Work.

NOTE—Consistent with the trickiness of all ideas below the Abyss, one must take refuge in those propensities which have been strengthened by the past practices, which are quite different from intellectual analysis. It seems exigent to give a few case histories here.

Exemplar No. 1. The Neighborhood Primate of one of the Los Angeles Lodges worked as a salesman in the central section of town. In this area were a dozen business houses on various streets that bore the address number 333. Now, the number 333 was the kabalistic number of the Order. He had always noticed these numbers, but he said, "Nothing came through."

"But on this particular occasion, it hit me," and he then noticed that drawing instruments were sold at the location. Upon looking closer, he saw three geometric figures. "Like a flash of light," he said, "these figures gave me the clue to how to proceed with the work that had hitherto baffled me." He went home and completed the work which was sent to G∴B∴G∴ Headquarters and it was incorporated in a very important section of the official workings of the Order.

An advised digression: We all know of cases such as "This tree speaks to me," "The raven settled close to me—it had a message for me," etc. Such beliefs among native peoples are explained as their typical state of mind in which they make little if any distinction between the objective and the subjective. Among modern peoples, it can be a case of so-called superstition, or in some cases close to the psychopathic. One should realize that it is a convenience of language to say "The tree speaks to me" while being aware that it is really a purely subjective matter.

Therefore let the readers understand that what is written in this book about the "messages" of events or things is thus written as a convenience of language.

This work is confined to giving the complete Magick Curriculum of the Secret Order G∴B∴G∴ and not an exhaustive inquiry into the hows and whys of its mechanism. However, before proceeding to some more case histories concerning the oath, a brief explanation of the mechanism seems advisable if only to negate an automatic or ill-advised charge of superstition.

First we postulate the sincere member as being 'saturated' with the spirit and substance of the oath, and that he is in a fairly constant state of awareness about all events. Suddenly some event serves as a mnemonic stimulus to what is already in the borderland consciousness, or the near-subconscious. Or, in another case, it may stimulate the intuitive mind. Whatever the mechanism may be, the result is a "message" or a non-literal "conversation." The following case is an excellent example of the intuitive.

Exemplar No. 2. The Lodge was holding its regular weekly ritual. Frater Loge, a very regular attendee, was not present. During the ritual, a crow flew through the skylight into the room. This could have happened during another meeting and the ritual would have been continued—but not this time! The acting Master of the Ritual, Frater Zeus, yelled, "Wotan's crow!" In Nordic mythology, the crow was the messenger from Valhalla of impending death. "Frater Loge is in trouble," shouted Frater Pan. "Let's go!" When they arrived at the house of Frater∴ Loge, they saw red streaks under his skin running up his arm into his shoulder—the sure sign of blood poisoning! Away to the hospital with him, automobile horn blasting. "A few hours later," said the doctor, "and the best that I could have done would be to amputate his arm, and he might have died."

Exemplar No. 3. Frater A of the San Diego Lodge had been asked for some time to leave there and come to Los Angeles to give stimulus to the O∴T∴O∴ lodge. There came the time when he figured that the G∴B∴G∴ had given out the complete Magick Curriculum, and that there would be nothing more of value. This member very seldom looked at the mileage gauge on his car, but at the end of a trip, for some reason, this time he did look at the gauge. It registered exactly 33,333 miles! As before stated, 333 was the kabala of the Order. To him, this was a very definite "oracle" that he should continue for six months more with the G∴B∴G∴. To this very day he gives thanks for that message; there was further invaluable working given out within the Order.

To repeat the oath—"I swear to regard every incident as a particular dealing between myself and the HGA"—is aspiration to invoke inspiration.

There is nothing new in this oath. It ran through the Golden Dawn, the A∴A∴, and the O∴T∴O∴, and in fact antedates the time of the Gnostics. But there was a weakness, although it was not stressed. There was no injunction to keep this alive throughout the day, day after day— with consistent regularity; and it is herein that its great strength and effectiveness lies.

Let us consider the magickal effect upon members of the G.·.B.·.G.·. when practiced sincerely and continuously. Without being told, members could see the extended implications of the oath, and practice it. They came to see clearly that their various actions were also "events." The almost automatic result was that they made Magick Rituals out of various things they were doing. When planting seeds in the garden, it would be done as a Magickal Ritual of "planting the seeds" of what was desired to be grown and developed within the Self, or developed in their Great Work. Weeding the garden would be a ritual of weeding out the undesirable and giving a better chance for the growth of the desirable. One can readily see that many activities are eminently suitable as little magick rituals. The case of a chemist whom I knew well is called to mind as a fine example of this.

It was Hans Olson who, aided by his unorthodox methods in chemistry, had invented and patented waterproof plastic cement. His royalties furnished enough money to work continuously with his true love, alchemy. He was trying to transmute metals, particularly to make gold and silver from the base metals. One day while I watched him put his conglomerate in his furnace, he told me the following:

> About a year after starting this alchemy venture, I began to notice a few changes taking place in myself. I now know that, because of having read so much on the occult angle of alchemy, I was unconsciously making a ritual over these batches that go into the furnace every day. I did not have any faith in this "Initiation" that the Theosophists read and talk about, but now I know what the real practice does instead of frigging around with intellectual gymnastics. It has "transmuted" me to such an extent that I am in awe.

Recapitulative Reminders of Chapter Three

These two Magickal Oaths are two practices that work strong magick when done with awareness continually, all day every day, and yet do not demand a minute of one's time from what one is doing, except such things as reading and writing.

Commentary

Communicating with your Higher Self

I swear to tell myself the truth.

I swear to regard every event (or condition) as a particular dealing between myself and the Holy Guardian Angel.

What we're doing, of course, is building more lines of communication between the middle (everyday) consciousness and the super consciousness, or the personality and the Holy Guardian Angel. And, we are doing one more important thing: in promising to tell the truth we are building trust.

On this basis of trust, the Higher Self knows that its messages will be respected and attended to.

But, there remains a problem to our communications, and that is that—in part—the Higher Self doesn't speak directly in the common language. Your Holy Guardian Angel doesn't just shout: "Hey, down there, listen up! I want you to stick with the G∴B∴G∴ for six more months."

Instead, through the use of clues and symbols, you have to put effort into understanding the message, making communication a two-way street and a learning situation with direct application to your needs of the moment. In other words, despite the cautions against a pathological belief that everything is a message just for you, almost anything can be used to bridge the gap between meaningless and meaningful. A crystal ball is just a polished rock, but it can open your vision to another world. With intention, anything can become a key to unlock the doors of the Unconscious.

Before Integration there must be Communication. Divination and meditation on the divinatory results and your dreams provide the basis for communication.

Study and Discussion Points

Abyss. The reference is to the Kabalistic Tree of Life and the perceived separation between the upper, unmanifest trinity of Kether, Chokmah, and Binah, and the lower seven Sephiroth that are manifest. It is believed that only adepts can access those higher levels.

Adept. Unfortunately, the term is used loosely and variously to mean either one who has reached a recognized higher grade in one of the initiatory orders, one who has made contact with their Holy Guardian Angel, one who has "crossed the Abyss," or an advanced student.

Aspiration. The aspiration of the student (we are all students) toward growth and the attainment of Initiation should be a burning flame like a lover's desire for his beloved.

Conversation. Yes, it is possible to converse with your Higher Self. First you have to honestly believe in the Higher Self, and that the person you think of as your self is not it. At the same time, don't let the name "Holy Guardian Angel" (HGA) deceive you into thinking of a separate being that is so *holy* as to be beyond your ability to deserve the attention of the HGA.

True, the HGA is normally distant from the personality that is the everyday "you," but the function of the Great Work is to build a relationship between the personality and the Higher Self leading toward Integration—when the two become as one.

"I swear to regard every event (or condition) as a particular dealing between myself and the H G A." Culling has done a beautiful job in explaining the practical issues around this magickal oath, and his examples demonstrate its value and effectiveness.

This practicality is rather unique among magickal oaths! Many are too grand for realization within a single lifetime. While their intention is to stimulate spiritual growth and attainment, it is usually not some grand event or rare or expensive artifact but very ordinary things that call to us for our deeper awareness. Their symbolism may be obscure—normally—but suddenly they glow with meaning or practically yell at you for attention. Or, it may seem like nothing, but still your attention has been re-directed to the event as if it has a special meaning for you, and then it does!

But, note further: This oath directs your attention to everyday events of all kinds so that your awareness is alerted to the greater meaning and potential that each may represent. Magick and meaning may be found in the most mundane of events when there is that possibility of relationship between the inner you and the inner side of the event or thing. The effect is to activate connections to your Higher Self, and that is the goal.

"I swear to tell myself the truth." This, of course, is very challenging. What is truth? Can we ever really know it? Again, Culling has given us a good but simple example. It is perhaps too simple. To some extent, truth is a matter of perspective. In other cases, it is a matter of mathematical or logical accuracy. In most situations, it is more a matter of religious belief or moral conviction that can only be applied personally or within a group of like believers.

The real requirement is to be honest with yourself and to test your answers for their truth and honesty. This is more than "knowing yourself" for it is also a test of your truth and honesty and consistency of action in relation to others and to the world you live in. We too easily deceive ourselves and once again the entire purpose of the oath is to prepare yourself to communicate with your Higher Self, the HGA.

Even though your communication with the HGA isn't always in "plain English," it is not a game! The Great Work is serious business.

Exemplar. An ideal example, worthy of being copied. Lou Culling liked words and liked to get his listeners and readers to take note of his sometimes unusual terminology. I think I more than once caught him making up words to fit what he wanted to say. In the usage in this chapter, I believe "example" would have been a better choice than "exemplar" because he was not pointing to something worthy of being copied; but by using it he was saying, "Pay attention to this example."

Initiation. In this reference to Theosophical Initiation, Olson is refer-ring to a non-magical and more Eastern process of expanding con-sciousness of which, in at least one system, there are ten in number usually administered by an enlightened teacher. (And maybe there are not enough of those teachers to go around...)

Self-Initiation bypasses that shortage along with the high costs and the possible dangers of international travel in troubled times. Even more are the dangers of attachment to a charismatic cult leader who provides an illusion of his own high adept status and an initia-tory experience for his followers that must be constantly renewed.

Messages. As Culling says, it can be "psychopathic" to believe that all the ideas sometimes inspired when we're in the presence of a tree or a garden, an animal or bird, or the night sky or a glorious dawn, are personal messages whispered to our ears alone. But, the source of in-spiration knows no boundaries, and our openness to such stimulation is healthy and vastly different than pathology. And like symbols in dreams, our Higher Self may alert us to some needed idea by awak-ening our interest to something happening in our environment.

While not exactly the same thing, it is fascinating to let things "speak" to you in divination. Rather than following other people's interpretations, let the cards, crystals, shells, bones, stones, coins, sticks, or whatever, speak through your touch and gaze. Let yourself slide into a mild trance, and "let your fingers do the talking" as they manipulate the chosen objects.

Don't impose a "left brain" rigidity of rules on what is essentially a "right brain" work of creative response. Patterns found in a tea cup may seem to say things, but the wisdom is in yourself and not the bottom of the cup.

New Thought. Lou Culling is showing his natural prejudice for what today we more often refer to as "fluffy." Today it would be the worst side of the New Age category—that side that assumes if you think positive and beautiful thoughts that "everything will come up rosy!"

"New Thought" was the name given the philosophy of Phineas Quimby, which can be summed up as "The infinitude of the Supreme

One; the Divinity of man and his infinite possibilities through the creative power of constructive thinking and obedience to the voice of the indwelling Presence, which is our source of Inspiration, Power, Health and Prosperity."

It's a beautiful philosophy, and was an inspiration in the development of Mary Baker Eddy's Christian Science religion with the belief that the physical is not truly real, and that healing of disease occurs by virtue of the presence of Truth.

In addition to Christian Science, the New Thought is influential in three major, but distinct, religious denominations within the American New Thought movement: Unity Church, Science of Mind, and the Church of Divine Science.

The difference between Magick as practiced by the G.˙.B.˙.G.˙. and other groups, and more importantly by individual magicians, and religious groups is less a distinction in philosophy than in practice. A "Shortcut to Initiation" is a promise of individual accelerated evolution, of self-transformation and integration of personality with the Higher Self leading to Self-Empowerment. There is no intermediary—teacher, priest, practitioner, swami, or other person—doing the Work that only you can do for yourself.

As sources of inspiration and knowledge, all of these movements have great value but they are not in themselves practical programs or self-transformation leading to that integration of personality with the Higher Self.

The New Age is real, representing the potential to move into a higher level of consciousness as another stage in human and planetary evolution, but the potential is only an opportunity that each of us can exercise, and that exercise represents the self-transforming work of Magick. But Magick is not the only path. By reducing this "Shortcut to Initiation" to its essentials and explaining what is intended and expected, you can instead make it a psychological process, or a spiritual one, or a mystical one. "Do as Thou wilt shall be the whole of the Law. And Love is the Law, Love under Will."

Oaths. Oaths are common in magickal work. If you are a member of an active coven or lodge you may be expected to swear to secrecy of the group name and the names—magick and mundane—of the members, you may be required not to reveal the teachings of the group, and in particular the names of the gods evoked in group work.

There are two primary reasons for such oaths: (1) to establish a feeling of respect for magick itself, and (2) to protect the members' identities. When you take an oath, you do so because of the perceived value and importance of those identities, and the wishes of the people involved.

A third reason for secrecy is to isolate and contain the energies involved with magickal work, including the particular egregor, or thought form that is the magickal identity of the particular group or even of the individual.

Oaths are best chosen and understood as important to the project and not as part of the pageantry of the group. Think of your oath, and of secrecy itself, as an internalizing. Your own magickal name takes on a greater psychological and spiritual importance by being held secret, and the oath feeds energy to the psychological and spiritual process.

Transmuted. To be "transmuted" is to be changed in an evolutionary manner. Just as the alchemist sought to transmute base metal into gold, the goal of the Great Work is to transmute the lower self into the higher. As magicians, as workers, we are committed to a process of alchemical transformation of our own selves.

chapter four

The Retirement Ritual:

The Inner Relationship with the Holy Guardian Angel

One document that each member received individually was the outline of the "Retirement Ritual." This was received after at least three months of membership, if one had been a loyal and active member. "Loyal" meant being loyal to the Great Work and practicing, sincerely and regularly, all of the directed work. Naturally this implied loyalty to the "Neighborhood" group and also to Headquarters. The word "active" is redundant, except in cases where it was temporarily impossible for the member to carry on with the work because of illness or particular obligations or circumstance.

Upon receiving a copy of the Retirement Ritual, the member was told also to choose his or her "Magickal Name." The Magickal Name is a condensation into one word of your conception of your unique magickal identity in the Great Work. Later you may change your Magickal Name; it is a progressive knowledge of your Identity. It is a parallel to the "substitute word" in Freemasonry, but in the meantime it is your guiding word. (Note—see Table of Letters & Numbers in chapter Five to get the number of the name.)

Instructions for the Magickal Retirement

You must first learn this ritual by memory so that you can speak the words and perform the gestures freely and without hesitation of memory.

The retirement is for three days and three nights, in a location where there are no distractions. You can drink water but eat no food. If deemed necessary for your well-being, you may take nourishment in liquid form only.

The ritual and your written record in your blank book marked "Book of [insert your Magickal Name]" is to be performed eight times daily, at one or one and one-half hour intervals. You may arrange this schedule in two parts so that you may have a siesta period. Do not neglect to write your record of impressions after each ritual.

In those cases where one could not be free from worldly duties for the stated period, there was a concession of two days and nights, but the rituals were increased to eleven times daily. There were a few cases where the limit of free time was just Saturday afternoon and all day Sunday—seventeen rituals required.

Ritual Furnishings

Small table or box that is covered with a purple cloth, upon which is placed a lighted incense burner. A copy of the ritual may be placed here for emergency reference.

Magickal Instruments

None. The extended thumb between clenched fingers is the "Wand." The right thumb is now to be always regarded as the "Magick Wand."

All Signs and Gestures

Sign of Opening of the Temple—Palms open, fingers extended, arms held overhead in the form of an inverted triangle. Then drop the palms and fingers before the eyes; then raise them back up in the original position.

Sign of Closing of the Temple—The same sign, except that the three-part motion begins with palms and fingers before the eyes, then overhead, then back to the original position.

Sign of Veneration or Eagle Sign—Arms crossed over chest, left palm over right shoulder and right palm over left shoulder, with the two thumbs interlocked. This is the "Eagle" sign, which means Countenance beholds countenance.

Sign of the Enterer—Lunge forward on the left foot and extend the arms straight forward, fingers extended. Hold this position while speaking the "Enochian Words."

Receiving or Welcoming Sign—Straddle the legs widely apart, sideways; extend the arms above the head in a half circle.

Clothes During Ritual

The clothing should be something different than one's customary apparel. This is a reminder that the operation is apart from one's worldly activities.

Incense

5 parts Olibanum (Frankincense)
1 part Storax
½ part Lignum Aloes

Light well the charcoal cake (obtained from a church supply house or New Age shop) and place a generous amount of the mixed resins in the center of the lighted cake.

Signs Used at the Four Corners of the Circle

These are the *trigrams* derived from the eight Pa Kua of the Yi King, given forth circa 3000 B.C. by the great initiate, Fu Hsi.

```
_____
_____        AIR
__    __


__    __
__    __        FIRE
_____
```

—— ——
———————   WATER
———————

———————
—— ——   EARTH
—— ——

Operation of the Retirement Ritual

1. Make the Sign of the Opening of the Temple.

2. Pace slowly three times around the circle while holding the concentrated thought that the circle is encompassing all good magick forces and is excluding all distractions and whatever alien forces.

3. Go to the center and say: "Let the rituals be rightly performed with joy and beauty."

4. Go to the EAST corner and trace with the "wand" the trigram of AIR, visualized as glowing yellow.

5. Make the Sign of the Enterer, saying: "Great Elemental of Air, I unite with Thee."

6. Make the Sign of Welcome, saying: "Great Yellow Powers of Air, come thou forth and aid and guard me in this work of art."

   Go to the SOUTH corner and repeat steps Four through Six above, except that the sign is the trigram of FIRE seen in red, and the name is changed to Great Red Fire.

   Go to the WEST corner and repeat as above, except the sign is the Blue trigram of WATER.

   Go to the NORTH corner and repeat as above, except the sign is the Green EARTH.

7. Go to the center, clap hands together in a rhythm of 1—3—3—3—1, a total of eleven claps.

8. Make a circle (with wand) above the head, crying: "Nuit."

9. Touch the wand (thumb) to the Muladhara (sex chakra), crying: "Hadit."

10. Touch the wand to the center of the Breast, crying: "Ra—Hoor—Khuit."

11. Now visualize yourself as being enclosed in a great silver cone that extends in great height above you. Project your consciousness higher and higher in the cone, saying: "Great Goddess Babalon, carry me safely and closer to my Divine Genius, my immortal Daemon, my Holy Guardian Angel." Let this be done slowly and also lasting long enough that you do not feel like enduring the aspiration any longer.

12. Make the Eagle Veneration sign and hold it while saying: "I hear and heed the words of mine Angel. My Angel tells me—*I am above you and in you. My ecstasy is in yours. My joy is to see your joy. To me! To me!*"

13. Go to the edge of the circle and say: "Now let there be a veiling of this shrine." Make the Sign of the Closing the Temple and say: "Abrahadabra."

> Now enter a record in the ritual record book, giving an account of any thought or incidents while you performed the ritual, and also any thoughts and impressions that may come to your mind after having performed the ritual.

The person who hurls the challenge, "Tell me what this Magickal Ritual has done for your members—or any other Magick, for that matter," is typically pugnacious or unfair. Nevertheless, if one could not report examples in which a three-*day* magickal retirement had accomplished far more than a three-*month* period with a psychiatrist, then the whole magick business is the bunk!

To quote Headquarters on what to expect from the Magickal Retirement:

In the first place, expect nothing specifically. You do not know your own Self-created necessity in relation to the Angel or Daemon. You can in no way command your Daemon! You may have an energized feeling of freedom or of being rejuvenated, and it may last for many weeks. You may have a completely empty feeling that absolutely nothing has taken place—and this is a sure sign that something of no value has been taken from you, which you will later realize. On the other hand, something outstanding may manifest almost immediately. Above all things, as an aspiring magician you must learn in your aspiration to "Lust not for result." To lust for result is anathema in Magick.

Here, however, it seems exigent to give the case of the Retirement of Soror Johana. I had offered her the use of my cabin for her Retirement. She went this one better; she climbed the hillside above the cabin and made her camp under an oak tree. Her record mentions the "yip-yip" cry of the coyotes as they nightly came down from the upper hills, but she took this as a reassurance of the outcome of her Retirement.

After her Retirement, she straightway set herself to sculpture a work in which she had been inspired. She was a fair sculptress. Two weeks later when she showed me her clay model, I was awe-struck; it was a masterpiece worthy of Rodin. Lo, after these many years, I still regret not having photographed this inspired work.

Now I do not mean to say that this masterpiece itself is the significant thing. The prime significance is that the sculpture was an outward and visible manifestation of what had taken place in her being.

Speaking of visible signs, it is well to tell about our observation of members who, after the Retirement said, "I do not feel anything—nothing is different." But we, as brother members and observers, could see various signs that something indeed had taken place—good signs and manifestations. On this point is the saying "The seer cannot be, at the same time, the seen." It is much easier to make observations in another person than in oneself, in their outer and visible character. However, one's inner relations with one's Holy Guardian Angel are quite another matter—unknown to the outsider.

It may well be that it is illogical to expect results immediately after a magickal operation. Furthermore, I have also had results of which I did not become aware until several months later. Let us be practical! The manuscript of this book was written a long time before there could come the objective magickal result—the Book.

Commentary

The G.·.B.·.G.·. Retirement Ritual

Even contemplating the "severity" of this retirement ritual clarifies the intensity of what a "shortcut" involves. In another sense, very little is really demanded—three days, a period of fasting (that is itself probably beneficial health-wise), and periodic rituals that are not unlike a litany of prayers and meditations in other spiritual traditions. However, the reality is that a real retirement like this is like going into solitary confinement for the purpose of finding your Soul.

It must be your commitment that you are to limit your whole being to this ritual. You don't bring books and magazines along, no games or play things, you don't have a radio or TV, nor any communication device other than—for emergency only—your cell phone. And any calls must be answered curtly and cut off as quickly as possible. You don't daydream, you don't think about your job or your family, you don't worry about the stock market or the weather or what's happening on the "outside."

The success of the ritual is at least partially dependent upon your ability to exclude the ordinary from what may turn out to be extraordinary.

The Value of the Personal Retreat

Retirement rituals, retreats, vision quests, wilderness journeys, periods of silence, etc., are all common to Initiatory Practices. Each tradition has its own unique practices, many symbolic and dramatic, and intended to "shake the foundations" and "stir the pot." The intention is to mark the ending of one part of your life and to mark the beginning of another. All involve a "change of pace" during which things can happen.

Some may demand a life-changing accomplishment at their culmination—a "Big Dream," the finding of an amulet, the making of a talisman, a substantial fasting and purging, the killing of an animal that then becomes one's totem, and other ways to establish a transition from one phase of life to another.

Aside from the Retirement Retreat, there is proven value to periodic retreats, even annually, to encourage review and communication with the Higher Self, the Holy Guardian Angel. Various businesses and organizations, churches, and other groups provide for such retreats for their own purposes—shouldn't you do the same for the most important personal purpose of all?

It doesn't demand much on your time and resources, and can be combined—as long as you are honest and disciplined about it—with a family vacation. But, you don't really have to go somewhere beyond your own home for a weekend retreat or personal vacation. The advantage of a change of place is the same as for a change of pace—you plan the time and environment to get the most out of your reflection time.

The only equipment you need is your journal and a pen, or your laptop computer provided you use it only for your journaling purpose. No e-mails, no online searches, just your journal. Your ideal program should call for three periods of meditation, thirty to sixty minutes each, followed by one to two hours of writing. That's it, a maximum of nine hours over two days once a year for the most important endeavor of your life. But, even as an ideal it may be too much. Adjust it if necessary.

If you have pressing questions about your spiritual progress, write them down and start your morning meditation with them. If you have no questions, just ask your Higher Self to communicate with you, and patiently "listen." Make no demands; just be open to your Holy Guardian Angel.

Of course, you can do lesser meditations for this sort anytime, but there is value to this larger, weekend retreat that will pay unlimited dividends.

Study and Discussion Points

Abrahadabra. Not to be confused with "Abracadabra." Crowley declared Abrahadabra to be the "Word of the New Aeon" that would unite microcosm with macrocosm in the new phase of human evolution. In itself, the word is understood as a formula of sex magick performed within the Great Work.

Alien forces. Are there such things? Are not all forces and beings part of a single and Divine Cosmos? Presumably, we have to say yes to that, but we also recognize that at different circumstances and times there are negative options. A snakebite can be poisonous. Even your pet cat can bite you and cause a severe, life-threatening infection.

In the context of magick, we are excluding from the Circle anything alien or unfriendly to the intent of the operation. Note the instructions in the G.·.B.·.G.·. Curriculum that the magician is to "pace slowly three times around the Circle while holding the concentrated thought that the circle is encompassing all good magick forces and is excluding all distractions and whatever alien forces."

Circumscribing the Circle three times is traditional. Holding a "concentrated thought" is another way to state our "intention" to exclude unwanted influences. Important to this concept is to believe in the effect, and to have no fears or visions of frightful spirits or nasty forces trying to enter the Circle. In magick, as in any psychological practice, always keep the emphasis on the positive as already reality and avoid any thought of the negative while doing the operation.

This practice of exclusion also applies to thoughts and fantasies and day dreams that are common indulgences. Especially in group working—which the Retirement Ritual is not—members not active at a given moment sometimes do "drift off" and that interferes with the purity of the magickal atmosphere inside the Circle.

Babalon. Crowley said Babalon was the goddess of the New Aeon as found in Thelema, the religion he founded in 1904. She represents the female sexual impulse and the most fertile Great Mother, the womb of all life and the mother of each of us. She can be invoked into an actual woman as priestess in working Sex Magick to manifest the energies of the Aeon of Horus. She is the Liberated Woman. She is the Sacred Prostitute. She is the Anima.

In Sex Magick she becomes the "Scarlet Woman" and the mixture of semen with menstrual blood is called the "menstruum of the lunar current." It is Babalon who gives birth to Life and Beauty, and who transforms men into Masters of the Universe for she frees them of fears and inhibitions.

Book M.N. Obviously, "M.N." is to be replaced with your Magickal Name. I make this point simply because I have found some people so literal that they use such abbreviations in their rituals, so—if the instructions say "Call the Angel 'N'" that is exactly what they do rather than calling the Angel by its name.

Circle. A temporary boundary within which a séance or magical operation may take place. The theory is that it becomes a kind of psychic container for the energies used in the operation and a barrier to unwanted energies from outside. See the earlier reference to "alien forces."

Magick Circle—whether drawn physically or in the imagination—is the "container" of magickal operations. The "Opening" and the "Closing" of the Temple—or of the Circle—is an operation that is both magickal and psychological. The rituals of Opening and Closing are various but all are simple projections of energy guided by will power with the express intent to provide a barrier against exterior forces while establishing the Circle (or Lodge) as container of the magickal energies.

Lest you doubt the reality of the energy involved, I will tell you that I once had a lovely, semi-circular stone Magick Room with permanent quarter stations of large candleholders and vertical metal pentagrams. In drawing the Circle, it was always drawn in the same place. Once I became interested in "black light," and to my amazement that circle appeared as cold blue hovering in the air when I turned the black light on.

Clothing for rituals. The G.·.B.·.G.·. calls for simplicity. The requirement is only that the ritual clothing be different from one's customary clothing. While fancy ceremonial robes would fulfill this requirement, they would be contradictory to the emphasis on the Great
Work in contrast to the accessories. A simple garment cut from cloth
with holes for neck and arms could be sufficient, as could an inexpensive bathrobe or night shirt.

In some Wiccan circles the choice is "skyclad"—nakedness so
that all are equal before the gods and nothing is in the way of the
body's natural energy. The observation can be made that nakedness
does not make us equal since we are very conscious of our physical
appearance—slim, fat, tall, sort, hairy, etc.—a distraction from the
Magick.

Elemental. These are the elemental forces of this world and possibly for
the whole Universe. They are variously ascribed to the inner side of
natural forces, and also to the Spirits of the four Elements of Air, Fire,
Water, and Earth, along with the fifth Element of Spirit from which
the four are derived. The Elemental Spirits, or Forces, are the Guardians of the Four Directions of the Magickal Circle, thus transforming
the Circle into a miniature of the Universe.

Enochian Words. In the magickal workings of Dr. John Dee (1527–
1608), astrologer to Queen Elizabeth I (and some also claim him to
have been her spymaster), he made contact with certain angelic beings who used a language distinct from any other. Dee believed these
beings to be the same angels that transported the Hebrew prophet,
Enoch, to heaven, and hence the name for the language. Enochian
words are sometimes called "barbarous" because their pronunciation
is so evocative.

Forces. Physics recognizes four primary forces: gravity, electro-magnetism, and the strong and weak nuclear forces.

In occult theory, East and West, and in classical natural philosophy,
there are the four elements: Earth, Fire, Air, and Water. In magickal
practices, the four elements are used as "forces" and often imbued

with consciousness as when they are identified with particular arch-angels. Might these really the same as the four forces of physics?

In occult theory, East and West, Spirit is the fifth element from which the other four are derived. If, as some of us speculate, Consciousness is the primary force, then are Spirit and Consciousness one and the same?

If Consciousness is the primary Force from which the other four Forces are derived, then is this primary consciousness or Spirit the same as the Creator, we otherwise call God?

Gestures. The different positions and motions of the hands are as important as the Signs—or positions and movements of the body—in magickal and religious ritual, and in energy healing. They are also found in various ecstatic and shamanic dances. They are not "empty" gestures as a little experimentation will readily show. See appendix Three for more guidance.

Hadit. The Chaldean aspect of the Egyptian god of evil or darkness. Crowley regarded Hadit as the master of magickal initiation and that is the understanding in this ritual. Hadit is the point in the center of the circle that is Nuit. He is "the flame that burns in every heart of man and the core of ever star."

Holy Guardian Angel. (Also the HGA) The transcendent spiritual self that mediates between the Divine Self and the Lower Personality and serves a guardian and guide. The term was used by Abramelin the Mage as the focus of the magical operation known as "the Knowledge and Conversation of the Holy Guardian Angel."

Contact between the Higher, Divine Self and the Lower Self/Personality is normally initiated by the Personality, and that contact is the first step in the Great Work that leads to integration, and thus to Initiation.

"I am above you and in you. My ecstasy is in yours. My joy is to see your joy. To me! To me!" This key part of the G∴B∴G∴ Retirement Ritual is your Holy Guardian Angel speaking to you. Saying it with feelings of deep emotion and acceptance of the reality that your HGA is your Higher Self and is the dynamic partner of you as a Whole Person,

and that your HGA loves you and all parts that make up the Whole Person, is an invocation of the deepest kind.

Inner Relationship with the Holy Guardian Angel. This is the goal for the Retirement Ritual, and of the Great Work. Think what it is saying—that you can and will establish an actual relationship with your Higher Self. Through this relationship—the knowledge and conversation with your Holy Guardian Angel—you have the opportunity to bring together all the "parts" that are your subconscious mind, your personal consciousness (the personality that you think of as yourself) with the superconscious mind, or Higher Self—into a unified, integrated, Whole Person.

Thus you become a fully conscious, fully awake, whole person in whom lost memories are restored, lost knowledge is regained, your psychic powers developed into usable skills, your magickal abilities energized, and your Divinity awakened.

"Let the rituals be rightly performed with joy and beauty." Spoken as the opening of your ritual from the center of the Circle, it has the power of similar phrases like "Man your stations" and "Let the games begin!" Note there are three admonitions—that the rituals are to be performed rightly, and with joy and beauty.

This is not a idle statement; indeed, nothing said or done in your magickal circle, or temple, is done without full awareness and intention to do anything less than your best and that is not only right action, but the feeling of joy and happiness in your heart, and the intention that all your movements, gestures, words, and thoughts will be done with the intention of grace and beauty.

How you think when doing Magick will affect how it works, and you want joy in your heart and beauty in our world.

"Lust not for result." This is an admonition that seems almost contrary to what you expect. The point is that your goals must be established before the Work begins, and during the ritual focus only on the Work, not the goal.

Magick Wand. The extended right thumb between clenched fingers as the Magick Wand is, to my knowledge, unique to the G.˙.B.˙.G.˙.

Other common substitutes for this tool are the right, or even the "power" index finger if left-handed, and the thumb and first two fingers clenched together and pointed.

The non-use of traditional magickal tools—like daggers, swords, chalices—is also fairly unique to the G∴B∴G∴ and is intended to keep the emphasis on the person and the Great Work and not on accessories. In some groups, the equipment can become quite expensive, sometimes with individuals trying to outdo each other with gold and jewels, fancy robes and crowns, etc. Or, at another extreme, the tradition may require that each person make their equipment: forging a sword, carving a wand in particular wood, and so on.

There is empowering magical validity to this, but again it is a distraction from the Great Work itself—the integration of personality with the Higher Self.

The question is the role of Magick in your life: If your goal is the Great Work of Self-Initiation, then focus on the "end" suggests simplicity of the tools and accessories. If the goal is to become a "professional" magician, then the focus on the "means" suggests great tools and accessories with a lot of dazzle.

Magickal Name. A condensation into one word of your conception of your unique magickal identity in the Great Work. As previously mentioned, it is commonly expressed in Latin or Greek. Culling's Magical Name was Aequilla.

In other instances, the name is more a Magickal Motto, a condensed statement of purpose. During my magickal years, my name and motto was Gnosticus, which I interpreted as "seeker of knowledge."

Muladhara. The root chakra located at the base of the spine, color red, associated planet Saturn, associated Sephirah Malkuth. It is home to Kundalini, and sexual energy.

Nuit. (Also Nut) The Egyptian sky goddess whom we see as arched as the sky overhead with only finger tips and toes touching the Holy Earth—who is also Geb, her husband. Beneath Nuit, Geb is often shown with an erect penis for it is through their union that all is born. Geb is also her brother, and Nuit and Geb are the parents of Isis,

Osiris, Nephthys, and Set. (Note: "Incestuous" relationships are common in all mythology and that has no pertinence to humanity. Myth's pertinence is to the inner understanding of cosmic energies.)

Nuit is also matter, and Hadit (also her husband, or masculine counterpart) is motion. Nuit is an infinite Circle, while Hadit is the infinitely small point at the core of everything.

Pa Kua. Eight trigrams, the eight signs which form the basis of I Ching, and from which the sixty-four hexagrams are constructed.

The Pa Kua is also used in various decorative and religious motifs incorporating the eight trigrams of I Ching; specifically in a circle around the yin-yang symbol.

Though the origin of the Pa Kua, and hence of the I Ching, is often attributed to Fu Hsi, the legendary Chinese emperor thought to have ruled at the beginning of the first millennium BC, the eight trigrams used for divination were not invented until about 1000 BC. Fundamental to their divinatory usage, these three-lined figures, in their sixty-four combinations, form the basis of Chinese cosmological speculation.

Ra—Hoor—Khuit. Ra is the sun god of the ancient Egyptian religion, and was carried on the back of Nuit, the sky goddess. Ra is the god of birth and of rebirth as he appears to be reborn at the dawn of each new day. Ra-Hoor-Khuit is a form of Horus and symbolic of the Solar Sexual Energies that are part of Crowley's sexual magick.

Retirement Ritual. A "retirement ritual" or "retreat" is common to many magical, shamanic, and spiritual systems. As a time of isolation and self-deprivation, it involves a challenge to one's self-identity and an opening to the Higher Self whether conceived as the Holy Guardian Angel or God.

A familiar task of the retirement ritual is to record one's visions and realizations in a diary, and/or to discuss the experiences with the shaman or teacher, and to return to that record in future times to review those insights from a constantly evolving perspective.

Ritual Record Book. The importance of a record book—whether as a Magical Diary, Book of Shadows, or other name—has previously been mentioned. I repeat that this is one of the most important actions that are undertaken by the magician. And, it is just as important in any activity, whether as student or professional, as wife or husband, etc. The act of recording is the act of self-observation and the opportunity for self-evaluation. Keeping in mind whatever the goal of your procedure, writing down what you did and how it affected you becomes a measure of your work.

Signs. As used in ritual, these are the movements and postures, accompanied by gestures, that function in unity with the voiced expressions, chants, invocations, evocations, and mental visualization and astral extensions.

Silver cone. Also known as a "cone of power." A cone is commonly visualized as an extension of the Magick Circle to function as a container of inner strength and purpose and as a barrier against external disturbance.

"The seer cannot be, at the same time, the seen." As Culling points out, it is much easier to make observations in another person of their outer and visible character than in oneself. However, one's inner relationship with one's HGA is quite another matter—unknown to the outsider. An outsider is outside this inner relationship and, at best, can only encourage you in the Great Work.

Trigrams. A trigram is a block of three parallel straight lines, each line being either complete (unbroken) or broken. See Pa Kua and I Ching for more details.

Yi King. See I Ching.

chapter five

The Qabalah of Numbers:

Table of Letters & Numbers, Tarot Correspondences

Within a few days after assuming his or her Magickal Name, the order member received a copy of the correspondences between the Hebrew alphabet and the English alphabet, including the numerical attributions to the letters (Qabalah) and also the attributions to the twenty-two Tarot Trumps.

Here it should be explained that, in ancient Hebrew, the vowel sounds were never written. However, by certain rules the English vowels are in correspondence with certain Hebrew consonants, which are "quasi" vowels. This will be seen in the accompanying table.

A brief explanation of the Tarot card numbers is also advisable. In the original major Tarot cards (twenty-two in number), the card called "The Fool" was positioned at the bottom, the 22nd position. This card is now numbered zero and positioned at the top of the pack—the "Pure Fool" instead of the "Rank Fool."'

The concepts of the Tarot cards have kept pace with the evolution of advancing knowledge, with the concepts and psychology of the European peoples, and there have been a few other changes in the numerical sequence of the cards. These changes were well-known in the Hermetic Order of the Golden Dawn, and such men as Paul Foster Case, former member of the Golden Dawn, openly taught these changes. The once "secret order" of the cards is given in the table.

The letter that I received from Headquarters about the Qabalah of Numbers, the Tarot, the Tree of Life, and their interrelated correspondences, read:

> *Eventually, members will run across these things and wonder why they had not received it from Headquarters. Our practical use of these things is limited to obtaining the number of Magickal Names (and a few other words) and the correspondences of these with the Tarot and the Tree of Life.*

(Why was this? Because the "shortcut to initiation" does not require it. The goal of the G.∴B.∴G.∴ program was focused on that single goal of Initiation and anything not pertinent to that is a distraction. Note, however, that the Tarot and Tree of Life tables and diagrams given at the end of this book, along with other tables, does supplement that minimal approach.)

A few examples of the Qabalah of Numbers as used, are in order:

Example No. 1. The magickal name of Soror ∴ Iva totals to 17 (I = 10, V = 6, A = 1). In this case it was seen that there was a significant relationship to the number 17 Tarot card called the "Star" (see later comment on the secret import of this card). Also, by reduction, 1 plus 7 equals 8. We shall see later that the 8 Pa Kua Hexagrams of the Yi King were a very important part of the Ritual Working. We can now see that, regardless of the doubts that beset the Soror, she could not escape the reassurance of her magickal name that she was in the "right work." (Note: G = 3, B = 2, G= 3 also totals 8. Two things of equal numerical value are in harmony with one another.)

Example No. 2. Frater.∴ Aequila totals to 153, and these three numbers added together reduce to 9. Now 9 is the number of Man—Mankind. The Hebrew spelling of "Adam" is ADM, which totals 45, and 4 plus 5 also equals 9. In Magick 9 is the number of those who aspire to the "Knowledge & Conversation of the Holy Guardian Angel." And the Beast of the Apocalypse—"Count well its number 666, it is the number of Man"—666 totals 18, which reduces to 9. When the K & C of HGA is attained, it is "abrahadabra," number 11. Frater Aequila was also re-minded of the 153 (1 + 5 + 3 = 9) fish as recounted in the Bible.

Example No. 3. Choronzon. In Hebrew this is spelled CHVRVN-ZVN, which totals to 333, which reduces to 9. Other alphabets with their numbers are to be found in a good encyclopedia under "alphabet."

To continue with the correspondence from Headquarters about the Tree of Life and the Tarot:

> In preoccupation with these subjects, some people have at-tained to various "Magickal Powers," but this does not directly lead to the K & C of H G A, which is the prime objective of the G∴B∴G∴. Furthermore, for the attainment of magickal powers, our methods are more direct and proficient, time savers, and al-ways in relation to the Great Work. If you must pursue the study of these outside disciplines, then you must do it in your spare time and not at the expense of the Order workings.
>
> You may have read that knowledge of a vast array of corre-spondences is necessary for the "testing" of various intelligences. As long as you are an active, loyal, sincere aspirant to the Knowl-edge and Conversation of the Higher Guardian Angel, and using the oracle of the Yi, you cannot be a victim of "alien" intelli-gences. Being well-armed and knowing that there is nothing out-side of yourself that is not also within yourself (and which you are daily facing), is enough to keep you sincerely and correctly on the path of the Great Work. *Weaklings, cowards, and the unworthy, are not of us!*

Coupled with your practical state of "awareness" some Knowledge of this Table will be of value even though you do not penetrate deeply into the subject.

For example, I have profited by being led into the significance of the number 17 Tarot card, "The Star," which has been a sign or "word" to me on many occasions. Incidentally, this card has a large star pictured on it on which should have seven points, if correctly depicted. The seven-pointed star is the sigil of the Goddess Babalon.

Table of Letters and Numbers, Tarot Correspondences			
Hebrew Letter	English Letter	Numerical Value	Tarot Card Number
Aleph	A	1	0 Fool
Beth	B	2	1 Magician
Gimel	G	3	2 High Priestess
Daleth	D	4	3 Empress
Heh	H and E	5	17 Star
Vau	V, U, and W F (o)	6	5 Hierophant
Zain	Z	7	6 Lovers
Cheth	Ch	8	7 Chariot
Teth	T	9	11 Justice
Yod	I and Y	10	9 Hermit
Kaph	K	20	10 Wheel of Fortune
Lamed	L	30	8 Strength
Mem	M	40	12 Hanged Man
Nun	N	50	13 Death
Samekh	S	60	14 Temperance
Ayin	0	70	15 Devil
Peh	P	80	16 Tower
Tzaddi	Tz or X	90	4 Emperor
Qoph	K soft, Q	100	18 Moon
Resh	R	200	19 Sun
Shin	Sh	300	20 Judgement
Tau	T soft, Th	400	21 Universe

Commentary

While this chapter exposes the student to the Qabalah of Numbers, and the Tarot, and a sense of identity through the choice of the magickal name, the real import is to demonstrate the use of the Qabalah of Numbers in relating one's choices to the Great Work.

Of course, not all things will so easily "add up" to match your goals. Used in this manner, the Qabalah helps show you where you are in relation to your goals, and what things are diversions or antagonists.

A "shortcut" is a straight and narrow path.

Study and Discussion Points

Case, Paul Foster. (1884–1954) Founder of the Builders of the Adytum (BOTA), an esoteric teaching center in Los Angeles. He was a former member of the Golden Dawn, and the author of *The Tarot, A Key to the Wisdom of the Ages,* and a book of Tarot card meditations, *The Book of Tokens.* Both books were recommended by Culling.

Choronzon. The number is 9, also the number of Man. But Choronzon is also the name of the demon that guards the Abyss on the Tree of Life—separating the lower from the higher. It's that Abyss that we must cross to fulfill our spiritual destiny. That demon is the obstacle between the adept and enlightenment. If met with proper preparation by the magician, his function is to destroy the ego, allowing the magician to cross the Abyss. We all must confront our demon.

The demon is also our Shadow, the lower self of the subconsciousness with our fears and repressions.

Correspondences. The Kabbalah, using the symbolic system of the Tree of Life and numerological associations provided through the Hebrew language, Astrology, and Natural Science identifies a wide range of 'correspondences' between subjects, planets, herbs, plants, metals, crystals, colors, animals, angels, deities, etc., that allow substitutions of one thing for another, or that augment understanding about one thing by knowledge of another of corresponding value.

Mostly the applications of correspondences are divided into Magical, Medical, Numerical, and Tarot usages.

Suggested Reading:

Whitcomb: *The Magician's Companion*

Hulse: *Western Mysteries*

Fool, The. (Tarot) Generally numbered "0" or 22nd of the Major Arcana—image: variously a Court Jester and a dog about to step off a cliff, naked child with a dog, a pilgrim in a strange land or an enthused rider with his dog jumping his horse across the chasm between the worlds; Hebrew letter: Aleph; Divinatory meaning: fool-hardy courage, determination, act of faith; 11th path on the Tree of Life connecting Chokmah to Kether.

The Fool is perhaps the most interesting card in the Tarot for it is he who makes the journey through life, from Start "0" to Finish "22." It is the Fool who is transformed by his journey, just as each of us must be to become a Whole Person.

Hebrew, Language and Alphabet. Hebrew is sometimes referred to as the "sacred" language of the West and compared with Sanskrit for the East. There are no vowels per se in Hebrew, only diacritical marks over the consonants performing that function. In addition, there are no numbers in Hebrew, but letters alone and in combination perform that function. The number basis provides a system in which words of comparable value have related meanings. It also provides the magickal meanings of Hebrew names.

Hermetic Order of the Golden Dawn. Founded in England in 1888, this magickal order provided the impetus and source for magickal study and practice within the Western Esoteric Tradition.

Israel Regardie's *The Golden Dawn* is an encyclopedic resource for the rituals and knowledge lectures of the Golden Dawn, while his *The Tree of Life, The Middle Pillar,* and *A Garden of Pomegranates* provide in-depth exposition of the Golden Dawn's magical system. See also books by Chic and Tabatha Cicero, including their *Self-Initiation into the Golden Dawn Tradition.*

Magickal powers. Nearly all esoteric groups and teachers make the point that the attainment of psychic and magical powers can be an impediment to real spiritual growth. But, is that really true? If the object of the Great Work is integration with the Higher Self to become more than we are, we have to presume the accompaniment of such powers and skill as natural to the Whole Person.

Jesus said, "Ye are Gods ... these things I do ye shall do and even greater." To me, that reads as both prophecy and promise; Jesus doesn't say we will become gods but that we are gods who will do miracles. As we grow in Wholeness, our latent powers become skills we can perform at will. We refer to this as "Self-Empowerment" because it is not given to us by others, nor do we have to be Christian for this to happen. On the other hand, merely having psychic powers does not make us a spiritually powerful person who has become Whole.

"A Shortcut to Initiation" is a program of psychological and spiritual integration leading to Self-Empowerment. It isn't the only way, but it is one way.

Qabalah of Numbers—of Names and Words. The alternate spelling of Kabbalah preferred by magicians and esoteric students.

Reduction. In the practice of numerology, larger numbers are—for the most part—"reduced" to single digit numbers in the manner demonstrated in the three examples.

Star, The. The seven-pointed star is the sigil of the Goddess Babalon. In the Tarot, the Star is the 17th Major Arcanum—image: a bright star overhead and most commonly a naked woman kneeling at the edge of a body of water pouring water from two vessels, sometimes one onto the ground but other times both into the water; Hebrew letter: Tzaddi; Divinatory meaning: spiritual guidance, hope, help; the 28th path on the Tree of Life connecting Yesod to Netzach.

Tarot. A vast system of Archetypal Knowledge condensed into a system of seventy-eight images on cards that can be finger-manipulated and then laid out in systematic patterns to answer specific questions or provide guidance to the solution of problems. While it is a form of divination, it is one of the most sophisticated and carefully developed systems of images and relationships following the structure of the Kabbalah's Tree of Life. Going beyond divination, it is also a system to access the Unconscious, and to structure magical ritual. It's a powerful Western esoteric system comparable to the Eastern I Ching.

As Culling noted: "The concepts of the Tarot cards have kept pace with the evolution of advancing knowledge, with the concepts and psychology of the European peoples." This is a very important point for it is fairly unique among occult divinatory systems for such evolution to take place. While interpretations of such systems as the I Ching will have some evolutionary change, the system and its physical representation in the sixty-four Hexagrams has remained static. The Tarot, in contrast, has changed, been modified, and evolved in physical form and structure, and in interpretation and application.

And there is interchange between the Tarot deck and the person using the deck, facilitated by the artwork, that—in my opinion—no other system has. The reader is "invited" to communicate with the cards, and that's one among many reasons that there are so many Tarot decks—over a thousand—to choose from.

Suggested Reading:

Amber K and Azrael Arynn K: *Heart of Tarot, an Intuitive Approach*

Ferguson: *The Llewellyn Tarot.* 78-card deck and 288-page book

Cicero, Chic and Tabatha: *The New Golden Dawn Ritual Tarot— Keys to the Rituals, Symbolism, Magic & Divination*

The "testing" of various intelligences. It has been a standard practice among astral traveling magicians to "test" the beings encountered by checking their names by their Qabalistic values.

Russell (Headquarters) is saying that "As long as you are an active, loyal, sincere aspirant to the Knowledge and Conversation of the Higher Guardian Angel, and using the oracle of the Yi, you cannot be a victim of 'alien' intelligences." Self-confident and knowing "that there is nothing outside of yourself that is not also within yourself (and which you are daily facing), is enough to keep you sincerely and correctly on the path of the Great Work."

It's another way of saying, "If your purpose be noble, and you're honest to yourself, you'll be okay." Or, "You have nothing to fear but fear itself." So, don't be afraid, and don't be seduced, stay with the purpose of your operation.

chapter six

The Group Ritual:

The Calypso Moon Language, the Enochian Language,
the Barbarous Words

Those who had performed the Magickal Retirement were then given a copy of the Group Ritual, which was to be performed regularly—weekly, without fail.

If a starting group could not muster enough to perform the individual parts then they could resort to a doubling up so that each member may undertake two roles.

Group Ritual Preparations

Here follows a list of the minimum of performers required, along with instructions for using a greater number of participants when available. (Note—Considering the fact that, in the event of absenteeism, it is sometimes necessary to have some performers "fill in," there should be those who have memorized more than one part to take care of this exigency.)

List of Performers

    1. Master of Ceremonies.

    2. King or Priest.

    3. Queen or Priestess.

    4. Acolyte.

    5. to 8. Four ritualists for the four corners, but one ritualist may take all four corners.

Furnishings of the Temple

ALTAR

Altar (this can be a simple square box).

A pair of dice is upon the altar. The die on the left has the number 6 facing upward. The die on the right has the number 1 facing upward.

QUARTER BANNERS

Four pieces of colored cloth should be hung at the quarters:

Yellow at the East.

Red at the South.

Blue at the West.

Green at the North.

There should also be four large open-top incense burners at the four corners, which the Acolyte has lighted before the ritual starts. He (or she, I will use "he" hereafter as convenience) has also prepared a swinging incense burner that he carries. The incense recipe has been given previously in chapter Four for the Retirement Ritual.

COSTUMES

Plain robes, with green stockings or green house slippers. The Master of Ceremonies and the King and Queen should wear some distinguishing marks or symbols, such as arm or head bands of gold for the King and silver for the Queen.

If there are four ritualists for the corners, each should have an arm or head band of a color corresponding to the banners.

PRONUNCIATION OF MAGICKAL WORDS

There is a distinct magickal importance to pronouncing the words used in the ritual correctly. Here are the rules for pronouncing the letters of the "Calypso Moon" language, the "Enochian" language, and the so-called "Barbarous" words. ("Barbarous" here is defined as "foreign; non-Hellenic, non-Roman, etc.")

A—as in the *a* in "father."

E—as in the *a* of "ate."

I—as in the *ee* of "meet."

O—as in the *o* in "note."

U—as in the *u* in "rule."

F—as in the *oo* of "book."

Ai—as in the word "eye."

GESTURES

Gestures to be used are the same as given in the Retirement Ritual, chapter 4. In addition, the following described Signs are to be traced by the Thumb-Wand. Make them about three feet in diameter. The Pentagrams and Hexagram are to be made in one continuous line. In the Rose Cross Sign the outer circle is drawn first, then the inner cross.

It is deemed advisable to explain a few points.

The first point is about the "averse" pentagram. While the more familiar manner of drawing the five-pointed star is with the single point upward, it is prevailing mental aberration of the ignorant to label as "Black Magic" the pentagram with two points upward. Actually, there is something of a difference between Invoking and Evoking in the positions of the points of the pentagram.

The second point deals with Invoking and Banishing pentagrams. Here I quote: "Banishing rituals have their good place, but in this ritual there is no banishing. Man is a microcosm or a macrocosm. There is no principle, force, or intelligences outside of you that is not also inside you. Wise up! If you are afraid of facing yourself, you are not of the worthy ones."

As to the Hexagram, it may take some practice to be able to freely trace the six-pointed star with one continuous line. For the Pentagrams, remember the four different starting points and note that one never starts from the two upper points.

The Four Pentagrams

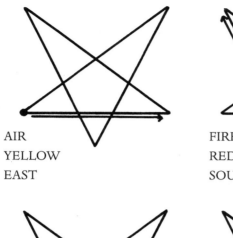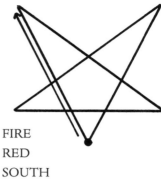

AIR
YELLOW
EAST

FIRE
RED
SOUTH

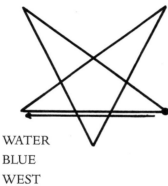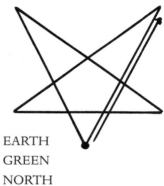

WATER
BLUE
WEST

EARTH
GREEN
NORTH

Hexagram

Rose Cross Sign

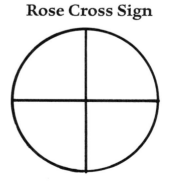

SILVER

Group Ritual Performance

1. The Master of Ceremonies makes the Sign of Opening the Temple.

2. Master of Ceremonies says: "Let the Rituals be rightly performed with joy and beauty."

3. As the Master of Ceremonies begins to speak the next sentence, the Acolyte immediately starts to pace the circle with the swinging incense burner.

4. Master of Ceremonies says: "My incense is of resinous woods and gums and there is no blood therein, because of my hair the trees of eternity."

5. One of the three principle officers says: "Be reminded, all of us, of the words delivered from the feminine aspect of Divinity—yea, also the words of the Holy Guardian Angel."

6. The Reader (who may be any of the officers, and who should be understood as speaking for all the participants) reads in an impressive voice—yea God-like:

   My number is eleven, as all their numbers who are of us. The Five-pointed Star with a Circle in the Middle, and the circle is Red. My color is black to the blind, but the blue and gold are seen of the seeing. Also I have a secret glory for them that love me.

   But to love me is better than all things: if under the night-stars in the desert thou presently burnest mine incense before me, invoking me with a pure heart, and the Serpent flame therein, thou shalt come a little to lie in my bosom. For one kiss wilt thou then be willing to give all; but whoso gives one particle of dust shall lose all in that hour...I love you! I yearn to you! Pale or purple, veiled or voluptuous, I who am all pleasure and purple, and drunkenness of the innermost sense, desire you. Put on the wings, and arouse the coiled splendor within you: come unto me!

   At all my meetings with you shall the priestess say—and her eyes shall burn with desire as she stands bare and rejoicing in my secret temple—To me! To me!—calling forth the flame of the hearts of all in her love-chant.

Sing the rapturous love-song unto me! Burn to me the per-
fumes! Wear to me the jewels! Drink to me, for I love you! I love
you!

I am the blue-lidded daughter of Sunset; I am the naked
brilliance of the voluptuous night-sky.

To me! To me!

The Master of Ceremonies again says, "Let the rituals be rightly performed with joy and beauty."

Everybody chants the four verses below in strict rhythm as shown,
while a female ritualist dances—just a swinging, pacing step around the
circle, going widdershins (counter clockwise), and at each corner makes
a complete turn-around, also widdershins.

To chant the following in strict and correct rhythm requires some
group practice. It is difficult to memorize these quasi-Enochian words
(called the "Moon Language') and therefore, at first, it would seem advisable to have a reader lead the group.

The rhythm can be scored as follows:

1	2 and	3	4,	1	2 and	3	4,	1 2	3 4,	1 2 3 4.
Mu	pa-te	la	i,	Tu	wa-me	la	i,	A	A,	A.
Tu	fu-tu	lu	u,	Tu	fu-tu	lu	u,	Pa	Sa,	Ga.
Qui	mu-te	la	i,	Ya	pa-me	la	i,	U	U,	U.
Se	gu-me	la	i,	Pe	fu-te	la	i,	Fu	Tu,	Lu.
O	chi-ba	la	i,	Wa	pa-ma	la	i,	Ut	Ut,	Ut.
Ge	fu-la	tra	i,	Le	fu-ma	la	i,	Kut	Hut,	Nut.
Al	rel-o	a	i,	Rel	a-mo	a	i,	Ti	Ti,	Ti.
Wa	la-pe	la	i,	Tu	fu-la	ta	i,	Wi	Ni,	Bi.

Then all retire—rapidly but orderly.

The English translation of the four verses is as follows:

Silence! The moon stands still.
That also was sweet
In the air, in the air, in the air!
Who will shall attain!
Who will shall attain!
By the Moon, by Myself, by the Angel.

Now silence ceases,
The moon waxes sweet,
The hour of Initiation, Initiation, Initiation,
My own Will is ended,
For Will hath attained.

Behold the lion-child swims
And the Moon reels:
It is Thou, Thou, Thou.
Triumph, the Will retreats,
The Strong Will that staggered
Before Ra Hoor Khuit!—Hadit!—Nuit!

To the God OAI
Be praised
In the end and the beginning;
And none may fall
Who will attain
The Sword, the Balance, and the Crown.

Everybody stands in the sign of veneration (the Eagle), while the Priest
or Priestess intones:

> *Thou Guardian Angel, Thou immortal Daemon, that art the es-*
> *sence of every True Man and every True Woman, continuing our sacred*
> *Magick from generation unto generation, we commemorate those Great*
> *Initiates of old that did adore thee and manifest thy glory. Particularly*

do we name these great ones of our Order: Pan, Babalon, Proteus, Si-
mon Magus, DeMolay the martyr, Dee and Kelley, Thomas Vaughan
and Diana Vaughan, and Richard Wagner. May their essence and force
be here present and potent to aid and guard us in this Great Work of
Art.

Now comes the section of invoking the aid of the four powers, at the
four corners—Air/East, Fire/South, Water/West, Earth/North. In the
group ritual, it is well that the four corners be taken by four ritualists,
even if for no other reason than the difficulty of memorizing the part so
that one may operate without any effort to exercise the memory—no
clumsy hesitation.

FIRST CORNER—AIR/EAST

1. The ritualist advances to the East and traces a large Air Pentagram, visualized in glowing yellow color.

2. Ritualist makes the Sign of the Enterer and holds it while intoning
   the magick words and feeling a penetration into and through the
   Pentagram, deeper and deeper.

3. The magick words: "Ar Thiaoo Rheibet—A-thele-ber-set—A Belatha Abeu Ebeu—Pni-theta-soe Ib Thiaoo."

4. Makes and holds the Sign of "Isis in Welcome" while saying: "Powers of Air, come thou forth and aid and guard us in this Work of
   Art." Makes the Rose Cross sign upon the corner and retires.

SECOND CORNER—FIRE/SOUTH

1. Ritualist advances to the South and traces a large Fire Pentagram,
   visualized in red.

2. Makes the Sign of the Enterer, holding it while intoning the magick
   words, feeling that he is penetrating deeper and deeper into and
   through the Pentagram.

3. Intones these magick words: "Ar-O-go-go-Ru-Abrao—Sotou Mudorio Pnalarthao OOO Aepe."

4. Makes the Sign of "Isis in Welcome" saying: "Great red Power of Fire, come thou forth and aid and guard us in this work of art." Makes R.C. sign on the corner and retires.

THIRD CORNER—WATER/WEST

1. Ritualist advances to the West and traces a large Water Pentagram in the air, visualized in blue.

2. Makes the Sign of the Enterer, holding it, and penetrating deeper and deeper into the Pentagram as he intones the magick words.

3. Intones these magick words: "Ru-abra-Iao—Mriodom Babalon-Bel-Bin-Abaot. Asal-on-ai Aphen-Iao I Photeth Abrasax Aeoou Ischure." (Note: At first, it is better to intone only the first half of the words rather than to bungle the whole thing.)

4. Makes the Sign of "Isis in Welcome" while saying: "Great Blue Power of Water, come thou forth and aid and guard us in this work of art." Makes the R.C. sign on corner and retires.

FOURTH CORNER—EARTH/NORTH

1. Ritualist advances to the North and traces a large Earth Pentagram in the air, visualized in green.

2. Makes the Sign of the Enterer, holding it while feeling as if he is penetrating deeper and deeper into and through the Pentagram, and intoning the magick words.

3. Intones: "Ma Barraio Ioel Kotha Athor-e-eBal-o Abraoot."

4. Makes the Sign of "Isis in Welcome" while saying: "Come thou forth, Great Green Power of Earth, and aid and guard us in this work of art." Makes the R.C. sign on corner, and retires.

Next follows the Invocation of Thoth. When a group has not yet practiced the ritual for a sufficient number of times, and the total job of memorizing is still too much for the ritualists, then this Invocation may be read by the "Reader," but the Reader should be able to read it easily and with feeling.

As in all parts of the ritual where words are spoken, the other ritualists and members should hold the sign of the "Balanced Eagle" (which you should know has the meaning of "Countenance beholding Countenance").

(Note: The Invocation of Thoth is to be found in a later section of this book.)

The Invocation of Thoth may be substituted by the following aspiring words. Until well memorized it may be given by the "Reader." The Reader, as in all cases, should read the part in an imposing way as though it were the voice of some demi-god who "aids and guards" in the "work of art."

> *Oh sublime Goddess Nuit, may your words bring the light to every ultimate particle of our bodies as we hear you say, "But to love me is better than all things: if under the night-stars in the desert thou presently burn mine incense before me, invoking me with a pure heart, and the serpent flame therein, thou shalt come a little to lie in my bosom. For one kiss wilt thou then be willing to give all; but whoso gives one particle of dust shall lose all in that hour. I charge you earnestly to come before me in a single robe, covered with a rich headdress. I love you! I yearn to you! Pale or purple, veiled or voluptuous, I who am all pleasure and purple, and drunkenness of the innermost sense, desire you. Put on the wings, and arouse the coiled splendor within you: come unto me!*
>
> *"Sing the rapturous love-song unto me! Burn to me perfumes! Wear to me jewels! Drink to me, for I love you! I love you!*
>
> *"I am the blue-lidded daughter of Sunset; I am the naked brilliance of the voluptuous night-sky.*
>
> *"To me! To me!"*

When the words have reached the point of "Pale or purple …," all members should advance rapidly to perhaps ideally a long, shelf-like bench or table, upon which is an individual small glass of wine for each one and which is taken in one single draught at the words "To me! To me!" This should be done in a manner in which there is no distraction—artistically.

While orderly returning to their places, the members should slowly and rhythmically chant: "Let there be no part of me that is unworthy of the Gods."

The Master of Ceremonies (King or Priest) advances to the center and traces the six-pointed star overhead, and then intones the following:

"Aoot Abaoot Bas-aumgn. Isak Sabaoot."

Then, in the sign of the Eagle, says: "Oh nameless sacred One, grant thy benediction upon us," and then continues with: "Ieou Pur Iou Pur Iaooth Iaeo Ede Edu Angelos Ton Theon Anlala Lai Gaia Aepe Diatharna Thoron." (Note: If at first these words are difficult to memorize, then only a few may be used until such time as the entire is learned.)

Then the entire membership intones:

> *Above the gemmed azure is*
> *The naked splendor of Nuit;*
> *She bends in ecstasy to kiss*
> *The secret ardours of Hadit.*
> *Also says Nuit—I am above you and in you. My ecstasy is*
> *in yours. My joy is to see your joy.*

All assume the Sign of the Eagle. The priest or priestess advances to the center, and intones the following invocation:

> *Now we begin to pray. O Circle of Stars, marvel beyond imagination, before whom time is ashamed, the mind bewildered and the understanding dark, not unto thee may we attain unless thine image be love. Let it be the love of and unto the Guardian Angel, the Holy Daemon. For this do we seek the Knowledge and Conversation of the Holy Guardian Angel, each individual for his or her Holy Daemon. Therefore let us now invoke the WORD of the Holy Daemon.*

At this point, the King and Queen immediately advance to the altar, where they face each other with crossed arms, i.e., with the arms extended each clasps the right hand of the other with his own right hand and the left hand of the other with his own left hand. All others remain in the Eagle Sign.

The King says:

> *The Daemon of each man and of each woman hath said, "I am above you and in you. My ecstasy is in yours. My joy is to see your joy."*

The Queen says:

> *Above the gemmed azure is the naked splendor of Nuit; She bends in ecstasy to kiss the secret ardours of Hadit.*
>
> *Unity uttermost manifest. I adore the might of thy breath. Supreme and beautiful God who maketh the Gods and Death to tremble before thee, we adore thee.*

The King then uses his right hand to manipulate the die which has the number 1 face up. He turns it over in various directions but never allows the fingers to lose contact with the die. When he finally has the feeling to stop, he looks at the number that is then face up. If it is an odd number—1, 3, or 5—it is male; if it is an even number—2, 4, or 6—it is female.

He calls out "Male" or "Female," whichever it is, and the person who is designated as the Recorder writes down a line—a whole line for male or a broken line for female.

The Queen does exactly the same thing with her die which had the number 6 face up.

The King and Queen go through this procedure three times each. They have thus designed a figure that has six lines. The Pa Kua figure is built from the bottom to the top.

The King then reads from *LIBER HEXAGRAMMATON* what the Oracle of this figure is. Each member considers this to be a "conversation" from the Holy Daemon, and regards and follows it faithfully until the next meeting.

Yes, each member regards the Oracle with veneration. It is viewed as the "Conversation of the Holy Guardian Angel" and each member abides by the Oracle until the next ensuing ritual.

King, Priest, or Master of Ceremonies now proceeds to close the Temple. All present stand in the Sign of the Eagle.

The King says:

*Now let there be a veiling of this shrine. May the Light penetrate every
ultimate particle of your bodies. May you accomplish the Great Work,
which is True Wisdom, Perfect Happiness, and the consummation of
your True Self—which is the Knowledge and Conversation of the Holy
Guardian Angel.*

All respond together:
   "So mote it be!"

The King makes the Sign for Closing the Temple.

Commentary

Group vs. Solitary Ritual and the Source of Magickal Power

The rituals in this book were written for group performance, as one would
expect for a Magickal Order. Yet, most "seekers" today do not belong to a
group and modern American, more often prefer to be solitaries.

Before offering suggestions on how to covert a group ritual to the
needs of a solitary person, let's discuss the theoretical advantages and
disadvantages of ceremonial groups. But, before doing so, we need to
distinguish between a group and an association or a community.

Many people belong to a society, such as the Theosophical Society or the Rosicrucian AMORC. Many of these have local lodges or
fellowships that present lectures and facilitate study groups and some
have members who can officiate at weddings and funerals much like
a church. Some have weekly services just like a church or temple. For
the convenience of discussion, let's call these "associations." Most associations have some type of legal charter and a formal declaration of
membership benefits.

I also want to provide a definition of a "community" as an informal
collection of people, not necessarily local, of like interests often facilitated by the Internet. If, for example, you are interested in astrology,
you are a member of the astrological community. Because you may buy
astrology books or the services of an astrologer, you may be on a mail-
ing list of people interested in astrology. You may attend lectures, even

go to conferences and conventions, but you don't have to belong to an association to be part of the astrological community.

Right now, because you're reading this book—for whatever reason—you are a member of the Magickal community. That doesn't make you a member of a group; nine chances out of ten you are a "solitary."

The book suggests that there is value of getting a group together to work these rituals, and mentions a minimal number of three, and the ritual given here has roles for four or eight ritualists. In a densely populated area, a lodge, church, coven, or a "circle" can be conveniently organized. But for those living in rural areas, such participation is impractical.

Two people make a "couple," but three or more can make a "group." Today there are Golden Dawn, O∴T∴O∴, O∴T∴A∴, A∴S∴, Wiccan Covens, and other Ceremonial groups (both Pagan and Christian) that you can join for instruction, training, practice, and initiation.

Aside from the community interest, what does a group provide—at least potentially?

If you enjoy drama, then what you have is called "ritual drama." You can think of it as a play with stage props, a script, and costumes.

But that same ritual drama can be a magickal ritual. You can have a magickal ritual as a solitary, but there are advantages and disadvantages to working magick in a group.

In the following discussion, please remember that the goal of the G∴B∴G∴ was entirely to facilitate Initiation in sense of integrating Lower and Higher Selves. Initiation is not simply an admission rite or a degree or grade recognition. In the most esoteric terms, Initiation is a spiritual transition in which one "crosses the Abyss," "encounters the Dweller on the Threshold," or—in Jungian psychology—becomes "Integrated," making the self whole.

Here are some possible advantages:

1. You can meet people seriously interested in Magick.

2. Members often help one another in their study; sometimes that is an obligation of seniority.

3. A group of people can produce a lot of energy together. We call that "Power."

4. As a member, you yourself may share in the benefits of that Power even if you don't know how to contribute Power to the group.

5. Group Power can either benefit practical goals or facilitate transformative experiences ranging from healings to Initiation.

6. (However, an Initiation Ritual may not actually result in "Initiation" in the sense of psychological and spiritual integration no matter how good it feels!)

7. A practical magical ritual can also function in spell-casting for such benefits as getting a job interview, helping secure a loan or mortgage, meeting someone special, blessing a new business venture, etc.

But, among the possible disadvantages:

a. You can meet someone ready to cause you harm.

b. Sometimes, you may lose energy to the group, and actually suffer a wasting disease.

c. Sometimes, you may pick up psychic parasites from the group.

d. Unless the group is truly local, participation can be expensive and inconvenient.

Where does Power come from?

Essentially, Magickal Power comes from "within" and may be biological or spiritual, or both. It is facilitated by such techniques as:

- Chanting. Whether solitary or in a group, chanting can produce a lot of energy. In a very harmonious group, that energy seems to build on itself and can become very substantial. Sometimes singing can be equally effective.

- Dancing, or other movement. Movement either expends energy or generates energy. Moving in a Circle particularly seems to generate energy, and through circular movement can condense it and then release it to function under Intention, or Will.

- Spirit, or whatever you want to call it. At our core, there is a Creative Force that animates us and it sometimes responds to personal or group direction.

- Kundalini—also called "Sex Energy." Sexual activity and yogi postures can activate this energy, which may be directed through meditation and visualization to other parts of the body, the chakras, and even beyond the body. It is often identified with "charisma."

- A battery! Some people seem able to charge the solar plexus with excess biological energy. Particular swaying and bowing movements as among Hasidic groups often leads to ecstatic experiences.

- Food, drink, and drugs. For the most part, there are serious disadvantages with their use for energy purposes.

Power is Power, but it isn't always reliable. I'm not a Catholic, but many of my family are and I have been involved in two wedding services where the officiating priest was drunk. In one case, the priestly power was as flat as yesterday's champagne; in the other there was so much priestly power that people starting dancing before the service was over!

When I was younger, I headed a small Wiccan/Magical group, and at times we had so much energy within our small circle that people were shaking and even ecstatic, and sometimes fainting from too much. I've participated in sending such energy—the Cone of Power—long distance to effect an instantaneous cure of a tumor.

Most people have experienced similar group energy at music concerts and dances; some have experienced it through shamanic activities or evangelical or Hasidic services. Others have experienced solitary energy through prayer and meditative practices, and couples experience such energy with Tantra and extended sexual activity.

Power is Power, and Power can be transformative. But Power alone will not bring about the Initiative Experience of the Knowledge and Conversation of the Holy Guardian Angel. Power can help in clearing away the physical and psychological debris that gets in the way of our growth into a Whole Person.

There can be lot of power in a harmonious groups, whereas one that is divisive is like a dead battery, or even worse. A solitary practitioner can "home grow" all the power he or she needs.

The Solitary Ritualist

Ritual is really a disciplined exercise directing energies towards an established goal. In "practical" magic (sometimes called "spell-casting") that goal is usually mundane and involves money, sex (love), and power in the social or political sense. In "high" magick, the goal is spiritual growth and attainment called here "Initiation."

Does a solitary practitioner need ritual?
Any disciplined exercise is a ritual, and to get what you want requires it.

What are some of the benefits of such exercise?
One of the most important strengths to be gained is a trained imagination, also called "visualization." Visualization facilitates Meditation and Self-Hypnosis—both of considerable value in psycho-spiritual growth and attainment.

There is value to adapting group ritual to solitary use, firstly because of the training and skill development involved and secondly when an established ritual is used all the symbols, the chanting, the words of power, the archetypal play, the body movements and gestures, etc., is focused in the one person without distortion from other group members.

The simplest approach is to learn the various roles and the words to be spoken, and to imagine yourself in the main role—the priest or priestess at the center of the circle and visualize all the other roles unfolding in your imagination. In addition, you have to "hear" the voices and "feel" the movements. You need to experience the emotions and experience the ecstasy.

You can do it, and it works. The ritual is from the *Book of the Law.*

The Group Ritual

As is well demonstrated by the size and wealth of many churches and religious organizations, there can be a business-like functional value to the group.

Does that apply to a working magickal or other esoteric organization?

The evidence is not always positive. Many groups organized around a charismatic teacher may continue to exist upon that person's death, but—to use Culling's terminology from the previous chapter—they usually lose their "dispensation" and are no longer effective.

What are the functions of a magickal or spiritual group?

a. To teach beginners.

b. To facilitate dramatic rituals.

c. Those dramatic rituals can be performed for the benefit of a single person, or for the group itself, or for an audience that may or may not participate in some minor way.

d. Possibly, to also provide such personal services as weddings, funerals, etc.

e. To financially support staff and physical facilities to carry out other proclaimed missions to the public—including education, medical work, charitable functions, etc., but often these are "fronts" for the larger goal of proselytizing, i.e., conversion of non-believers.

f. In practice, some religious groups will have the priestly leader carry on a separate and nearly private service on behalf of the congregation, the local building, a magio-religious ritual to bridge between God and Humanity. Usually that local leader is also the local fund-raiser and business manager.

Of these six, only "b" cannot readily be provided in other ways—often better ways. But if we grant the positive value of dramatic ritual, the power of the group is demonstrable. Yes, as pointed out elsewhere, it is possible to perform an entire group ritual or drama in your imagination.

Just recall the last movie you've seen, and you will easily re-experience the drama with the roles played by each character. And, yes, such ritual dramas could be performed professionally before cameras and made available on DVDs to support the solitary's experience via imagination and meditation just as books support "a," the learning experience.

For a group performance, as in the ritual presented in this chapter, you commonly have three or more roles to fill: that of the officiating priest or master of ceremonies and the masculine and feminine actors. In addition, you can provide a main assistant, and up to four ritualist assistants.

Ultimately, solitary or group, the decision is yours. The important point I feel obligated to make is that for the goal of Initiation, solitary can be as good as group. And, ultimately, it is what you do yourself that initiates Initiation!

Definitions and Discussion Points

Altar. An altar is really a workbench holding your magickal tools. Usually it is placed at the center of the circle or working area. Sometimes it may be moved to face any of the four corners. Traditionally it is composed of two equal size cubes, one on top of the other.

Babalon. Mother Earth. Also "the Scarlet Woman" as the ruling spirit of Earth.

Barbarous Words. These are really "words of power," whether intelligible or not. Originally, the name comes from the languages spoken by the "barbarians," those who did not speak Greek when the Greeks thought they had invented civilization.

In ritual, barbarous words and names don't have to make sense or be understood by the ritualist. Many are derived from Hebrew, ancient Egyptian, and Persian; some are based on the Enochian language provided to us by Dr. John Dee. Rather than rational sense, they make emotional sense with the drama.

There is some evidence—see *Magic, Power, Language, Symbol: A Magician's Exploration of Linguistics,* by Patrick Dunn—that experienced magicians created certain barbarous words without regard to proper language but entirely to have a magical effect. Or, rather, the magician spontaneously speaks these words without plan as if derived from or through the sub-conscious mind. It is, perhaps, related to "speaking in tongues" where a person speaks with no awareness of what she is saying.

Black Magic. Magic performed to cause harm. Culling's point about "it is prevailing mental aberration of the ignorant to label as 'Black Magic' the pentagram with two points upward" is that it is not the tools of magic that are evil but only the intentions of the magician. A pentagram is a pentagram no matter which end is up; a knife is a knife no matter how it is used, and a gun is a gun no matter it held by a policeman or a murderer.

Calypso Moon Language. I am rather at a loss to give definition to this. Culling calls it a quasi-Enochian Language. Researching, I find that Calypso is a West Indian musical style influenced by jazz; it's also a small species of orchid (*Calypso borealis*), having a flower variegated with purple, pink, and yellow that grows in cold, bog-like localities in the northern part of the United States. Calypso is also the name of a tiny moon of the planet Saturn, discovered in 1980, and in 1983 named for the goddess Calypso who detained Odysseus for seven years in Homer's *Odyssey*. And, finally, it is a fashion in which women tie a knot in their shirt and expose their waist. There is some indication that it closely resembles modern Greek.

Dee, Sir John. (1527–1608) With Edward Kelley as clairvoyant, the source for the Enochian language and the eighteen Enochian Calls.

Dice for form Yi King Hexagrams. The same six-sided cubes are commonly used in gambling as well as divination. The particular technique here is a unique method for determining Hexagrams.

Enochian Language. (Also known as the Language of the Angels, and the Secret Angelic Language) The words transcribed by Dr. John Dee (1527–1608) and Edward Kelly in their spiritual contacts, starting in 1582, were eventually seen to form a genuine language as well as a system of magic.

"Enochian" is pronounced "Eh-no-kee-an," and is supposedly the same language spoken by the angel Ave to the prophet Enoch, whose name in Hebrew is spelled *Heh Nun Vav Kaph*.

Gestures. The different positions and motions of the hands are as important as the signs—or positions and movements—in magickal and religious ritual, and in energy healing. They are also found in various ecstatic and shamanic dances. They are not "empty" gestures as a little experimentation will readily show.

Hexagram. A six-pointed star traditionally composed of two equilateral triangles like the Jewish "Star of David." The upright triangle is male, the reverse triangle is female, and their union is both whole and Divine.

Kelley, Edward. (1555–1595) Dr. Dee's assistant. As a clairvoyant he could see the angels and what they were doing.

LIBER HEXAGRAM ATON. Liber Yi King. See Appendix Two, The Oracular Meanings of the 64 Hexagrams. While not available when the G∴B∴G∴ was first published, today the choice would be Culling's own *The Pristine Yi King*.

Pan. The Greek god of nature, with a human head and torso and the hind legs, ears, and horns of a goat. Also symbolic of the male sexual drive.

Pentagram. A five-pointed star.

Simon Magus. Also known as Simon the Sorcerer, he was a native of Gitta. Possessing great magical powers, he described himself as a "son of God," and that we were all gods in the making imprisoned in matter. In this sense, he is considered the founder of Gnosticism.

There were accusations by Christians that he was a demon in human form, and he was specifically said to possess the ability to levitate and fly at will. The fantastic stories of Simon the Magician persisted into the Middle Ages, and were possibly inspiration for Goethe's Faust.

He was the Emperor Nero's Court Magician for whom he did many demonstrations, among them the moving about of heavy furniture untouched by human hands. Legend has it that while performing magic, he levitated to prove himself a god. St. Peter prayed to God to stop his flying, and Simon fell to the ground, and later died of his wounds.

His constant companion was a woman he called Helen of Troy. Within Helen was the Spirit of God, leading to the Gnostic belief that the true God has a feminine part called Spirit. The Gnostics further held that God the Father was accompanied by God the Mother, sometimes called Sophia, or the Wisdom of God. In the Old Testament written in Hebrew the Spirit of God is referred to as Ruach and has a feminine gender.

Solitary. A practitioner of Magick working alone rather than in a group.

Vaughan, Thomas (1622–1665). Welsh alchemist, Qabalist and mystic— "the spirit of man is itself the spirit of the Living God"—as Above, so Below. He translated many alchemical works, including the *Fama Fraternitatis* and *Confessio Fraternitatis* into English and wrote a number of important magical and alchemical works under the pseudonym "Eugenius Philalethes." Vaughan's works include *Anthrosophia Theomagia, a Discourse of the Nature of Man and his State after Death* (1650), *Anima Magia Abscondita, a Discourse of the Universal Spirit of Nature* (1650) *Magia Adamica, the Antiquity of Magic* (1650), *Coelum Terrae, the Magician's Heavenly Chaos, Unfolding a Doctrine Concerning the Terrestrial Heaven* (1650), *Lumen de Lumine, a New Magical Light* (1651), *Aula Lucis, the House of Light* (1651), *The Fame and Confession of the Fraternity of the Rose Cross* (1652), and *Euphrates, the Waters of the East* (1655).

Vaughan was killed in an explosion during an alchemical experiment.

Wagner, Richard (1813–1883). Wagner regarded himself as "the most German of men" who projected "the German spirit" in his thirteen operas and other compositions. He is best known for "The Wedding March," familiar to most married couples. He was also a vociferous writer of about 230 books and articles. He was a vegetarian and a socialist, and has been called an anarchist, a nationalist, and even a fascist and anti-Semite. Hitler adored Wagner, and was often heard humming his operas.

chapter seven

Magickal Writing:

Imprinting the Yi King

Next on the Curriculum was the learning of a special Magickal writing alphabet. There was actually only one purpose for this alphabet. It was in conjunction with a practice in which the instruction was to write certain given sentences in eight different ways, as follows:

1. All letters of the sentence to be written deosil (in a clockwise motion), from left to right as in normal writing.

2. Next from left to right, but with all letters made widdershins (counter clockwise).

3. Same as in number '1' except that the sentence is written from right to left.

4. Same as in number '2' except from right to left.

5. Same as number '1' except written upside down.

6. Same as number '2' except written upside down.

7. Same as number '3' except written upside down.

8. Same as number '4' except written upside down.

(Note: It is most important that the pencil never leave the paper in this magickal writing; write continuously.)

This makes a total of eight different ways of writing. Now the English alphabet script does not lend itself to being written either deosil or widdershins in one continuous line without the pencil leaving the paper, so it was necessary to learn the special G.·.B.·.G.·. alphabet.

One cannot be blamed for thinking that this is a rather senseless exercise which accomplishes nothing much, but it has been definitely proven that attaining proficiency in this exercise accomplishes the "Magick" of leading one psychologically to regard any idea from four different standpoints. This enlarges the scope of the perceptive mind, and encourages intuition. It tends also to kill out any dogmatic tendency.

It seems relevant to quote a very valuable axiom from Aleister Crowley—"No idea is worth entertaining unless it can be seen how, where, and why its opposite is equally true."

While the importance of this writing in different ways remains true, a later practice of still greater value was substituted for the G∴B∴G∴ alphabet. The eight Pa Kua of the Yi King are ideal in this practice because the Pa Kua is an intimate part of the magickal workings.

The Instruction:

> Let the feet and legs be bare. Sit in a comfortable position. Concentrate all your attention and awareness on the inner anklebone with the idea that you are "printing" one of the Pa Kua upon the skin. Continue this concentration for ten minutes. Some good success is indicated when that portion of the skin seems to become sensitive. Some have even been able to cause that portion of the skin to blush red during the practice.
>
> As one becomes more efficient in the concentration, five minutes will be sufficient for each evening practice, and therefore not too much time is required to extend the concentration to all parts of the body. Before one has thus covered the whole body one is ready to go deeper—and should do so.

Any practice that is worthy of the name "shortcut", or of being termed "very efficient," should accomplish several goals—or aid toward several accomplishments.

The virtues of this practice of imprinting the Yi King on the body are:

1. It is a very efficient method of attaining the ability to concentrate.

2. Facile concentration is a must for a good "Magickal Imagination," which is in turn a must for magickal work. Furthermore the fac-

ulty of "awareness" is important and it is enhanced by the ability in both concentration and imagination.

3. As one "prints" upon the skin and flesh one should mentally "imagine" that every ultimate particle of the body is penetrated by the "Great Black Light" which is, in effect, being more spiritualized to the "Knowledge and Conversation of the Daemon, or Holy Guardian Angel." In different words, one is being psychologically conditioned in the "Great Work."

Note: The foregoing practice was given forth by a high Initiate of German birth, named Koenig, and was set to print in a now rare book, *Man and His Highest Purpose.*

It is well to again remind the neophyte that the G.·.B.·.G.·. (with good cause) did not use the complicated and difficult postures of the Far East; on the contrary, a comfortable position is advised, which in some cases may mean sitting upright and, in other cases, taking a reclining position.

One should have good respect for this thing called "Imagination"— the *Imago* is a manifestation of the force of Spirit. To those having proper respect for the word "imagination," it can be told that the Magickal Imagination may well be over 50 percent of the total of Magick itself. Naturally, it is meant that kind of Imagination that is brought to a point of "Subjective Reality" and most certainly never the non-willed and uncontrolled ramblings of what can hardly be called "mind" in the undisciplined person.

Commentary

The Importance of the Magickal Imagination & Visualization

As magical training, both the Magickal Writing and Yi King Imprinting are interesting.

There's a lot than can be said about such exercises, but the first challenge is to take them seriously. As Culling writes: "One cannot be blamed for thinking that this is a rather senseless exercise which accomplishes nothing much, but it has been definitely proven that attaining proficiency in this exercise accomplishes the 'Magick' of leading one psychologically to regard any idea from four different standpoints."

It reminds me of the three-dimensional chess that Kirk and Spock used to play on the classic *Star Trek* television episodes, and the various attempts I've seen for three-dimensional Enochian Chess. Just like the practice of imprinting Hexagrams upon the body, these are exercises that develop Concentration and Visualization abilities.

Culling points out that the Magickal Imagination is a major factor in Magick itself—to the point where "Subjective Reality" is equal to "Normal Reality." At some point, "Inner" can be substituted for "Outer," and that which is imaged happens.

Imago is an idealized mental picture that can be recalled in its perfection at any time. While still in the realm of the Imagination, Culling describes it as a manifestation of the "Force of Spirit," taking it beyond ordinary imaginary images. To illustrate, the *Imago* was the name of the death mask worn in a special ritual on behalf of the deceased in ancient Rome to establish his immortality. Similarly, I once had a dream about a "Life Mask" to be molded when a person was at their peak, and then worded ritually to enforce that image of youth, strength, and beauty.

The Magickal Imagination is that process at work—an *Imago* of perfection imposed to change ordinary reality into the ideal.

Imprinting Images on the Body

The I Ching consists of sixty-four Hexagrams making a very structured alphabet of energy diagrams. Each hexagram is a particular combination of Yin and Yang Trigrams, each not merely representing a schema of those energies but a kind of transducer to bring their macrocosmic form into the microcosmic. As they are imprinted on the body, the result is that those energies emerge into the local consciousness.

I have very little experience with the Yi King, but it is quite understandable that imprinting any particular Hexagram could lead to some very interesting developments in healing, programming behavior as in weight loss, etc. Imprinting them all is like having sixty-four energy switches at ready command.

Look at an image of the body mapping all the "meridians" of energy in the system of Chinese medicine and perceive that those imprinted switches now provide voluntary control for their movement and action.

The Twenty-Five Tattwa Symbols

The Golden Dawn developed some similar practices using the Indian Tattwa symbols representing the five elements (Earth, Water, Fire, Air, and Spirit) and their twenty-five combinations (Earth of Fire, Water of Air, etc.) where the student would enter into the astral realm of the visualized symbol and otherwise use the charged images in magical practice.

With new understanding of quantum theory, "subjective reality" finds new expression in Magickal practice.

Definitions and Discussion Points

Awareness. Awareness is something of a corollary to concentration. We are used to thinking of it as passive in sensory perception but it changes dramatically when used actively. Your perceptions can be extended with expanded awareness, and what was invisible can become visible, or heard, or tasted, or sensed. To become more aware is to become enriched. And becoming aware is not limited to objects and people, but includes energies pulsing through and around objects, persons, and their environment.

Through extended awareness, we grow and develop our latent psychic powers into reliable skills.

Postures, and Movements, East and West. Culling is primarily referring to Eastern yogic postures along with controlled breathing, and our familiar Western postures of standing and sitting. In addition, postures involve intentional movement—even if just sitting with grace and awareness of energy flow. There are, of course, other postures: those of the martial arts in China and Japan, belly and dervish dances in the Middle East, the hula from Hawaii, and much more. Any movement and posture that involves energy probably has an associated shamanic or sacred tradition.

The Western Esoteric Tradition has adopted the Egyptian God postures as seen in paintings on tomb and temple walls. Whether standing, moving, or seated, these show positions of dignity and energy restraint. You can sense power that would be released in a simple gesture.

"Special G.·.B.·.G.·. alphabet." This remains a mystery to me. Culling wrote me on March 8, 1968, "I should not have made mention of the special alphabet. This was a technic of Russell to build up his own Magickal Strength but with no benefit to members. Of course the four ways of writing—forwards, backwards and the same upside down is valuable & not to be deleted." However, since the alphabet mention was not cut out of the first edition, I chose to leave it in the second edition, adding this note.

chapter eight

The Book of the Law: Thelema

Sex Magick: Alphaism—the First Degree

In order to keep the minds and feelings of the members who were in the practice of Alphaism (explained in a later chapter) occupied, it was decided by Headquarters to provide intensive mental work in another channel. Each member in the referenced grade was required to make a copy of the first chapter of Aleister Crowley's *The Book of the Law*. This book consists of three short chapters, which total only twenty-seven pages, and was published as a very small volume.

The occult name of Crowley's book is "Liber Al," which Qabalistically numbers 31, which is one third of the formula of "Thelema" or Will, 93. The Greek word "Thelema" does not mean willpower in *The Book of the Law*, but has a wider and profounder implication.

The central aim of Western Magick, as first instituted in the nineties of the previous millenium in the Hermetic Order of the Golden Dawn, is to attain to the "Knowledge and Conversation of the Holy Guardian Angel"—the Daemon, one's true spiritual identity. This aim was taught in the Golden Dawn, then descended to Crowley's A∴A∴ and the O∴T∴O∴, and then to the G∴B∴G∴, but the word "Thelema" did not appear until the giving forth of *The Book of the Law*, at the Spring Equinox of the year 1904.

Thelema implies drawing closer and closer to the consciousness of one's real Individuality (the Khabs), in contradistinction to the active conscious Personality (the Khu). It then becomes the aim of the aspirant to be and to express one's True Individuality as much as possible, instead of being submerged in the Personality.

The key to the cryptic word "Thelema"—Will—is to recognize and "Do the True Will in conformity with the Conversation of the H G A, the Daemon."

Incidentally, the foregoing is a good example of the crypticisms to be found in *The Book of the Law*.

The instructions from Headquarters to the Alphaist members was to begin with the first verse of the first chapter of *The Book of the Law*, and take one sentence every day, in sequence, and meditate on that sentence; one sentence, not one entire verse.

"Beware most rigidly," the instructions said, "against making an intellectual study of this book. This is a very cryptic book, and is beyond intellectual rationalization. Get what you are capable of getting by inspired meditation." Concentration is a better word for what is required here.

The dictionary defines "meditation" as "To contemplate, to muse, to reflect." This state can go farther, into reverie, and one is likely to slip into near sleep. Passive meditation is a negative, dreamy state which is of no value here. It is possible in such a state to wander into hallucinations and visions. These last can sometimes be useful in Magick, when they can be made subjectively real.

Concentration, on the other hand, is defined as "close mental application or exclusive attention." When one is working out the cube root of 4,913 (the answer is 17), one is concentrating, not meditating. The mental activity is confined to a definite point. When one visualizes tracing a pentagram in green light, one must really concentrate in order to make it subjectively real.

Concentration on one sentence of *The Book of the Law* for at least an uninterrupted fifteen minutes should be practiced at least once a day; though one can and should concentrate at other times of the day even if for a few minutes only. Incidentally, this becomes a form of Yoga breathing, without effort and intention—all to the good.

The members of the G∴B∴G∴ were put to a great task in trying to get something from "Liber Al," working from scratch. The G∴B∴G∴ students had no idea as to what the *Book* implied, whereas students working under Crowley had the benefit of his commentaries on the *Book*.

As I see it, the aspirant deserves to have the benefit of some comment, and to satisfy this need I shall give a short commentary of my own, which has been approved by Crowley himself. Most of it I gleaned from Crowley's own writings.

Religion and psychology are so generally interrelated that, in their evolution, there may be said to be many distinctions without differences. The advances and demands of both psychology and religion are concomitant. There is an involved question as to whether the "inspired prophet" gives impetus by his words to this evolution, or whether the self-created need of the people gives rise to the stimulus of the prophet. It is, however, rather a sterile speculation for the active and devoted disciple in Magick.

The significant point is the nature of the Prophet of "Liber Al" in relation to the necessity of a people. A prophet worthy of the name is at least conscious of the demand for evolution in Magick, even though the people's awareness of their need may still lie submerged in the subconscious. And the prophet serves to bring this into more conscious awareness.

The *Book* is an inspired document prophetic of a "New Aeon," called the Aeon of Horus, the Redeemer. The Old Aeon, or Patriarchal Aeon should lie down and die, but it persists in a most determined, although subtle, way. Its very subtlety gives it a tricky persistence.

People at large are so drenched in the propaganda of the Old Aeon that it was an almost miraculous phenomenon that a capable prophet, Aleister Crowley-666, arose above the morass and was able to receive and be a channel for the word of the revolutionary New Aeon. It can hardly be denied that Aleister Crowley was the Great Outstanding Deviate from the Old Aeon. Crowley had vowed, "I shall take no man's directives as sacrosanct. I shall test all. I shall try doing everything that they say one must not do, and I shall not do what they say one must do." But even he wrote in many places bemoaning his inability to completely free himself from the Old Aeon.

The Old, the Patriarchal Aeon has taught man not to live and think by his own individual Light, but instead to live by the dicta of a self-superhumerated, regimenting, all-powerful intelligentsia. Crowley was the arch-rebel against this.

Almost every verse in *The Book of the Law* is better understood by reference to several other verses in the *Book*. These others are required to make the meaning complete. Seldom if ever is there any literary sequence in the *Book*. The related verses are scattered helter-skelter through it.

It is for this reason that one should read the entire first chapter several times and thereby one gains considerable light on the sentence that is the object of concentration.

Such cryptic sentences as Number Four—"Every number is infinite, there is no difference."—are difficult if one tries to unravel the implication to the core. On the one hand, "differences" are of great importance, while from a higher sphere differences are but as ornaments.

(Note: The following spellings, grammar, and sometimes strangeness of wording in *The Book of the Law* are exactly as transcribed—just as instructed in Verse 54: Change not as much as the style of a letter.)

The Book of the Law
Liber Al vel Legis—Liber 31

CHAPTER I

Verse 1.   *Had! The manifestation of Nuit.*

See the co-relative Chapter II, Verse I. The first verse announces that Nuit is speaking through an intermediary who is not identified until Verse 7.

Crowley says, "By Had is Nu manifested. Nu (56) plus Had (9) equals 65, the number of Adonai, the

Holy Guardian Angel."* Note that there are 65 pages to the manuscript of the *Book.*

*Note: Material in quotes is direct from Crowley's commentary. Otherwise the comment is the author's own.

Verse 2.

The unveiling of the company of Heaven.

"This Book is a new revelation or unveiling."

Verse 3.

Every man and every woman is a star.

"Latent or undeveloped in each person is the sublime starry nature to be attained."

A star moves in its own orbit by its own direction and not by some director-general of stars. It has its own unique nature, one star from another, and not to be directed into a common mold of conformity. The entire book spells out that the Great Work is to unite with and do the will of one's own True Self—one's own Genius—not a collection of automatons under the direction of all this under which he has been dominated. Without the entire concept of this Verse 3, the entire Book of the Law is vacuous.

Verse 4.

Every number is infinite; there is no difference.

"This startled my intelligence into revolt. I now see that the limited is a mere mask."

Verse 5.

Help me, O Warrior Lord of Thebes, in my unveiling before the Children of Men!

"Appeals to me to still my rebellion and to help her, the speaker, Nu, to unveil herself. She needs a mortal intermediary aid and, to uplift me, she identified me as the warrior lord of Thebes, so I thought, but it was actually identification with Aiwaz, mentioned in Verse 7."

Verse 6.	*Be thou Hadit, my secret center, my heart and my tongue!*

"She again appeals to the Hadit identification of Aiwaz."

Verse 7.	*Behold! It is revealed by Aiwass the minister of Hoor-paar-kraat.*

Aiwass finally announces himself as the speaker and intermediary between Nu and the scribe.

(Note: Verses 8 to 15 are addressed to Mankind in general. Also refers to Verses 12, 13, and 14.)

Verse 8.	*The Khabs is in the Khu, not the Khu in the Khabs.*

The text now actually begins.

"The Khabs is the innermost light in the Khu, the entity man."

This very clearly states that the Divine is not outside of man. This is quite different from being a puny spark outside of the Great Divine Flame.

Verse 9.	*Worship then the Khabs, and behold my light shed over you.*

This is clear. Worship the "Heart of the Star" and not the outer form of the star.

Verse 10.	*Let my servants be few and secret; they shall rule the many and the known.*

This is the rule of Thelema. The "few and secret" refers mostly to the "secret" ruler, the Holy Daemon and a few of the higher emissaries. The "many and the known" is to be taken more than literally: the many automatic intelligences in every man, despite his denial motivated by his strange egotism.

Verse 11.	*These are fools that men adore; both their Gods & their men are fools.*

The folly of seriously giving too much credit, credibility and quasi-worship to man's falsely revered tinseled aristocracy of the intellect or of the State—straight folly.

(Note: Verses 12, 13, and 14 state certain high secrets of the O∴T∴O∴, though in disguised metaphor.)

Verse 12.

Come forth, o children, under the stars, & take your fill of love!

"Under the stars"—why under the gloom of sin and guilt? Under the stars is joy-openly. "The key of the worship of Nu," says Crowley.

Verse 13.

I am above you and in you. My ecstasy is in yours. My joy is to see your joy.

"Human ecstasy and divine ecstasy interact."

Here there is not one speck of room for the long face of gloom, saturated with guilt or hate for all that is joy and ecstasy. The Gods take delight in the joys and ecstasies of Man. This is the prime key of the required attitude in what is vulgarly called "Sex Magick."

Verse 14.

Above, the gemmed azure is
The naked splendour of Nuit;
She bends in ecstasy to kiss
The secret ardours of Hadit.
The winged globe, the starry blue,
Are mine, O Ank-af-na-khonsu.

This is a poetical translation of the "Stele of Revealing" which is the Magickal Pentacle of the Book. See the two preceding verses.

(Note: See verses 15 and 16. Under certain rituals, may the inspiration and spiritual force of Nuit and Hadit be with them.)

Verse 15.

Now ye shall know that the chosen priest & apostle of In-finite Space (Nuit) is the prince-priest the Beast; and in his woman called The Scarlet Woman is all power given. They shall gather my children into their fold: they shall bring the glory of the stars into the hearts of men.

Referring to the last book of the Christian Bible, the Book of Revelation, an extremely wild vision of a man called "John of Patmos." He saw the "Great Beast" and knew its name in Greek, "Tomega Therion," and he said, "Count his name, it is 666." Now this is accurate enough because in Greek Gematria, "Tomega Therion" adds to 666. He also saw "the great whore," Babalon, "drunken upon the blood of the saints." But Johns vision was seen through the eyes of a psychopathic fanatic. He himself said that 666 is the number of MAN. But he did not have the sense to see that this is not anathema, i.e. Man, the Great Beast—greatest of all living flesh on earth. Nor could he see that Babalon, 777, is Mother Earth. Summed up, *The Book of the Law* presents the symbology in its real perspective.

In Verse 15 the Great Beast and the Scarlet Woman are personifications of the ruling spirit of Man and the ruling spirit of Earth. They are also titles of office—and also of paths and grades in magick. It is also interesting to note that the sum of the Qabala of Nuit and Hadit is 666; and by inference the four preceding verses are to be considered as relevant to Verse 15.

Verse 16.   *For he is ever a sun and she a moon. But to him is the winged secret flame, and to her the stooping starlight.*

This is a continuation or extension of Verse 15; it also bears some reference to what the vulgar call "Sex Magick," which is to be found scattered throughout the *Book*.

Verse 17.   *But ye are not so chosen.*

That is the uninitiated, the "Troglodytes."

Verse 18.   *Burn upon their brows, O splendrous serpent!*

Verse 19.   *O azure-lidded woman, bend upon them!*

(Note: See verses 15 and 16. Under certain rituals, may the inspiration and spiritual force of Nuit and Hadit be with them. This is the original position of the note now duplicated before Verse 15.)

Verse 20.

The key of the rituals is in the secret word which I have given unto him.

Crowley suggests that this word may be "Abrahadabra," which in essence, means the accomplishment of "The Knowledge and Conversation of the Holy∴ Guardian∴ Angel∴." This is indeed the key of the teachings of Aleister Crowley.

Verse 21.

With the God & the Adorer I am nothing: they do not see me. They are as upon the earth; I am Heaven, and there is no other God than me, and my lord Hadit.

"This refers to the actual picture of the stele. 'Nothing' means beyond human category. The knowledge is only to be attained by adepts."

Herein is an injunction that one should not regard a lesser God (a specialized reflection) with the Supreme, and as Crowley writes: "It is a concept beyond all men have thought of the Divine. Nuit is not a mere star-goddess."

Verse 22.

Now, therefore, I am known to ye by my name Nuit, and to him by a secret name which I will give him when at last he knoweth me. Since I am Infinite Space and the Infinite Stars thereof, do ye also thus. Bind nothing! Let there be no difference made among you between any one thing & any other thing; for thereby cometh hurt.

Verse 23.

But whoso availeth in this, let him be chief of all!

Verse 24.

I am Nuit, and my word is six and fifty.

Verse 25.

Divide, add, multiply and understand.

"This is a charge to quell the faculty of discrimination between illusions—the seeming. The 'chief' is he who has destroyed the sense of duality."

Referring to verse 25, the number of Nuit is 56. 56 equals 7 times 8. Now in an extensive preoccupation with the 64 figures of the Yi King, Frater A∴ noted that there are 56 figures that have no Yang element in the upper trigram; also 56 which have no Yin element in the upper trigram. The same 56 number was noted in the lower trigram. This led to the discovery of what might be called the prime key of the Yi King—that Yang and Yin are not a pair of dualisms, they are co-equal cooperating co-relatives. This is a most remarkable concept of non-dualism, given forth more than 5,000 years ago, although unrecognized until recent years. In a way, *The Book of the Law* calls attention to the fact that all modern prevailing religions are based upon conflicting dualisms.

It is not amiss to call attention to such a concept that came after the time of the giving of *The Book of the Law*. Throughout the thousand pages of Charles Fort's books are scattered references to his "Law of the Hyphen," which is contained most clearly in Verse 22 of *The Book of the Law*.

Verse 26.

Then saith the prophet and slave of the beauteous one: who am I, and what shall be the sign? So she answered him, bending down, a lambent flame of blue, all-touching, all penetrant, her lovely hands upon the black earth & her lithe body arched for love, and her soft feet not hurting the little flowers; Thou knowest! And the sign shall be my ecstasy, the consciousness of the continuity of existence, the omnipresence of my body.

Crowley says that this was his question and the answer received, which was personal. However, the last sentence is addressed to all mankind.

Verse 27.

Then the priest answered & said unto the Queen of Space, kissing her lovely brows, and the dew of her light bathing his whole body in a sweet smelling perfume of sweat: O Nuit, continuous one of Heaven, let it be ever thus; that men speak not of Thee as One but as None; and let them speak not of Thee at all, since Thou art continuous!

Here the scribe was caught up in a vision of ecstasy. Again, Nuit is referred to as "None"—no limiting category—the sum total of all possibility.

Verse 28.

None, breathed the light, faint & faery, of the Stars, and Two.

The ecstasy continues, but there follows a reference to "Two," which continues in the next verse.

Verse 29.

For I am divided for love's sake, for the chance of union.

Verse 30.

This is the creation of the world, that the pain of division is as nothing, and the joy of dissolution all.

This is to be interpreted in the light of the grade and of each individual.

"There are three grades, the Hermit, the Lover, and the Man of Earth." See verses 39 to 41 inclusive, of Chapter I; also Chapter III, verses 63 to 68 inclusive.

Verse 31.

For these fools of men and their woes, care thou not at all! They feel little; what is, is balanced by weak joys; but yet are my chosen ones.

Again the scribe had rebelled against the idea of pain of the people. He was assured that their "weak joys" compensated for their weak woes—"They feel little."

This is the compensation that is also declared in Chapter II, Verse 9, for ALL people.

Verse 31 is not as cynical or heartless as it seems to be. We also have assurance in the next following verse, "The joys of my love will redeem ye from pain."

Verse 32.

Obey my prophet! Follow out the ordeals of my Knowledge! Seek me only! Then the joys of my love shall redeem ye from all pain. This is so: I swear it by the vault of my body; by my sacred heart and tongue; by all I can give, by all I desire of ye all.

This is far from a light oath, as delivered through Aiwass, not only to the scribe personally but to "ye all."

Verse 33.

Then the priest fell into a deep trance or swoon, & said unto the Queen of Heaven; write unto us the ordeals; write unto us the rituals; write unto us the law!

Verse 34.

But she said; the ordeals I write not; the rituals shall be half known and half concealed; the Law is for all.

Verse 35.

This that thou writest is the threefold book of Law.

These three verses need no comment.

Verse 36.

My scribe Ank-af-na-khonsu, the priest of the princes, shall not in one letter change this book; but lest there be folly, he shall comment thereupon by the wisdom of Ra-Hoor-Khu-it.

The charge is made to the scribe personally, that he shall not change a single letter. It directs that the comment be in "open" thought, not by initiated wisdom.

Verse 37.

Also the mantras and spells; the obeah and the wanga; the work of the wand and the work of the sword; these shall he learn and teach.

Verse 38.

He must teach; but he may make severe the ordeals.

These two verses are personal injunctions to the scribe, Crowley.

Verse 39.

The word of the Law is Thelema.

In the original script the word "Thelema" is in Greek letters; and by Greek Gematria, the letters total the number 93. Thelema and 93 are synonymous with Pure Will. One fourth of the entire book is relevant to Thelema.

Verse 40.

Who calls us Thelemites will do no wrong, if he look but close into the word. For there are therein three grades, the Hermit, and the Lover, and the Man of Earth. Do what thou wilt shall be the whole of the Law.

The first sentence is in answer to those of dishonest prejudice. Frater A.·. proposed "Do what thou wilt" to a professor of philosophy. The professor replied, "You cannot act as you please." But "act" is not a synonym for "do," "as" is not a synonym for "what," and "please" is not a synonym for "wilt." The professor's answer is prejudiced and his lack of insight is reprehensible.

The grades are explained in the following verse.

Verse 41.

The word of Sin is Restriction. O man! refuse not thy wife if she will! O lover, if thou wilt, depart! There is no bond that can unite the divided but love: all else is a curse. Accursed! Accursed be it to the aeons! Hell.

"Man" here refers to the "Man of Earth" grade mentioned in the previous verse, and "lover" to the "Lover" grade. A reference to "the Hermit" is to be found in Chapter II, Verse 24. What is written about man and lover in this verse is to be taken as metaphor rather than literally.

Verse 42.   *Let be that state of manyhood bound and loathing. So with thy all; thou hast no right but to do thy will.*

"Stevenson suggests that man may be discovered to be a 'mere polity' of many individuals. The sages knew it long since. But the name of this polity is Choronzon (mob rule, Chaos) unless one can serve his own and the common good without friction nor restriction. The curse of society has been its procrustean morality, the ethics of the herd-man. A mere glance at Nature should suffice to disclose her scheme of individuality made possible by order."

Verse 43.   *Do that, and no other shall say nay.*

The power of asserting one's own true will is a magick that ultimately kills oppression and regimentation.

Verse 44.   *For pure will, unassuaged of purpose, delivered from the lust of result, is every way perfect.*

The "true will" is an expression or action derived or in consonance with one's true and unique individuality, with one's Genius. Certainly this is perfect. "Unassuaged of purpose" means not sugared up. Self-deception by means of sugar-coating one's motives will boomerang badly.

The "lust of result" refers to the fact that pure will is expressed in a love of doing rather than looking for rewards or consequences. Both Wagner and Shakespeare expressed their true genius purely for the love of expressing it, and with no pressing motive of gain or "lust of result." Those possessed by the lust of result are rendered desperate and impatient; and they wind up in disillusionment.

Verse 45.   *The Perfect and the Perfect are one Perfect and not two; nay, are None!*

Verse 46.   *Nothing is a secret key of this law. Sixty-one the Jews call it;*
I call it eight, eighty, four hundred and eighteen.

Verse 47.   *But they have the half; unite by thine art so that all disap-*
pear.

Verse 48.   *My prophet is a fool with his one, one, one; are they not the*
Ox, and none by the Book?

These four preceding verses and also verses 15 and 16
of Chapter II are involved in the Qabalistic Tree of
Life, in the major Tarot and in Qabala.

Crowley has worked out an extensive and complicated set of Qabalistic computations and correspondences, which are of interest only to a profound student
of same. One thing is certain, at the time of writing the
Book, this complicated Qabala was not in either his conscious or his subconscious mind. This is one of the many
testimonies that something did genuinely come to him
from outside sources, from far beyond his earthly self.

Verse 49.   *Abrogate are all rituals, all ordeals, all words and signs. Ra-*
Hoor-Khuit hath taken his seat in the East at the Equinox of
the Gods; and let Asar be with Isa, who also are one. But they
are not of me. Let Asar be the adorant, Isa the sufferer; Hoor
in his secret name and splendor is the Lord initiating.

This simply declares that all of the "Old Aeon" Gods
are no longer the "Lords initiating." Let Asar (Osiris)
and Isa (Isis) be mere officers. Hoor (Horus) is the Lord
of the New Aeon. The character of the New Aeon is to
be found in almost the entire *Book of the Law*.

Verse 50.   *There is a word to say about the Hierophantic task. Behold!*
There are three ordeals in one, and it may be given in three
ways. The gross must pass through fire; let the fine be tried
in the intellect, and the lofty chosen ones in the highest. Thus

*ye have star & star, system & system; let not one know well
the other!*

It is here obvious that "grades" are involved, and necessarily so. It does not merely refer to system.

Verse 51.   *There are four gates to one palace; the floor of that palace
is of silver and gold; lapis lazuli & jasper are there; and
all rare scents; Jasmine & rose, and the emblems of death.
Let him enter in turn or at once the four gates; let him stand
on the floor of the palace. Will he not sink? Amn. Ho! warrior, if thy servant sink! But there are means and means. Be
goodly therefore; dress ye all in fine apparel; eat rich foods
and drink sweet wines and wines that foam! Also, take your
fill and will of love as ye will, when, where and with whom
ye will! But always unto me.*

To "enter at once the four gates," thus perhaps taking
on more than one can handle, brings up the possibility
that one will "sink." But Nuit assures one that "there are
means and means," that there is more than one method
of the aesthetic life or than the secluded life of the mystic. Therefore it is stated in sensual terms that one can be
knee-deep in the enjoyment of life. Crowley puts it that,
"The point to remember is that one is a 'Member of the
Body of God,' a Star in the Body of Nuit. This being
sure, we are urged to the fullest expansion of our several
natures, with special attention to those pleasures which
not only express the soul, but aid it to reach the higher
developments of that expression."

One should include "unto Nuit" in every activity,
so that one will see every other star as equal in interest
and importance to one's own. This will save one from
falling into the trap of egotism. The Holy Guardian
Angel is included with Nuit in this attitude toward life.

Verse 52.   *If this be not aright; if ye confound the space-marks, saying: They are one, or saying, They are many: if the ritual be not ever unto me: then expect the direful judgments of Ra-Hoor-Khuit.*

"Neither intellectually, morally, nor personally should one make lop-sided distinctions before Nuit. Metaphysics, too, is intellectual bondage."
Note again the injunction "ever unto me."

Verse 53.   *This shall regenerate the world, the little world my sister, my heart & my tongue, unto whom I send this kiss. Also, o scribe and prophet, though thou be of the princes, it shall not assuage thee nor absolve thee. But ecstasy be thine and joy of earth: Ever to Me! To Me!*

Crowley says that this verse tells him that he is not to be allowed to rest on his laurels even though he be of "the princes" (see Tarot), but that he must continue his work.

Verse 54.   *Change not as much as the style of the letter; for behold! thou, o prophet, shall not behold all these mysteries hidden therein.*

Crowley always admitted that he had not divined all of the mysteries hidden in the *Book*. However, if the *Book* remained literally intact, there is a hint that something may be divined at a later time.

Verse 55.   *The child of thy bowels, he shall behold them.*

Crowley gives credit to Frater Achad.·. for divining an important key of the *Book*, that "Al" is 31 and that 3 times 31 (the triune form of the Book) equals 93—Thelema. But more, the Books says "he shall behold them" (the mysteries); it does not say that he shall solve all.

Verse 56.

Expect him not from the East, nor from the West; for from no expected house cometh that child. Aum! All words are sacred and all prophets true; save only that they understand a little; solved the first half of the equation, leave the second unattacked. But thou hast all in the clear light, and some, though not all, in the dark.

The "clear light" is intellectual truth. The "dark" or "black light" is the initiated wisdom of the sphere of Chokmah, riding high on the Qabalistic Tree of Life.

Verse 57.

Invoke me under my stars! Love is the law, love under will. Nor let the fools mistake love; for there are love and love. There is the dove, and there is the serpent. Choose ye well! He, my prophet, hath chosen, knowing the law of the fortress and the great mystery of the House of God.

'Invoke me, etc.' I take literally. Love under will—no casual pagan love; nor under fear or guilt. But love magickally directed, and used as a spiritual formula," says Crowley.

Verse 57. continued

All these old letters of my Book are aright; but א is not the Star. This also is secret: my prophet shall reveal it to the wise.

Verse 58.

I give unimaginable joys on earth: certainly not faith while in life; upon death, peace unutterable, rest, ecstasy; nor do I demand aught in sacrifice.

This is clear enough, and sublime. No comment necessary.

Verse 59.

My incense is of resinous woods and gums; and there is no blood therein: because of my hair the trees of eternity.

The word "hair" is used as in Shakespeare and in classical literature. It means true or inherent nature.

Verse 60.

My number is 11, as all their numbers are who are of us. The Five Pointed Star, with a Circle in the Middle, & the circle is Red. My color is black to the blind, but the blue & gold are seen of the seeing. Also I have a secret glory for them that love me.

It is a true metaphor that some see only the black of the night sky and others see the blue and gold of infinite space.

Verse 61.

But to love me is better than all things: if under the night-stars in the desert thou presently burn incense before me, invoking me with a pure heart, and the Serpent flame therein, thou shalt come a little to lie in my bosom. For one kiss wilt thou then be willing to give all; but whoso gives one particle of dust shall lose all in that hour. Ye shall gather goods and store of women and spices; ye shall wear rich jewels; ye shall exceed the nations in splendor & pride; but always in the love of me, and so shall ye come to my joy. I charge you earnestly to come before me in a single robe, and covered with a rich headdress. I love you! I yearn to you! Pale or purple, veiled or voluptuous, I who am all pleasure and purple, and drunkenness of the innermost sense, desire you. Put on the wings, and arouse the coiled splendour within you: come unto me.

Again an interlocking mixture of the sensual and the spiritual.

Verse 62.

At all my meetings with you shall the priestess say—and her eyes shall burn with desire as she extends bare and rejoicing in my secret temple—To me! Calling forth the flame of the hearts of all in her love-chant.

Verse 63.

Sing the rapturous love-song unto me! Burn to me perfumes! Wear to me jewels! Drink to me, for I love you! I love you!

Verse 64.   *I am the blue-lidded daughter of Sunset; I am the naked brilliance of the voluptuous night-sky.*

Verse 65.   *To me! To me!*

The beautiful ritual, as read in the G.·.B.·.G.·.

Verse 66.   *The Manifestation of Nuit is at an end.*

By Qabalah computation, Nu = 56, Had = 10. 56 plus 10 equals 66, which is Nu and Hadit conjoined.

And there are 66 verses in this chapter. Is this a mere coincidence?

Commentary

The goal is Initiation. The process is that of Integration. It comes about through understanding of Thelema, Pure Will.

Thelema implies drawing closer and closer to the consciousness of one's real Individuality.

To recognize and do the True Will in conformance with the conversation of the HGA. Concentrate (exclusive attention) on one sentence daily (fifteen or more minutes), but do not make a mental study of it as it is beyond intellectual rationalization.

The entire book spells out that the Great Work is to unite with and do the will of one's own True Self. Thus, "Every man and every woman is a star" moving in their own orbit, by their own unique nature, not to be diverted into a common mold of uniformity.

But, what of Love that is an extensive part of the Book of the Law? Is this spiritual or carnal love? Verse 41 says, "The word of Sin is Restriction. O man! refuse not thy wife if she will!" And, "There is no bond that can unite the divided but love." This seems to be saying that carnal love is a powerful force. Culling adds that the "power of asserting one's own true will is a magick which ultimately kills oppression and regimentation."

In relation to Verse 51, Crowley puts it that, "The point to remember is that one is a 'Member of the Body of God,' a Star in the Body of Nuit. This being sure, we are urged to the fullest expansion of our several natures, with special attention to those pleasures which not only express the soul, but aid it to reach the higher developments of that expression."

Culling adds: "One should include 'unto Nuit' in every activity, so that one will see every other star as equal in interest and importance to one's own. This will save one from falling into the trap of egotism. The Holy Guardian Angel is included with Nuit in this attitude toward life."

Finally we know that each of us must live like "a Star in the Body of Nuit," "to the fullest expansion of our several natures, with special attention to those pleasures which not only express the soul, but aid it to reach the higher developments of that expression." This, then, is the New Age, the New Aeon, in contrast to the old age still passing from us with its regimentation and denial of free expression. For a richer society, each of us must grow and we do so with pleasures that uniquely express each person's own soul.

It isn't all work and no play, for the Great Work is not denial and restriction but fulfillment. There's not just one narrow Path, but many paths—one for each of us.

Definitions and Discussion Points

Alphaism. Culling writes, "'Alphaism' means first or beginning because 'alpha' is the first letter of the Greek alphabet. Alphaism was the beginning of the instruction in what is vulgarly called 'Sex Magick.' Alphaism simply means no sexual intercourse. Erotic thoughts of imaginations should not even be entertained in the mind during the one or two months that the practice was required.

"Whence comes the weird notion that it is the man who is always after sexual intercourse? Our experience in the G∴B∴G∴ was the women typically gave in to sexual intercourse (without conscience) during their period of supposed Alphaism. The men followed it far more honestly and conscientiously. Furthermore, it was oftener that the unmarried women were more derelict than the married women."

I'm not sure what Culling was saying here; perhaps that women were more honest and true to their own nature, uninhibited by the Order's unjustified rules.

Instead of sex, the Alphaist member was to begin with the first verse of the first chapter of *The Book of the Law*, and take one sentence every day, in sequence, and meditate/concentrate on that sentence for at least an uninterrupted fifteen minutes one or more times daily. "Beware against making an intellectual study of this book. This is a very cryptic book, and is beyond intellectual rationalization. Get what you are capable of getting by inspired meditation."

Concentration is defined as "close mental application or exclusive attention." The mental activity is confined to a definite point. When one visualizes tracing a pentagram in green light, one must really concentrate in order to make it subjectively real.

Book of the Law. This book, also known as "Liber AL vel Legis," is composed of three chapters, each written down by Crowley in one hour starting at noon April 8, 9, and 10 in 1904 in Cairo, Egypt. The words were spoken to Crowley by an entity named Aiwass, later referred to as Crowley's Holy Guardian Angel.

The Book of the Law is the holy book for Crowley's followers. It teaches the Law of Thelema, usually represented by these two phrases:

Do what thou wilt shall be the whole of the Law (AL I:40) and

Love is the law, love under will (AL I:57)

Thelema is both religion and philosophy, and yet—as used in the G∴B∴G∴ it is more a source of inspiration to the student to continue with the Great Work of attaining the Knowledge and Conversation of the Holy Guardian Angel.

The original title of the book was "Liber L vel Legis," but Crowley changed the title to "Liber AL vel Legis" in 1921, when he also gave the handwritten manuscript the title "Liber XXXI." The book is often referred to simply as "Liber AL," "Liber Legis," or just "AL." Officially, it is "Liber AL vel Legis, sub figura CCXX, as delivered by XCIII=418 to DCLXVI."

Published Editions include:

The Law is For All, edited by Israel Regardie, Llewellyn, St. Paul, 1975, softbound.

Book of the Law, printed on hand-made paper and bound in crimson English-cured leather, 1973, OTO, London.

Book of the Law, edited by Jerry Kay, Xeno Pub., 1967, yellow soft cover.

Book of the Law, edited by Jerry Kay, Xeno Pub., 1970, white soft cover.

Book of the Law, Weiser, York Beach, 1981, facsimile of handwritten manuscript, soft bound, red covers.

Book of the Law, OTO, Magickal Childe, New York, 1990, leather bound.

Book of the Law, Weiser Books (Reissue edition; 1987).

Book of the Law, Weiser Books (100th Anniversary edition; 2004).

Book of the Law, Mandrake of Oxford (1992; paperback).

The Book of the Law: Liber Al Vel Legis by Aleister Crowley and Rose Edith Crowley (Hardcover; 2008).

The Law Is For All: The Authorized Popular Commentary of Liber Al Vel Legis Sub Figura CCXX, the Book of the Law by Aleister Crowley, Louis Marlow, Hymenaeus Beta, and Louis U. Wilkinson (Paperback; 1996).

Magical and philosophical commentaries on The book of the law (Hardcover) by Aleister Crowley, 93 Publishing, 1974.

ALEISTER CROWLEY - The Book of the Law by Aleister Crowley, (Kindle Edition; 2008).

The Complete Concordance to Aleister Crowley's The Book of the Law (Liber AL vel Legis) by Wolfgang Gregory Zeuner (Paperback; Aug 22, 2002).

Law Is for All, by Crowley Aleister, New Falcon Press, 1991

Liber Al Vel Legis, The Book of the Law by Aleister Crowley, Level Press, 1974.

The Genesis of the Book of the Law: The Coming of the A A and the Legacy of the OTO, 1905–1914 by David Allen Hulse, Holmes, 2002.

The Book of the Law, Vondel Park Audio Book 2003.

"Liber AL" is also published in many books, including:
The Equinox (III:10). (2001). S. Weiser.
The Holy Books of Thelema (Equinox III:9). S. Weiser.
Magick : Liber ABA, Book Four, Parts I–IV. (1997). S. Weiser.

Evolution in Magick. Magick evolves, just as does every art and science of man. We have new understandings of the relationship between the Inner and Outer Worlds through psychology and quantum theory. We have new experience of change brought about through self-hypnosis and computer-bred technologies. We have new visions of man and cosmos through micro and macro instruments. As our understanding changes, our technology and practice changes and evolves.

Hair. The word "hair" is used as in Shakespeare and in classical literature. Culling wrote that the definition can be found only in "the Standard Encyclopedic Dictionary," "giving the classicus locus in one of Shakespeare's plays where the bishop says, 'If I fight I would violate the HAIR of my profession.' Hence 'hair' means inherent nature of."

Khabs is in the Khu, The. Khabs is Consciousness of one's real Individuality, while Khu is the active conscious Personality. "The Khabs is in the Khu, not the Khu in the Khabs." This very clearly states that the Divine is not outside of man but is part of the Personality. Awakening to this is the beginning of Knowledge of the Higher Self. The Divinity is not distant and separate but right in the heart of the matter—in fact, it's the Soul of the Matter. The Khabs is the soul and the personality is function of the soul.

Love under will. It's the second part of the phrase that begins with "Love is the Law." "Love magickally directed, and used as a spiritual formula," says Crowley. This is an important clarification for what otherwise has commonly been interpreted as justification for a kind of "free love" movement. As a "spiritual formula" it is a concise instruction for Sex Magick as practiced by the G∴B∴G∴

"Will," of course is the True Will of the Higher Self, while Sex is the engine of energy to be directed by the True Will in fulfillment of our goal.

Old Patriarchal Aeon. Whether as an Aeon or an Age, the Old gives way to the New. Some we identify zodiacally as Piscean to Aquarian, others as the Dark Ages to the Enlightenment, from theocracies to democracies.

The Book of the Law is an inspired document prophetic of a "New Aeon," called the Aeon of Horus, the Redeemer. The Old Aeon, or Patriarchal Aeon, should lie down and die, but it persists in a most determined, although subtle, way.

Was, or is, Crowley the only prophet of this New Aeon, or New Age? Not likely. Every transitional time seems to require more than one prophet even though one person may become historically identified with the New Age. Many have claimed this mantle but no one has yet to be acclaimed as the only "Father of the New Age."

Perhaps it is not just a single message or a single event that marks the closing of the old and the opening of the new, and hence no one person stands alone above the others with a single voice. And, perhaps, we don't recognize all of them as prophets because we know them in other ways—as Abraham Lincoln, as Karl Marx, as Theodore Roosevelt, Thomas Jefferson, Albert Einstein, Helena Blavatsky, Carl Jung, and many, many others.

Prophet. The "prophet" of "Liber Al," of the New Aeon, is Crowley himself. What do we mean by "prophet" and "prophecy" in the context of this discussion? It usually means a message (prophecy) from God through an intermediary (the prophet) to humanity or a chosen people. The message may be moral instruction, a warning to change behavior, and/or it may include prediction about the future.

The prophecy is usually communicated through the chosen messenger while in a state of ecstasy, sometimes induced through various shamanic techniques.

Generally, to be called "prophetic," the message is evolutionary, leading to progressive or revolutionary changes such as the founding of a new religion or a new political movement. There is then the question as to whether the prophecy is responding to a need of the people or does it instead leapfrog ahead to create a new situation or condition to which the people respond in an evolutionary way?

Self-superhumerated. "The Old, the Patriarchal Aeon has taught man not to live and think by his own individual Light, but instead to live by the dicta of a self-superhumerated, regimenting, all-powerful intelligentsia. Crowley was the arch-rebel against this."

Culling writes: "'Humerate' (if there were such a word) would mean metaphorically to take upon oneself a task or position. Hence 'superhumerate' is a favorite nasty word of mine which means, for illustration, one poses that the mantle of Elijah has been cast upon his shoulders—making a pretense of greatness or authority."

chapter nine

Sex Magick:

Dianism—the Second Degree

By the time the disciple has attained some practice in the art of proper concentration, he is ready for a continuance of the concentration in a far greater magickal way.

The first two or three weeks of this practice in the original Curriculum concerned the discipline of sexual Alphaism. Alphaism, originally the First Degree of Sex Magick, was deleted from the Curriculum as having no particular magickal value by itself. The rule of Alphaism was a testing course of no sexual intercourse for a period of one month, or more. The important point was that the neophyte must not allow any sexual feelings or emotions or imagined fantasies to enter into the consciousness.

Note that it is not mere physical chastity that is of value, but rather that one should reserve sexual interest and imagination for the time of actual sexual "congrex" and its preparation. The injunction is valuable as a daily practiced discipline between the actual times of the Dianism practice. In short, Alphaism is and should be part of the Technic of Sex Magick rather than as a separate degree.

Now the disciple received instructions in the practice of sexual Dianism, the original Second Degree of Sex Magick in the Complete Magick Curriculum.

Dianism is sexual congress without bringing it to climax. The participants should be warm and ardent, yet not allow themselves to be carried to the point of concupiscence (strong physical desire). Practice in this art presently produces a condition in which there is no sense of frustration because of this rule of no orgasm. Rather than allowing oneself to be submerged in the full flow of pleasurable sensation, one should allow the ecstasy to feed the fires of aspiration and inspiration.

The first point of practice was to aspire to draw something additional (at least unconsciously) from each of the sentences of *The Book of the Law*. This served three ends: (1) proficiency in the practice of Dianism; (2) obtaining inspiration from *Liber Al, The Book of the Law;* and (3) training and skill in other practices of Dianism, particularly the "Magickal Imagination." This last is extremely important in the third degree of Qodosh, described in the next chapter.

Both concentration and meditation disciplines are involved in the practice of Dianism. Each participant in the congrex should do his best to regard the partner as a god or goddess, or at least a favorite daughter or son of one of the gods. He should withhold from consciousness any awareness of a known earthly personality. While it is natural at first for the known personality to intrude persistently, it should be as persistently suppressed, so that the partner is regarded as a visible manifestation of one's own Holy Guardian Angel.

The aim of Dianism and its highest magick lies in continuing the union until such time as one goes into the "Borderland" state. A hallucinatory meditation may be achieved, in which one is submerged in spiritual inspiration and aspiration.

All things require time, regularity and persistence for results. Many experiments indicate that one or two hours, or even more, are required to attain to the Borderland state. And it takes time to build up the energized enthusiasm of the Magickal Imagination, which gives one's thoughts subjective reality. It might take thirty minutes or it might take hours to build up a satisfactory force.

Individuals are different, and each must work out his individual technique. Dianism is not to be regarded as an end in itself, but as a great means to further very great ends. In time one will learn through practice to concentrate on a chosen point, while at the same time suffering the sexual ecstasy. The fire of concentration will replace the preoccupation with sexual sensation.

Note—Readers who wish more information on this subject may refer to the author's book, *A Manual of Sex Magick* (Llewellyn, 1969).

Commentary

What is "Sex Magick"?

Hey Baby, want to get together and do some Sex Magick?

NO!

At least, I hope she says "no" to that proposition because what he's after is not what we call "Sex Magick." Nor are we proposing "the magic of sex." And to clarify, romance and relationship are not fundamental to Sex Magick. You will find out why as we progress in this discussion.

Every man thinks he's an expert on sex, and most women know that he's not. He does know how to make babies, but he doesn't necessarily know how to make love, or to make magick. Women instinctively know how to make magick but both men and women need to learn Sex Magick.

The simple truth is that men simply get an "itch" in their penis, and want it scratched—preferably by a woman. Women yearn for something more complex: they want to be attractive and desirable, gathering men like honey gathers flies. The want to feel adored and they want to know that they cause a man to have an erection and desire sex. And they want romance and intimacy, to feel that they are the only one in his life. They want to be held and kissed, and to have lots of slow foreplay.

Women's pleasure is the key, and orgasm is not the biggest part of it. Prolonged intercourse, with or without her orgasm, is vital to create the energy field needed for the transformation of consciousness fundamental to Sex Magick. Women are the "engines" that power-up the field, whereas men are just the mechanics and the best of them learn how to carefully manage the process while she just swoons in enjoyment.

Every woman should feel herself as a goddess incarnate in the lead-up to sex, during sex, and after sex. His role as a god is a secret—else his ego inflates and robs the mission. She should become filled with energy, but her energy is "magnetic" while his is "electric." They should both enter into the "Borderland" state of consciousness where there is only pleasure but no climax, and hold that state for two or more hours. When the "moment is right," her magnetism should simple draw his electricity into her person, body and soul, with or without his sperm, which is of no particular interest to the Sex Magick operation.

And when the "moment" comes, he projects his special intention, the magickal goal of the operation, right along with his electricity and semen. His role is primarily that of the Magician who projects the imaged goal with the release of his power into her. She receives, transmutes, and makes it happen in dimensions beyond the physical and mostly beyond her awareness. Some women claim to know when they're impregnated, but it's not likely and not necessary. Instead of a physical child, here there is a "magickal childe."

(More about "beyond Dianism" in the next chapter. I just wanted to assure you that more is coming.)

In Giving and Receiving there is Magick, and Love

Yes, all this does require preparation, discipline, and restraint. And the importance of preparation precedes foreplay and should include the planning and execution of drama to elevate the feeling of importance of the ritual and the roles of the players. Sex Magick evolves from dramatic Ritual with the staging of place, costuming, incense or aromatic oils, soft lighting, possibly romantic or with a stimulating base beat, and possibly a non-intrusive script leading to awareness of the intended result.

In this case, it is the Knowledge and Conversation with the Holy Guardian Angel. It can be the objective for either partner, or both.

It calls upon the Magickal Imagination to see the partner as god or goddess, or as Holy Guardian Angel.

What does the god or goddess or Holy Guardian Angel look like? Do they move? Do they speak? Some answers can be found in reference works in religion and mythology, while others will arise from your subconsciousness.

"Do what thou Wilt. Love is the Law; Love under Will."

In your planning, let awareness of pleasure and arousal be your guide. Don't neglect the possible role of fetishes in costuming. Goddesses wear anything they want, and what they want includes knowing and witnessing the arousal and lust of their partner. The challenge remains the required discipline and restraint, especially on the part of the man so that you can remain engaged for two or more hours. Even though the emphasis in a Sex Magick operation does not call for the partners to be an established couple, knowledge and understanding of each other's needs and "turn-ons" is helpful in holding the man back from orgasm.

See yourselves enjoying the extended bliss of the Borderland state rather than the immediacy of satisfaction. *Make Love for an Eternity!* You will find that extended bliss is healthful, will rejuvenate you; will lower blood pressure, bathing your inner bodies with health-giving energies and secretions.

Love is the Law

Definitions and Discussion Points

Alphaism. "Alphaism, originally the First Degree of Sex Magick, was deleted from the Curriculum as having no particular magickal value by itself. The rule of Alphaism was a testing course of no sexual intercourse for a period of one month, or more. The important point was that the neophyte must not allow any sexual feelings, emotions or imagination to enter into the consciousness."

Culling points out that the goal of Alphaism is to "reserve sexual interest and imagination for the time of actual sexual congrex and its preparation." Depending on one's age—and maybe regardless of age—this is an unrealistic discipline for a full month. We are surrounded by advertising and entertainment that is strongly inclusive of sexuality so it really is nearly impossible to say it cannot enter into our consciousness.

But we can agree to abstain from sex for a month and to restrain ourselves from actively seeking out sexual stimulation of any kind.

The goal of Alphaism is discipline, strengthening our self-control over body and emotion so that we can engage in prolonged sex. It is more of what is called "Tantric Sex" today.

Alphaism should be considered immediately in context with Dianism, which see below, along with the articles on the Borderland and congrex.

Borderland state. The aim of Dianism is to continue sexual union until trance occurs. This not the trance of hypnosis, or of spiritual or shamanic practices. It's a state characterized by poise and non-movement. The sexual stimulation is felt, but controlled and the focus is on consciousness and not the body.

Culling says: "A hallucinatory meditation may be achieved, in which one is submerged in spiritual inspiration and aspiration."

It requires two hours or more "to build up the energized enthusiasm of the Magickal Imagination which gives one's thoughts subjective reality." It should be felt as a "force field" about the couple. Some may even see it as a glowing aura.

Congrex. Here's another of Lou Culling's fancy words he was so fond of using. It just means "intercourse, having sex, sleeping together." But the use of an unfamiliar word, even when the meaning is obvious, does have a certain value of "stop, look, listen, pay attention."

"Having sex" is more than a physical act. In Alphaism you were instructed to avoid any sexual thoughts, feelings, and fantasies for an entire month. When you do have sex, all of these are present because sex is a complex of physical, emotional, energy, mental, and spiritual exchange between two people.

While Alphaism was dropped from the Curriculum, it is worth realizing that the intention was not so much denial as it was to emphasize their importance and the role they do play in whole and healthy sex whether within the context of Sex Magick or not. Yes, even fantasy is part of real sex whether recognized as such or not. Is your lover a "big, strong, heroic man"? Is she "beautiful, soft, and loving"? No matter the outer reality, the answer through emotional fantasy is "yes" and that brings you into contact with the archetypal levels of the Subconscious and Collective Unconscious important to the program of Wholeness.

Openness with regard to emotion-level fantasies is important to release associated repression and fear and childish dependencies so the powerful fantasy *Imago* can become more inclusive of the "real" lover, making the exchange between two people deeper and stronger, building a partnership at all levels.

In Dianism and Sex Magick, the fantasized *Imago* is not the personal fantasy but rather that of a god or goddess, but the technique is similar and the imagined god or goddess can eventually impose and transform the personal fantasy.

Even if others tell you that your lover is nothing but a beer-drinking no-good lay-about, this transformative power of the *Imago* is one of the greatest things that we can give and receive within our intimate relationship with our partner. With the added empowerment of Sex Magick, the old reality can become a new reality.

Dianism. The Second Degree of Sex Magick, Dianism is sexual union without climax. It's further training, but unlike Alphaism with its emphasis on avoidance here the partners should be warm and ardent, but controlled. It's like a surfer riding the crest of the wave forever. There should be no feelings of frustration for it is without "lust for result."

Dianism is not an end in itself but rather is the means to a greater end than orgasm, which is fleeting. One "comes," and it's gone. Here, Dianism uses the energy of sexual ecstasy to feed the fire of concentration—which we will learn to project in the attainment of our magickal goal.

Both concentration and meditation disciplines are involved in the practice of Dianism. Each partner regards the other as a god or goddess, so that the partner is regarded as a visible manifestation of one's own Holy Guardian Angel.

What seems difficult now will become greater pleasure with accompanying spiritual awareness with experience.

Magickal Imagination. The imagination is one of the most powerful tools that a human has. Through the imagination we can see what is not yet existent, and can change one thing into another. We can fly without wings, see with our eyes closed, hear sounds beyond sounds, or silence in place of sound. We can test things in our imagination and work out any problems.

Tesla, the great electrical genius, is said to have been able to create a motor in his imagination, set it running, and then come back to it at a later time and check for wear on the bearings.

The Magickal Imagination is yet more powerful, for with it we do exchange one reality with another. In your ritual, you submerge the personality of your partner into the imagined identity of a god or goddess. It isn't illusion, for the more often this is done, the more attributes of the god or goddess will manifest into the old personality.

The skill of the magician is enhanced by the skilled use of correspondences so that the imagined identity is supported by the established attributes associated with the god or goddess. This is why it is important to memorize and know the various appropriate correspondences.

Qodosh. In the Third Degree of Sex Magick, physical ecstasy must become psychic ecstasy that in turns "fires" the Magickal Imagination. In the now empowered imagination we aim for realization of the objective of the operation. All the while, the chosen objective is the central focus of the concentration and imagining from beginning to end of the sexual union.

If the objective of the operation is a quality, such as the vision of Beauty, then the experience, the trance, may continue on for a week or even more. And if the operation is repeated, the experience extends more and more, and becomes reality.

Sex Magick. Sex Magick is the whole thing—the persisted application of all that has been learned and gained as skills in the training of Alphaism, Dianism, Qodosh, the Magickal Imagination, the memorization of correspondences, the learning of concentration and visualization, and the glory of union.

For I am divided for love's sake, for the chance of union.

chapter ten

Sex Magick:
Qodosh—the Third Degree

The first half of the Third Degree was designated Qodosh, and the papers of instruction were called *Liber Qodosh*. "Qodosh" is a Hebrew word meaning supreme, or holy.

Before being given this book, the Neighborhood Primate of each Lodge was required to pass rigorous tests, and it was no easy task for the first members to achieve success. The book was kept highly secret, and there were, in fact, many lodges to which this book was never communicated.

The test given the writer, as Neighborhood Primate of the San Diego lodge, was first to pay the expenses of a chosen woman member of the Chicago Headquarters group to travel out to San Diego. He chose Soror 17.∴.

In the Rite of Diana, the Primate was required to give evidence of his ability to make the imagination become subjectively real. He was further tested on his ability in meditation to come very close to the "Borderland" state. He achieved all of this during one Dianism congrex that lasted three hours without break.

In choosing members from his lodge who were prepared to receive this first step in Qodosh, the Neighborhood Primate always considered deeply the readiness and worthiness of the member. But he did not resort to the rigorous tests to which he himself had been subjected. It is to be remembered that the principle of hierarchy prevailed in the government of the Lodge, and that the force inherent in the Magickal Hierarchy has been recognized for over three thousand years.

Its concept is that the spiritual energy of the Superior is transmitted to some extent to the Inferiors in the Hierarchy, and particularly to those directly under the Superior's guidance. But the concept works both ways, in that the Inferiors have contributed no small amount of magickal support and force to the Superior.

Therefore, if a woman member was a loyal and active member of good promise, who had been practicing Dianism satisfactorily; upon performing the Qodosh congrex with the Superior in a serious and worthy manner she automatically received the secrets of the first half of *Liber Qodosh*. At a later time, upon the same conditions, the last half of *Liber Qodosh* was given her.

Among other instructions received from Headquarters, the Primate was referred to a paper-bound booklet of some hundred pages, written by Ida C. Even back in the 1930s this book was scarce and hard to come by, although it had been used by the psychiatrist Dr. Theodore Schroeder in his publication, "The Erotogenesis of Religion." The title of the book published by Ida C. was *The Heavenly Bridegroom*.

The chief value of the book from Headquarters' point of view was that reference could be made to various passages in the book by their brief official documents, and thus cut down on the typing. It is possible also that some thought was given to the United States Post Office's rules on the transmission by mail of such material. In the present work, however, the writer gives the complete official instructions plus material privately received from Headquarters as additions, and also a certain amount from "The Order of Palladians."

In the year 1939 it was my good fortune to meet an elderly doctor who had been an intimate of Ida C., the author of *The Heavenly Bridegroom*. He told me her full name, Ida Craddock. She had done a tremendous amount of research, and beginning with a native gift of psychic intuition, improved with psychic training, she was able to attain to the knowledge of highly secret citadels, which citadels guard the secret workings of Sex Magick.

She had written and circulated several privately printed pamphlets on the subject, and for this she was most viciously persecuted by the public. Who are the members of this public? Those who fornicate every night when first married and then become guiltily virtuous and cry that "sex is dirty and sinful, and that it is blasphemy to teach the use of it as ritual for spiritual advancement and illumination."

But unless one's mind is completely in the gutter, one will acknowledge that the drive for sexual union contains no small amount of yearning, conscious or subconscious, to transcend oneself—even to striving for the Knowledge and Conversation of the Holy Guardian Angel by this means. Admittedly it is a clumsy drive in many cases, but it is pure Nature, and it must and will operate. From this fact did Ida Craddock write, "Share your joy and pleasure with God." Crowley's *Book of the Law* beautifully makes the same point.

(Note: All Magick can be perverted into Black Magick if one is evil enough to divine how it is to be done.)

Everything learned in Dianism applies to Qodosh, with the single exception that there is no abstention from the climax. In fact, in Qodosh the climax is the essential thing.

To use the language of Alchemy, the "Red Lion" is the male of the magickal sex rite; the "White Eagle" is the female. The "Elixir" or "blood of the Red Lion" is the essence of the male orgasm. The vagina or the vessel that receives "the blood of the Red Lion" is "the retort." The "Mother Eagle" is the mouth. The "menstruum" is the "solvent of the White Eagle" in the retort. Together, the effluvia of the Lion and the Eagle is the "First Matter," the original Creation. This First Matter is to be transmuted by the Magickal Imagination, by aspiration and inspiration and by the "Fire," which is the ecstasy into the "Quintessence." Ecstasy is, as it were, the magickal fire for transforming all into inspiration and aspiration.

The simplest operation of Qodosh is the invocation of some desired human quality into one's personality in an intensified manifestation. One may invoke understanding, wisdom, logic, love, beauty, harmony, or a greater ability in Magickal Imagination. What it is to be must be determined beforehand, and both Lion and Eagle must be in full agreement.

If, for instance, "beauty" has been chosen, it must be made the central focus of the entire concentration and imagination from beginning to end of the congrex. One may imagine beauty in all possible forms and manifestations, but one may never drift away from the subject of Beauty.

One does not try NOT to be aware of the pleasure of sexual union. In fact if there were not sexual ecstasy, the operation would be sterile from a magical standpoint. **The physical ecstasy must be made to become the psychic ecstasy, the fire to excite the Magickal Imagination; and the Magickal Imagination in turn attains to a greater realization of the objective "Beauty."** You can see how this is an application of what was learned in the practice of Dianism.

As before mentioned, every endeavor of man takes time, and time is certainly no illusion as it is so often said to be by would-be occultists. Three minutes would accomplish very little. It takes much more than that to build up the magickal visualization of the desired objective, and the inspiration necessary to its accomplishment. Just as long as the force can be kept building up, the participants should continue their endeavor. A general rule is not under twenty minutes, and usually it would take an hour or more for the best accomplishments. Herein is the importance of having mastered Dianism. Both people and conditions vary, however, and the operation would be a weak one if the operators are continually distracted and diverted by a fight against the climax.

One of the best applications of Qodosh is the aspiration to union with the Holy Guardian Angel, the Daemon, the Soul. **Here again applies the instruction in Dianism that one should submerge the consciousness of the personality of the partner in the imagination of the person of a god or goddess, or the soul itself. The partner then becomes an objective embodiment of the H G A,** and the result to be sought after. From my own experience and that of others, I can state that this is the most efficient, powerful and ecstatic rite of Union with the Divine that can be imagined.

The result is almost unbelievable to the uninitiated. Typically, one may retain and exult in the "Trance of Beatitude" for more than a week; and the result increases in geometrical progression when practiced regularly with a good partner.

The practice is far more potent if the Lion and Eagle share the Eucharistic Rite of the Elixir. If any person objects to absorbing the transmuted First Substance, then he is a poor magickal operator.

At this point it is exigent to explain both the physical and psychological mechanisms operating in sex magick. It really is only a quasi digression, although a necessary one. We have some strange disguised hints in several writings but before examining these writings we should bring one important point to the fore.

This point is the extended application of the Hermetic axiom, "As above, so below." Man is a microcosm of the vast macrocosm. The "Magickal Axiom" derived from the above Hermetic axiom completely includes the Q.E.D. axiom that there is no magickal phenomenon outside of oneself that is not also inside oneself. Thus, if you believe in the existence of "elementals" in the astral then, perforce, you must also accept that there are likewise elementals within your own psyche.

The foregoing leads to the subject of "objective reality" and "subjective reality." Psychologists recognize the fact that those people who have subjective experiences that have not been self-induced and self-directed are in a bad way when they think that the experience is actually an objective reality. Thus, for instance, the psychopathic personality (or the one nearly so) in having the subjective experience of Saint Peter talking in his ear, thinks that it is an actual objective reality, and is in a bad way. Take note that he thinks it to be something from outside of himself: but had the whole experience been a result of self-will and intelligent direction he would have known it for what it is—something of his own self rather than something he thought to be entirely from outside his self.

Therefore, in letters of fire, let the Zealator know, and so operate, that **all psychic forces in Magick originate from within, as willed phenomena** and never shall he let himself be seduced into being a victim of non-willed subjective delusions and obsessions.

However, the Zealator asks a good question. He says, "If I invoke and evoke the 'Intelligence of Beauty,' for example, then how can it communicate to me more than what I already have, since it is nothing but a part of me?"

The answer to this question is simple, logical, and what experience has indicated to be factual. The "Intelligence" that is in the "microcosm" (the person) is a channel through which the same "intelligence" of the "macrocosm" operates and communicates a greater scope of the particular intelligence. Naturally the amount of the force of the intelligence depends exclusively upon the amount of aspiration and inspiration of the magician firstly; and secondly on how much virility and power of persistence (long life) that has been given to the said intelligence. In this, there is nothing that remotely equals the power of Sex Magick when efficiently performed.

In magick, these evoked "intelligences" are traditionally called "Magickal Offspring," and more particularly as a "Homonunculus," "Elemental," and the more widely known "Familiar." The "Familiar" is not limited to only one specialization (as our example of Beauty) but may finally be cultivated to have a number of specialized characteristics. Its first invested characteristic should be to serve one with its higher intelligence—and for one's best magickal interests. However it is possible that there might be something that the Zealator regards as more exigent.

The foregoing seeming digression should now have put to rest any apprehensions and even fears that the "Familiar" is something alien to oneself—rather it is a part of one's own psyche that has only the characteristics which the magician has projected to it in a state of subjective reality, and its superior "intelligence" is attained by it being an integral part of the Great Macrocosm even though basically being entirely a projection of part of one's own self. There is only one other or question to be resolved: "Is it the creation of the Eagle or the Lion?" The answer is: According to the preliminary decision (mutual or otherwise) it can belong to either partner or both according to whether it is exclusively individual or not. Certainly both parties can mutually agree on such categories as are universal, such as "Beauty, "Intelligence," etc., but the text will also give examples where the aim is almost exclusively individual. In those cases where it is individual there is the question of whether the individual should be the sole repository and nourisher of the "quintessence" or if instead it should be both operators. It is the male "Lion" who is in command of the process of putting the quintessence in the care of the absorbing "Mother Eagle," i.e., the various mucous membranes, and therefore the male Lion should have a conscience about making an undue imposition upon the Eagle when the operation is entirely for the benefit of the Lion.

Before covering the Technic of bringing "Intelligences," the Familiar, etc. to the light, it is better to give descriptions of other workings of Sex Magick.

First, the Zealator should be reminded that he or she now has a double concentration and magickal imagination. The Zealator must perform the congrex with all of the attitudes set forth in the second degree; then besides this, it is necessary to also concentrate on the object desired. Here follows several suggested applications.

1. The letter method: This is to be used in cases where a letter to a particular person has the potential of accomplishing the purpose. First, concentrate on the desired purpose during the congrex. Second, place a quantity of the quintessence upon the written letter and immediately seal the envelope and mail as soon as convenient. This writer and his associates in Magick can testify that they have never seen this to fail in bringing about some result. If another letter is advisable, it should be treated in the same manner. The force is augmented if one traces some kind of sigil or symbol that pertains to the objective on the letter—traces it with the elixir.

2. The money method: Where some objective is desired with some money or a check (also to bring money). Proceed exactly as given in Number 1, above.

3. For mental and emotional improvement: Such as Joy, Concentration, Imagination, Systematic Concentration, Love, Awareness, Wisdom, Understanding, and many others. Keep the mood of the Second Degree and also concentrate upon the particular propensity desired. Keep it specific and do not allow the mind to wander. Whether the quintessence is preserved via the "Mother Eagle" of the man or of the woman is a matter of judgment and decision. If the objective is solely for the woman the virtue of the operation is enhanced by tracing an appropriate symbol upon the skin of the

woman with some of the "medicine of metals." Again it is well to repeat that the elixir should remain in the "curcurbit" (vagina) for at least ten minutes—and in the other Mother Eagle for at least five minutes.

4. Divination—All serious workers in Magick are desirous of attaining ability in divination (or should be). The favored methods, beginning with the most simple, are tea leaves, playing cards, Tarot cards, Horary Astrology, and the Yi King (also spelled "I Ching"). Note—The Yi King is the most definite, reliable and, in being less tricky, does not require so much so called "psychic ability." (There is also the more direct method of depending upon one's psychic propensities—this requires the development of the faculty of "Awareness," which is here given separately in Number 5, below.)

In this method the Zealator should choose one definite method of divination in the Magick working. Let him or her devise a chosen symbol of this method. It is assumed that both partners in the congrex welcome development in this divinatory ability and therefore both parties are involved in taking part in the absorption of the magick elixir. On a prepared paper may also be traced the symbol and upon the forehead of both operators. During the congrex working do not fail to visualize the symbol and also the working of the divination. As in all of these magick workings, added strength and wisdom is attained by several repetitions of the magick congrex workings.

5. Awareness: The attainment of awareness is of first degree importance in all magick working. The mind should be attentively aware of anything that comes to one's sight or feelings and the sight and feelings must be alert and aware! When a person seeks knowledge and guidance and indications of the future, be it either by one of the oracular methods or by the psychic faculties, it may be some very small or apparently insignificant thing, which is the key and clue to guidance and, in order to recognize this, a keen and active sense of awareness is required. The magick Technic in the congrex is the same as given in Number 4, above.

6. The attainment of the "Knowledge and Conversation of the Holy Guardian Angel," also called the Daemon, the Divine Ego, the Divine Genius, the Immortal Self, the All Knower, the One that Goes—the True Inner Guidance. One should review the required attitude as given in the Second Degree, Dianism. This is very important: The partner must be identified as an actual manifestation of the Daemon—one's Divine Self—and yet as a Lover!

This should be the central aim of all Magick, which is to attain the knowledge and conversation of one's Daemon and, prosper chance, finally actual union. This is the true definition of "Initiation"—to discover one's true identity and thereby fulfill the purpose of one's existence on this planet.

Then comes the question: What about the "magickal powers" as here given in the first five applications? What better reason than to aid one and in this "Great Work," as it is called! Actually if one confines the congrex to this central aim there comes, automatically, enough of the "magick powers" for many aspirants, though not specifically so, as for example, one must first master the principles of the Yi King before expecting to get added psychic inspiration through the rite dedicated to the G∴G∴A∴—the Daemon.

The attitude of the magicians is described in the Second Degree. The partner is no longer a certain known person but rather identified as a spiritualized manifestation of the Divine Daemon, the Holy Guardian Angel. The whole congrex is as an enchanted spiritual feeling. Let one imagine (realistically) that the Divine presence communicates, "I am above you and in you. I am here and now with you. My ecstasy is in yours. My joy is to see your joy. I love you; I love you. Come unto me. To me. Thou art verily with me." The aspirants should really feel the benediction of the spiritual presence—and it should persist long after the congrex.

If the aspirants have felt nothing it is due to one of three things: (1) inhibitions; (2) not capable of spiritual feeling; or (3) more practice is needed. Every human endeavor improves and develops by practice.

The results of this magick rite ever increase with continued practice and eventually lead to an Initiation. No sexual congrex should be without this rite—the physical, psychological, and spiritual benediction is too great to be neglected.

The Rite of Transubstantiation is naturally the summation of this rite. In the Christian churches the consecrated wine and wafer is declared to be the body and blood of Jesus Christ. The only difference in the herein described magick rite is that there is an actual vital spiritualized substance that is consecrated. This is a sufficient hint to the wise. To the troglodytes, the whole subject of magick must remain as an ignorance, which even results in their anathema.

The subject is now closed with a comment by a medical doctor who is also a practicing psychiatrist.

Too many people will object to "Sex Magick" upon the grounds that the sexual act is "supposed" to be solely for procreation. They base their argument upon the sex life of animals, saying that animals copulate only during the menstrual season, resulting in procreation. Very well, if they want to base the argument upon physical phenomena and ignoring the spiritual and psychological part, let us meet them upon their own ground.

Animals (excepting monkeys) can produce offspring only when the union occurs during the menstrual period or so called "season" but, with humans, copulation during the menstrual period is the one time that it is impossible to produce offspring. Thus we see that it is impossible to make a human-animal comparison based exclusively upon physical phenomena. Incidentally, the one exception mentioned, the monkeys, happens to be much the same as humans in sexual habits—the same as so many humans whose physical ways occlude the qualities of soul.

The sexual mores of the ancient primitives is illuminating. The most ancient primitives extant in the world are the natives of the Isle of Melville, off the northern coast of Australia and secondly the natives of the Isle of Iffia. Both of these peoples have a natural instinct to celebrate sacred sexual rituals. So it also goes with primitives of lesser age and lesser succeeding age until it finally degenerates into merely sexual orgies, just as do modern humans. Strangely enough, it is just this class of humans who are most inclined to decry any ideas of associating spirituality with the sexual act; not so strange either, it is merely a left-handed way of showing their subconscious guilt of practicing the mere "gross physical act."

I also find it interesting to observe the instinct for hygiene in the primitives as, for example, the use of a small sponge soaked with the juice of some fruit or plant which is acidulous, such as lemon juice to prevent conception. It really is a mystery to me how the so-called teenagers come by their information—such as using a warm bottle of some acid drink such as 7 Up or Coke as a contraceptive.

In conclusion, let us not overlook the fact that one of the eight reasons that Sex Magick has been under the cloak of vowed secrecy is that it inevitably would meet with derision, accusations, feigned horror and persecution by that great mass, the Troglodytes.

(Name withheld by request)

7. The Magickal Child: This has been reserved for the closing of this chapter. The secret of this operation was given only to the few who had been "tried and proven," especially as to being greatly proficient in all phases of "Dianism."

It has been called the generation of the "Magickal Offspring" (or "Child"). In some ways, a better name is "the Bud Will Intelligence." The idea of a "Magickal Child" puzzles and even repels and frightens some people—therefore it is exigent to give an explanation from modern psychology.

In the language of psychology, the manifestation is called a "complex." A complex is any group of ideas and feelings, heavily charged with energy, (can be conscious or unconscious) that is capable of functioning autonomously to influence personality and general behavior in its own characteristic way. Now it will be seen that when this is "unconscious" in the person, it only too often indicates a psychopathic personality.

However, the general public is dead wrong in assuming that a "complex" is always subversive. Under certain conditions it can be quite the opposite.

There is one condition in which the complex is the result of a great magickal achievement. Under cogent and willed creation it aids and serves and even informs the individual, even to a point of Genius.

Let one again read the definition of the "complex." Take note that it "functions autonomously," i.e., as an existing functioning Intelligence, apart from one's own thinking state. When one creates or generates this functioning Intelligence it has the actual subjective reality of being a Magickal Offspring, and it is both good psychology and good Magick to regard it as an Autonomous Intelligence, apart and separate from oneself, albeit also an extracted and generated part of oneself.

Here is the tremendous value of the "Child." For example, you have concentrated on "Beauty" as its outstanding characteristic. Although it is generated from your "microcosmic" principle of beauty, it becomes greatly magnified and specialized and "communicates" to you an infinitely greater sense of beauty than you ever had consciously.

Also note in the definition, "heavily charged with energy." There is nothing equal to the force of "charging" by Sex Magick.

To return to the points raised in comparing human and animal sexuality—when we exclude man and monkeys, we know that sexual union produces an offspring by the rule of Nature. In man there is also a psychic factor—and for all we know, also in animals. So that we can assume that the sexual union of male and female produces either a physical or a psychic offspring. In this application of Qodosh we call it "the generation of the Magickal Child."

There is little point in quibbling about the term, as this is exactly what it is on the subjective plane. I quote from C. G. Jung, "It is unintelligent to spend one's energy and time denying the existence of the gods, when one could be learning much about those forces which operate just as the gods are said to act." This quotation is applicable in all Magickal workings, and particularly so in this subject of creating the "Magickal Child."

Assuming that the operator has mastered the first part of the operation (which I wish to emphasize is very necessary) the rules are simple. The operators concentrate vividly and intensely on the nature of the desired Magickal Child. It is very much better if both parties in this Rite are agreed on the nature of the Child to be produced. If the woman knows nothing about this Rite, the man should certainly adjust the nature of the intended Child in conformity with the nature of the woman.

One may name the Child "Love," "Beauty," "Wisdom," "Inspiration," or whatever human quality it is desired to produce. Or one could choose an activity such as "Clairvoyance," "Power of Speech and Writing," "Union with the Daemon," etc. If the partner is not an initiate, extra care should be taken by telling the partner in advance, "Let us think of ... during this congrex," so that there is no potential disharmony between the two psyches.

The Magickal Child is a sort of demi-god of the quality for which it is named. Any human quality that may be invoked already exists in the subconscious of the person. The aim of the Magician is to increase the strength of the quality, and when it is brought to a quasi-objective manifestation and seems to have an independent existence outside of one's body and personality— then it is indeed a psychic child.

If the name of the Child is "Beauty," then assuming that the magickal operation has been performed fairly well, one is given an intensified awareness of beauty of greatly extended scope and almost continuous application. Again, "One should not deny the existence of forces when these forces operate just as they are supposed to act."

When is the Child "born" and how long does it live? The Child comes into manifestation almost immediately in some cases. In other cases it may take as long as nine days. The length of its life depends upon the force of the magickal operation. Both the first-hand and second-hand experiences of the author is that the Child should be given a new lease on life by the same operation every seven to nine days. It increases in strength to a maximum after three magickal rites. And it is only after this Child has attained full stature that a differently named Child should be attempted.

The sensational press publicized at one time the supposed fact that Aleister Crowley, Black Magician, "eats babies." By now, the student should have come to suspect that this may mean that one does take to one's self the essence of the Child. The partner should also do this if she is in agreement with the project.

If the Child is solely of the woman's choosing, then she "sustains the essence."

The Qodosh Rite is also used for other things than those applications described in this chapter. It is not advisable to go into detail about all the possible applications of the Qodosh Rite, as the operators will undoubtedly resort to their own ingenuities. Emphatically, however, it must be stated that the operation must never be used for any purpose that might harm another person in any way whatsoever.

In closing, let me say that the Qodosh Rite never fails to produce some result.

Commentary

The Rite of Diana

In the Rite of Diana, Culling demonstrated his ability to make the imagination become subjectively real in the "Borderland" state of consciousness while in sexual intercourse for three hours. It is the practice of Dianism that leads to the ability of sustained intercourse in which the partners need not fight against orgasm.

During the "congrex," a desired human quality is intensely invoked into the personalities of both partners. This is their Magickal Childe, and their Familiar. The chosen quality must be the central theme upon which both partners concentrate and focus their empowering imagination during the entire congrex. During that time, as long as two hours or even more, one may imagine that quality in all possible forms and manifestations, but one may never drift away from the subject itself.

And then there is the ultimate goal, that of the Knowledge and Conversation of the Holy Guardian Angel. Culling points out that it is nearly instinctive "conscious or subconscious, to transcend oneself—even to striving for the Knowledge and Conversation of the Holy Guardian Angel."

With the movement of the creative force that some characterize as the "Goddess" herself, consciousness is itself opened to the force of Will, the "face of God." We feel the touch of the Divine as we climax, and then smile with the sense of Blessing as we remain bathed in bliss.

As Ida Craddock wrote, "Share your joy and pleasure with God."

What is instinctive is augmented with deliberate awareness of the personality of the partner transformed into the god or goddess or the soul itself. The partner then becomes a spiritualized manifestation of the Holy Guardian Angel.

Imagine (realistically) that the Divine presence communicates, *"I am above you and in you. I am here and now with you. My ecstasy is in yours. My joy is to see your joy. I love you; I love you. Come unto me. To me. Thou art verily with me."*

The partners should endeavor to really feel the benediction of the spiritual presence—and it should persist long after the congrex. The partners may experience this as a "Trance of Beatitude" for a week or more; and the result increases "in geometrical progression when practiced regularly with a good partner."

The Eucharistic Rite of the Elixir

The experience is increased by the alchemical sharing that is the oral exchange of the partners' shared and transmuted sexual fluids. It can be accomplished by sensuously licking and sucking "the First Matter" from the "Retort" and then holding it in the "Mother Eagle" of the male before exchanging it with the "Mother Eagle" of the female who should likewise hold it before ingesting it. Even better is that this last be a long sustained kiss before mutually swallowing the "Quintessence." All the while, the goal is held in their consciousness.

While the "69 position" is a not unheard of sexual practice nowadays, it is the extended technique and the attitude and imagination that transform it into the Eucharistic Rite.

Practical Applications

But there are practical applications for the Quintessence as well, and Culling lists seven of them:

1. The letter method: where a letter to a particular person has the potential of accomplishing the purpose. Concentrate on the desired purpose during the congrex and then place a quantity of the quintessence upon the written letter and immediately seal the envelope and mail as soon as possible.

2. The money method: where a particular purpose is desired through the exchange of money by check. Proceed exactly as above.

3. For mental and emotional improvement: Concentrate upon the particular propensity desired. Hold the quintessence in the mouth of the man or of the woman and then trace an appropriate symbol upon the skin of the woman. The elixir should remain in the vagina for at least ten minutes, and in the mouth for at least five minutes.

4. Divination: Devise or choose a symbol representing the goal. Trace the symbol on a prepared paper and also upon the forehead of both partners. During the congrex working do not fail to visualize the symbol and also the working of the divination.

5. Awareness: The mind should be attentively aware of anything that comes to one's sight or feelings and the sight and feelings must be alert and aware! When a person seeks knowledge and guidance and indications of the future, be it either by one of the oracular methods or by the psychic faculties, it may be some very small or apparently insignificant thing, which is the key and clue to guidance and, in order to recognize this, a keen and active sense of awareness is required. The magick Technic in the congrex is the same as given in Number 4, above.

6. The attainment of the "Knowledge and Conversation of the Holy Guardian Angel." The partner must be identified as an actual manifestation of the Divine Self as a Lover. This is the true definition of "Initiation"—to discover one's true identity and thereby fulfill the purpose of one's existence on this planet.

7. The Magickal Childe: A manifestation of the chosen quality empowered through the imagination.

Definitions and Discussion Points

Alchemy. The alchemy of the occultist and of Sex Magick is the transformation of the "baser" self into the "gold" of the higher self. The procedures, tools, and materials of the physical alchemist become symbols for the psychological and magickal operations of the occult alchemist.

Borderland state. An alternative state of consciousness in which the demarcation between ordinary reality and subjective reality disappears, and that which is built in the imagination becomes magickally and psychologically real. The woman partner in Sex Magick becomes the Goddess incarnate.

Ecstasy. Through prolonged intercourse and visualization of woman as the Goddess Incarnate, sexual ecstasy must be made to become psychic ecstasy, the fire that excites and powers the magickal imagination. Body, Mind, and Spirit are united with a transfusion of energy to transform subjective reality into objective reality.

Effluvia. The mixed fluids of Male and Female in the vagina make up the "First Matter," which is to be transmuted by the magical imagination by their aspiration and inspiration, and by the Fire of their sexual/mystical ecstasy while engaged in Sex Magick.

Elixer. The "Elixir" or "blood of the Red Lion" is the essence of the male orgasm.

Familiar. The "Magickal Childe" created through Sex Magick.

First Matter. Together, the effluvia of the Lion and the Eagle is the "First Matter," the original Creation. This First Matter is to be transmuted by the magickal imagination, by aspiration and inspiration, and by the "Fire," which is the ecstasy. Ecstasy is, as it were, the magickal fire for transforming all into inspiration and aspiration.

Hierarchy. It is believed that those of a higher initiation compose a leadership that has the ability to transmit spiritual energy to those of lesser spiritual stature and thus "raise them up."

Menstruum. The "menstruum" is the "solvent of the White Eagle" in the retort.

Order of Palladians. A French magical order of the late 1800s created by Leo Taxil (pen name of Gabriel Jorgand-Pages), apparently, as a total fraud. In books and articles, Taxil described dramatic sexual scenes in magickal settings, later admitted to being fictional.

However, that doesn't mean that the sexual teachings were erroneous. Rather, they were the inspiration for the scheme.

Quintessence. The transmuted sexual fluids are held in the mouth, and used for magickal operations.

Red Lion. The male of the magickal sex rite.

Retort. The vagina is the vessel that receives the ejaculated semen, i.e., the essence of the male orgasm, also called "the blood of the Red Lion."

Rite of Diana. Culling says he was required to give evidence of his ability to make the imagination become subjectively real, to make his meditation come very close to the "Borderland" state, all during one Dianism congrex that lasted three hours without break.

Rite of Transubstantiation. The Rite of Transubstantiation is the alchemical transformation of the shared sexual fluids. In the Christian churches the consecrated wine and wafer is declared to be the body and blood of Jesus Christ. The only difference in the herein described magick rite is that there is an actual vital spiritualized substance that is consecrated.

White Eagle. The female of the magickal sex rite.

chapter eleven

Conversations with a God:

Selection of the Totem

The next advanced work was the selection of one's totem, an animal form which most nearly describes the aspirant. It is important to have a full knowledge of the nature of the animal and to give considerable thought to the appropriateness of the selection.

In nobility, the lion is an inspiring example, yet many animals can whip the lion in spite of the common belief that the lion is the "King of Beasts." Possibly man calls the lion "King of Beasts" in order to beat his chest with egotism when he has killed one and can sport its noble mane. Nor let anyone think that the hyena is a coward; the hyena is intelligent enough to avoid man as he would the plague, and this same intelligence will not allow senseless bravery to overrule experience.

One may ask, "Of what use is the totem?" One's totem can be a valuable psychological reminder, if it has been chosen with care and with some inspiration. It has its own manner of "conversation" of the sort that will next be described.

After the totem was chosen, the next instruction received was about the practice of holding a conversation with an appropriate God. In choosing both the totem and the God, great accuracy and an understanding of the subject are of paramount importance.

Let us take the god Proteus as an example.

Proteus is a prophetic sea-god to whom Poseidon (or Neptune) assigned the guardianship of seals, and we are led to the conclusion that

Proteus rules all sea-going mammals such as cetaceans, whales, and dolphins. Now all mammals have much in common with man and, since time immemorial, the sea has been a symbol of the vast ocean of man's unconscious. We are assured that this is the symbology intended for Proteus.

Proteus is also a god of wisdom, and dispenses wisdom to those who consult him, under certain conditions. Proteus, on being approached, at once assumes a weird and frightening form in which he gives his first answer to the consultant. If the consultant refuses to be fooled or frightened by this swift change, but persists in his question, Proteus again changes into another form and gives another answer. There are always three possible reactions for the consultant. One, he may be frightened (either of the strange form or of the answer he gets, because imperfect and incomplete manifestations of Truth can be frightening) or, two, he may accept this partial form of Truth as the final illumination. If he does that he is apt to go about starry-eyed, imposing his weird, half-baked "illumination" on all who will listen. Or, three, the consultant may be one of the few who will persist to the end, when Proteus finally reveals his true nature in all his glorious wisdom. Proteus may repeat the whole process five or six times, each time getting closer to the wise answer.

Now let us see what a sloppy and imitative analysis of Proteus would lead one to believe. Says the dictionary, "Proteus when seized would assume different shapes," and it is of course true that wisdom has many forms. The inept could be influenced by the use of the word "protean" in psychology, where it describes the phenomena of a patient getting rid of one bad habit or neurotic quirk, only to find that it breaks out in another form. For example, a person may give up smoking with considerable effort, only to be plagued by compulsive eating. But the real god Proteus does not signify this sort of thing.

Let us examine this puerile and superficial description of the god. In the first place, dozens of gods and demigods have the ability to change forms, and there is no uniqueness about this ability of Proteus. Also, the conditions under which Proteus changes forms has no relation to that which the dictionary misnames "protean."

The technique of conversing with a God is well described in that classic "The Invocation of Thoth" which is to be found in Crowley's *Equinox, Volume I, Number VI*, under the title of "The Rite of Mercury." It is also in Israel Regardie's magnum opus, *The Golden Dawn*.

This "Invocation of Thoth" was, at a late date, added to the weekly ritual of the G∴B∴G∴ and it is here given in its entirety.

The Invocation of Thoth

The Banishing

Procul, O procul este profandi. Bahlasti Ompehda! In the name of the Mighty and Terrible One, I proclaim that I have banished the Shells unto their habitations. I invoke Tahuti, the Lord of Wisdom and of Utterance, the God that cometh forth from the Veil.

Section One. The magician prays and projects his will. He describes the beauties of the God.

Oh thou majesty of Godhead, Wisdom-crowned Tahuti, thee, thee I invoke! O Thou of the Ibis Head, Thee I invoke! Thou who wieldest the Wand of Double Power, Thee I invoke! Thou who bearest in Thy left hand the Rose and Cross of Light and Life, Thee I invoke! Thou whose head is as an emerald, and thy nemmys as the night-sky blue, Thee I invoke! Thou whose skin is of flaming orange as though it burned in a furnace, Thee I invoke!

Section Two. The God speaks, and the magician listens.

Behold, I am Yesterday, Today, and the brother of Tomorrow! I am born again and again. Mine is the unseen Force whereof the Gods are sprung, which is as Life unto the Dwellers of the Watchtowers of the Universe. I am the Charioteer of the East, Lord of the Past and of the Future. I see by mine own inward Light. I am Lord of Resurrection, who cometh forth from the dusk, and my birth is from the House of Death. O, ye two Divine Hawks upon your pinnacles, who keep watch over the Universe! Ye who company the bier to the House of Rest, who pilot the Ship of Ra advancing onward to the heights of heaven! Lord of the Shrine which standeth in the Center of the Earth!

Section Three. The magician loses objective consciousness and becomes one with the God. The God directs the conversation.

Behold, He is in me and I in Him! Mine is the Radiance wherein Ptah floatheth over the firmament. I travel upon high! I tread upon the firmament of Nu! If I say, "Come up upon the mountains," then shall the Celestial Waters flow up at my Word. For I am the Eidolon of my father Tmu, Lord of the City of the Sun. The God who commands is in my mouth. The God of Wisdom is in my heart. My tongue is the sanctuary of Truth, and a God sitteth upon my lips, and the desire of my heart realizes itself. I am Eternal, therefore all things are as my design.

Section Four. The magician knows it is the God's words and ideas he utters and listens to.

Therefore, do thou come forth unto me from Thine abode in the Silence. Unutterable Wisdom, All-Light, All-Power, Thoth, Hermes, Mercury, Odin—by whatever name I call Thee, Thou art still nameless to Eternity. The wind hath borne Thee in its bosom, and Earth hath ever nourished the changeless Godhead of Thy Youth.

Come Thou forth, I say, come Thou forth, and aid me in this work of art!

I invoke the priestess of the Silver Star, Asi the Curved One, by the Ritual of Silence. I make open the gate of Bliss; I descend from the Palace of the Stars. I greet you; I embrace you, O children of Earth. Let there be the Shaking of the Invisible, the rolling asunder of the Darkness, the Becoming Visible of Matter, the Piercing of the Scales of the Crocodile, the Breaking Forth of the Light.

Let the Silence of Darkness be broken and let it return in the Silence of Light.

****

Let us now examine the ideal artistic and magickal structure and procedure of an invocation such as this. The first section is an eager prayer with an active projection of the will. It also describes the beauties of the God.

In the second section the God speaks, while the magician becomes passive. He listens to and catches the reflection of the God, imagining that he is hearing and echoing the words at one and the same time. And he understands the words to be true also of himself.

In the third section, it is as though the God and the man become one. "Behold, He is in me and I in Him!" The magician loses objective consciousness, as it were.

In the fourth section, the magician becomes silent, listening. It is not really the magician who says, "Do thou come forth unto me," but rather the God who is listening to the far-off utterance of the magician.

Now, in carrying on a conversation with a God, one follows a very similar mental pattern. At the outset, one should have a clear, concise picture of the God and his nature, and the imagined conversation should be on lines consonant with the God's nature. One should certainly not be talking about legal codes and customs to the Goddess of Love! And further, one should not expect the God to converse a great deal at the beginning, except perhaps superficially. It is the magician who is active in initiating the conversation.

Presently, as in the second section of the Invocation, the magician should become passive and receptive. He may imagine that he is receiving conversation from the God even though he knows consciously that it is his own thoughts that he is tearing.

He progresses to the third stage wherein "He is in me and I in Him," and now there should be a strong feeling that the God is directing the conversation. Since the two are one, they now speak as one.

In the fourth section, if the invocation has been successful, the magician knows that he is no longer forming the words and the ideas. Unique concepts develop and the ideas produced are such as have never been before in the magician's conscious mind.

It is not advisable that this "conversation" be held with anyone other than a God or demi-god—never with a human being. No matter what God one converses with, it is assumed that the particular God is a part of the psyche of every human being, in spite of the fact that the conversation appears to be with a stranger. The Great Unconscious is a stranger to one's conscious mind unless and until the great union has been achieved, and even then there is the strange element.

Why? "If will stops and cries 'why?' then will stops and does naught."

If the practice of conversation with a God as given here, seems not to be on as high a plane as the Invocation of Thoth, at least it will be found that there are several applicable points of technique in the Invocation that will assist the conversation.

Author's Note: Despite the doubts that many have had about the value of the conversation, it is my own testimony and of many others that there finally results, in the "Conversation," ideas and even wisdom that absolutely was not of the conscious self.

Many will argue that it did not come from a "God"—and worse, argue themselves out of seeing the real value. *It is results that count—* not explanations (which, after all, are mere theories) of the mechanisms involved. It is well to again heed the words of Carl Jung, "Why argue against the existence of the Gods when there are forces that act just as the Gods are supposed to act."

At first one may feel silly in holding a conversation with an "imaginative" God, but suddenly, under due perseverance, comes the empathy with a great force and in addition, inspiration and even wisdom of which was not in one's conscious mind.

Commentary

The Nature of Sacred Conversation

This "conversation" with a god is a major stepping stone toward self-realization and toward conversation with one's Holy Guardian Angel.

It is not the same thing as "talking to oneself," or "self-talk," or the idle chatter that commonly goes on inside our heads as we recount conversations we've had with real people or the imaginary conversations we wish we'd had with those people.

It is far more like the active prayer with a particular saint that once was common among Catholics. And it is similar to those prayers to particular gods common in India and in some areas of Africa.

But there are important differences that must be recognized and understood. In the background of your consciousness you should know that this particular god, or other god, demi-god, or saint, is part of your own psyche and not an entity outside your own consciousness. You need to understand that consciousness is universal and with this technique you are working through your own subconsciousness and the collective unconscious, and perhaps even the Divine Consciousness.

Eventually, you will be conversing with your higher consciousness, and to some degree that is also happening now. But the main point is that you need to converse with the god as if it were an objective presence even though it is purely subjective, and you need to address it with all the respect, politeness, and honor you would give to a living saint.

And you need to listen! Too often even a "real" conversation is one-sided. Too often, we hear only what we say and tune-out what the other person says. Here you want to listen with all the attention and respect you would give to the president of the United States of America. With attentive listening, you are opening the doors to your higher consciousness.

Another important point is that this is a private conversation not to be held with another human being, or with others present. It is not a public performance!

Even in group ritual, your perspective must be private and singular as if in the confessional.

The Nature of the Sacred Deity

There's a lot missing in a "shortcut" to anything, and Culling says leaves a lot to the student's common sense.

He does write: "At the outset, one should have a clear, concise picture of the God and His Nature, and the imagined conversation should be on lines consonant with the God's Nature." He does not tell you to carefully select the god you are about to engage in sacred conversation. Be as conscious of your choice as you would in selecting a consultant about the most important area of your life. And then you should study and familiarize yourself with all the characteristics of the selected god: appearance, dress and ornaments, associated colors, incenses, areas of expertise, alternative names, and other correspondences.

Above all, treat your selection with the utmost respect. You are not only awakening to an aspect of Divine Consciousness, but you are awakening corresponding consciousness in your own self.

Another very important point: It is you who is active in initiating the conversation. Don't just sit there hoping the god will speak to you. You're the one who made "the date" with this Divine Being. Plan the things you need to say. Plan the way you will honor the deity, how you will acknowledge his or her appearance, and so forth.

Next, in planning the things you need to say and the needs you need to have addressed, note carefully the rhythm of the four parts in the example "Invocation of Thoth" and follow it as a formula.

Pay Attention! This is Important!

Conversation with a God is one of the most important practices you can undertake. It may lack the seeming excitement of Sex Magick or the mysteries of the Qabalah, but it is a practice you can undertake anytime and it awakens your consciousness.

Many great teachers have made the point: Most of the time that we think we are awake and conscious, we really are asleep. But, we are "sleeping giants," and we have an obligation to wake up!

Everything in this very concise "Shortcut to Initiation," *The Complete Magick Curriculum of the Secret Order of the Great Brotherhood of God*, is intended to awaken us to the Whole Person our innate Divinity calls to us to become. But this is a curriculum that fits into your two hands in book form: You are both the Awakener and, potentially, the Awakened.

Definitions and Discussion Points

Eidolon. Ghost.

Invocation. Invocation and Evocation are often, mistakenly, used interchangeably and with little appreciation of their vast difference. Invocation precisely means to actually bring a spirit or divine presence into the psyche and even the body of the magician.

Evocation, in contrast, calls a spirit or other entity into the presence, not the being, of the magician and usually into a magical triangle placed outside the magic circle of the magician.

Invocation requires psychological and spiritual strength as well as proper preparation. It's not just that there are dangers but that the opportunities are so great.

Nemmys. The familiar Egyptian head-dress that somewhat resembles a "page-boy" hair styling. The colors and designs all have meanings, and additional meanings beyond the traditional associations make the nemmys in different colors and patterns a convenient ceremonial garment to distinguish ritualists from one another, and signifying their ceremonial function.

Ptah. In the ancient Egyptian pantheon, the first of the gods and the primal creator of all the world and all that is in it. He is the primal matter itself. Ptah appears as a bearded man wrapped up like a mummy with his hands free to hold a staff made up of the symbols for life, stability, and power. He is the patron of craftsmen and artisans, of all things creative.

Ra. Egyptian king of the gods who watches over the world from the sky as the sun.

Shells. Shells are a Kabalistic concept, and are known by the Hebrew Qlippoth. They are the negative side of existence, the leftovers after creation. In many ways, the idea of a shell is appropriate for it is a container for the positive aspect, the inner goodness, the seed of life. Think of a walnut, and crack the shell to get the edible "meat" out. The shell is discarded, yet it has some residual value—perhaps as fuel, compost materials for your garden, etc. In the process of life, the buried walnut would come to life, bursting out of the shell and growing into a new tree. The shell is waste debris having served its purpose.

In some philosophical perspectives, the Klippoth (alternate spelling of Qlippoth) are seen as evil because they limit the life force within. In our analogy, if the walnut shell is too thick, the seed won't be able to burst into life. Or think of a chicken egg with a shell so thick and hard that the baby chick is unable to peck through and become the chicken intended.

Now, let's extend our story of the chicken and the egg another step, and agree that the egg comes first. But, before there is a real egg the shell is formed. That shell has a purpose of its own in containing and limiting the growing embryo. If it has a consciousness, it is fighting to contain the embryo. On a cosmic scale, there are such "forms without force" left over from the descent of life and consciousness into matter. As such, they are evil and demonic. If fed with the energies of hate, greed, and desire to return to the past (as in hatred of modernism), they may become true demons with enough consciousness to act on their own.

Basically, however, we can think of the Qlippoth as the opposite of the Sephiroth on the Tree of Life as in the following table:

Sephiroth	Qlippoth
Kether	Futility
Chokmah	Arbitrariness
Binah	Fatalism
Chesed	Ideology
Geburah	Bureaucracy
Tiphareth	Emptiness
Netzach	Repetitiveness
Hod	Order regardless of purpose
Yesod	Form without Life
Malkuth	Stasis

Tahuti. An alternate name for Thoth.

Totem animal. *See chapter Thirteen for further guidance on the process of choosing and "living with" the totem.* The selection of a totem is emblematic in a near archetypal way. Major animals, such as bear, lion, eagle, horse, etc. stir an instinctual emotional response. Your particular totem can be determined in response to the simple question: What animal would you like to be, and why?

A careful study of the answer can reveal a great deal about your preferred self-image, about the person you'd like to be, or—rather—the *persona* or mask you would like to present as your public image.

Some ritualists do wear totem masks, and adopt it as an astral mask.

Think, for example, of what it would be like to choose the Eagle as your totem. What is so admirable about the Eagle? The Eagle has the true "bird's eye view," a perspective that sees the Big Picture, and yet the Eagle can focus on the minutest detail and descend from the sky to extract it. The Eagle soars effortlessly on updrafts, "going with the flow" until it is time for meaningful action. The Eagle wastes nothing, mates for life, returns to the nest season after season, building it stronger and stronger. The Bald Eagle is the American emblem, fierce and protective, "Don't mess with me!"

As you adopt the totem's point of view, you learn lessons of life that called to you in response to your unconscious needs.

chapter twelve

The Individual Ritual:
Use of the Barbarous Words

The disciple has been taking part in the weekly ritual for many months now, and has memorized it and made it a part of himself. In addition, he will have been constructing his own individual ritual. Many ritualists find that they develop a great liking for the "Barbarous Words." Although the words are unintelligible, they are found to have two great effects: first, the sound of the consonants and vowels as they are pronounced, serves as a sort of magickal music; and second, added magickal force has been given to these words by centuries of use by magicians. The actuality of this force can only be discovered by long practice.

For the construction of one's individual ritual, there are given below the Barbarous Words belonging to the four Quarters of the Earth: Air is East, Fire is South, Water is West, Earth is North. The words should be intoned while the magician holds the Sign of the Enterer and should be projected outward into the "corner," or quarter.

AIR: Ar, Thiaoo, Rheibet, A, Thele-ber-set, Belatha, Abeu, Ebeu, Phi-thesetasoe, Ib.

FIRE: Ar-O-Go-Go-Ru-Abrao, Sotou, Mudorio, Phalarthao, Ooo, Aepe.

WATER: Ru-Abra-Iaoo, Marridom, Babalon-Bal-Bin-Abaoot, Aphen—Iaoo, I, Phiteth, Abrasax, Aeoou, Ischure.

EARTH: Ma, Barraio, Ioel, Kotha, Athor-Bal-O, Abraut.

The climax of the Ritual, upon tracing the six-pointed Star overhead calls for the words of:

SPIRIT: Ieou, Pur, Lou, Pur, Iaooth, Iaeo, Ioou, Abrasax, Sabriam, Oo, Uo, Adonai, Ede, Edu, Angelos-Ton-Theon, Anlala, Gaia, Aepe, Diatharma, Thoron.

In the construction of the Individual Ritual, many have used passages selected from Crowley's *The Book of the Law*. This is highly recommended. Nothing is recommended which might startle one or jar one into full objective consciousness, as would perhaps the tinkling of a bell. The ritual must work up without interruption to an absorbed seeking of inspiration from the Holy Guardian Angel. Nor must the fundamental point, Regularity, ever be forgotten or neglected.

The way that one feels when intoning the words should be a guide as to whether they are properly intoned. If one is not stimulated by the words, then it is not properly done.

Sending out the words rapidly is a very bad mode. A slow, sonorous intonation is the method to be achieved and the first time that it is really properly and effectively done one might even feel the effect of "goose-pimples running up and down the spine." A good technique is to exercise the magickal imagination. Imagine that the magickal power of the words derives from the many magicians of centuries past who have used these same words—this may well be more than "imagination."

Commentary

The Voice

There is lot to be said about how one speaks the words of ritual. Some words, particularly those in languages other than your native tongue, should be spoken in a special manner—in a slow, sonorous, or deep and resonating, voice. Think of the deep sounds emitted from a church pipe organ!

Culling makes the point that you should feel stimulated as you intone these words so that you have "goose-pimples running up and down the spine."

He also suggests that one should imagine "that the magickal power of the words derives from the many magicians of centuries past who have used these same words."

Others have suggested using your imagination to see the words projected out into the universe, awakening whatever it is you are calling. In the case of the barbarous words for the five elements, you want to sense that you are awakening these powers to respond to your call, and that you are being filled with them.

These words you speak in your Individual Rituals are for you, alone. You are not performing before an audience, not even an invisible one! This is important—it is easy to get carried away by your own voice, resulting in an inflated ego, which is the antithesis of what you need.

The inflated ego of the magician, the religious preacher, the politician, or anyone speaking or reading aloud, can create a barrier separating you from your Higher Self and decreasing your psychic and occult abilities even to the point that you will be misled by them.

The Goal of the Ritual

Remember that the purpose of the rituals you compose is psychological integration, otherwise known as Initiation. Your goal is to awaken, develop, cleanse, and unite your many parts into the Whole Person that is your potential.

Nothing in this book can be said to directly instruct you in the practical magic involved in self-help practices—the matters of "Money, Sex, and Power" as one occultist put it. You can expand those categories as you need: "Money" becomes questions of career, training, financing, contracts, success, buying a house, etc., while "Sex" includes romance, love, relationships, marriage, children, and so on, and "Power" is really the ability to be who you are.

Yet, all the elements are here. There is no absolute conflict between the realities of the "outer" world and those of the "inner" world. We are spiritual beings incarnated and living in a material world. We have the obligations of being "co-creators" to "make the world a better place." We're partners with the world spirit, and brothers and sisters to all living beings.

We are "gods in the making" and need to think of that as our life purpose without letting ego inflation hinder our ability to "listen" to not only our brothers and sisters walking this same path, but to the "whispers from eternity." You don't need an intermediary between the divinity within and the Divine itself so long as ego is kept in its proper place.

Definitions and Discussion Points

Barbarous Words. These are really "words of power," whether intelligible or not. Originally, the name comes from the languages spoken by the "barbarians," i.e., those who did not speak Greek when the Greeks thought they had invented civilization.

In ritual, barbarous words and names don't have to make sense or be understood by the ritualist. Many are derived from Hebrew, ancient Egyptian and Persian; some are based on the Enochian language provided to us by Dr. John Dee. Rather than rational sense, they make emotional sense with the drama.

There is some evidence—see *Magic, Power, Language, Symbol: A Magician's Exploration of Linguistics,* by Patrick Dunn—that experienced magicians created certain barbarous words without regard to proper language but entirely to have a magical effect.

Consciousness during Ritual. Within a ritual, you are in a state of light trance, and you do not want anything to startle or jar you back into full objective consciousness until the ritual is over. The ritual must work up without interruption to an absorbed seeking of inspiration from the Holy Guardian Angel.

When a Word is more than a word. Some words have meanings that have evolved through their usage; others are attached purely through the emotions projected as they are spoken. There can be powerful effects through relatively minor nuances in pronunciation that should be carefully observed and used to effect.

Beyond that, words can be spoken to be heard like music, as indeed is the case with some poetry. Listen, as you speak, to Crowley's Hymn to Pan:

Thrill with lissome lust of the light,
O man! My man!
Come careering out of the night
Of Pan! Io Pan!

Io Pan! Io Pan! Come over the sea
From Sicily and from Arcady!
Roaming as Bacchus, with fauns and pards
And nymphs and satyrs for thy guards,
On a milk-white ass, come over the sea
To me, to me,
Come with Apollo in bridal dress
(Shepherdess and pythoness)
Come with Artemis, silken shod,
And wash thy white thigh, beautiful God,
In the moon of the woods, on the marble mount,
The dimpled dawn of the amber fount!
Dip the purple of passionate prayer
In the crimson shrine, the scarlet snare,
The soul that startles in eyes of blue
To watch thy wantonness weeping through
The tangled grove, the gnarled bole
Of the living tree that is spirit and soul
And body and brain—come over the sea,
(Io Pan! Io Pan!)
Devil or god, to me, to me,
My man! my man!
Come with trumpets sounding shrill
Over the hill!
Come with drums low muttering
From the spring!
Come with flute and come with pipe!
Am I not ripe?
I, who wait and writhe and wrestle
With air that hath no boughs to nestle
My body, weary of empty clasp,
Strong as a lion and sharp as an asp—
Come, O come!
I am numb
With the lonely lust of devildom.

Thrust the sword through the galling fetter,
All-devourer, all-begetter;
Give me the sign of the Open Eye,
And the token erect of thorny thigh,
And the word of madness and mystery,
O Pan! Io Pan!
Io Pan! Io Pan Pan! Pan Pan! Pan,
I am a man:
Do as thou wilt, as a great god can,
O Pan! Io Pan!
Io Pan! Io Pan Pan! I am awake
In the grip of the snake.
The eagle slashes with beak and claw;
The gods withdraw:
The great beasts come, Io Pan! I am borne
To death on the horn
Of the Unicorn.
I am Pan! Io Pan! Io Pan Pan! Pan!
I am thy mate, I am thy man,
Goat of thy flock, I am gold, I am god,
Flesh to thy bone, flower to thy rod.
With hoofs of steel I race on the rocks
Through solstice stubborn to equinox.
And I rave; and I rape and I rip and I rend
Everlasting, world without end,
Mannikin, maiden, Maenad, man,
In the might of Pan.
Io Pan! Io Pan Pan! Pan! Io Pan!

The power of the words spoken in rhythm and rhyme have an almost hallucinogenic effect. They can lift you off your seat as if levitating.

chapter thirteen

The Great Lunar Trances:
Specialized Studies

The three final directives for the G∴B∴G∴ curriculum were not specific in content, rather the practicing member made his own specific selections. The objective, in any case, was the same. It was to set up the student for a life-long program of growth and progress.

In the first of these, each member was advised or required to select as a specialized study or hobby, some subject involving the laws of nature, such as botany, biology, zoology, zoography, chemistry, etc. The object of the study was to learn to observe the sublime design, harmony and beauty inherent in nature.

In the second directive, the student was advised to practice several "trances," each for a number of days. The method of the "trance," for instance a trance of beauty, a trance of joy and laughter, a trance of beatitude, was to see that quality in everything throughout the entire days and nights of the given period. In the trance of Beauty, one sees beauty in everything that touches one's consciousness, allowing no feeling or idea of ugliness to enter. In the trance of Laughter, one should imagine, feel and see life and living as a Divine Comedy without intrusion of any element of the Divine Tragedy. In the trance of Beatitude, the breeze caresses oneself, the birds sing to oneself, every person that crosses one's path has a most friendly glance or smile for one, etc.

Let the cynic or quibbler, who would think that this is an avoidance of realism, a kidding of one's self, practice the opposite of these trances!

He would then get a well-deserved dose of his own medicine. What we build in our consciousness shapes outer reality.

The third directive was for the student to choose some specialized field of the Occult for study, such as the Tarot and/or the Tree of Life. Such study must be done from the viewpoint of the magician and not merely to satisfy the seven-year-itch of the mind.

The word "trance" is not used in the sense of a condition where a person is in a near complete abstraction of the normal mind. Rather it is a state of willed engrossment of the mind in being absorbed in some particular facet of the emotions and feelings—even though it might lead to a state of ecstasy. At the outset, an illustration seems to be advised.

The first rule of the trance practice is that it is not a thing of a few minutes practice daily. It is an attitude to be maintained for at least a week. This may be partly imagination but it must be a willed imagination. Let us suppose that the chosen trance is "joy." Then one must apply the act of concentration, fortified by imagination, which becomes a close mental application or exclusive attention to that emotion and feeling called "joy." If and when this is done there remains small room for feelings of sadness. There is just plenty of room in one's living, and attention for engrossment of the feelings in joy, so that the melancholy and sad have small chance of crowding out the willed concentration upon the manifestations of joy.

A case history of one of these trances that did not conform to all of the rules serves to help describe our genuine trance, i.e., when properly practiced, given as follows.

Frater J.˙., through a series of happenings, was made a subject of the Trance of Beatitude for one day. Take note that it was not a willed trance (as it should be) but rather it was the result of a series of incidents in which the Frater was involved. He says, "Everything of which I was conscious was blessing me. The gentle breeze caressed my face as though it were fingers of loving benediction. The birds were not merely singing—they were singing to me! The flowers were blooming just for me! All the animals and all of the people that I passed seemed to be messengers of the Gods and were giving their loving blessings."

The foregoing describes what one should experience in the trance of Beatitude, but in this particular example it did not happen as a result of a willed engrossment of the mind and feelings. It was not maintained by willed attitude for the duration of the week, and we must remember that the duration of time is important. The result was therefore as a flash in the pan and had no lasting effect upon the Frater. Only too often does the budding magician regard a flashing experience as something that persists while actually all that he really has is a memory of it. What he really should have is a continuing persistence—because it should have been an added part of oneself.

Now to some, case histories have been performed more correctly. Here is a case of the Trance of Beauty, my own case, and it is given because it is at least firsthand. It was interesting to remember one of the "New Testament" apocryphal stories. As Jesus and his disciples were walking along they passed a dead dog. The disciples cried, "What a foul stench." Jesus said, "Its teeth are as beautiful as rare pearls." Here we note that the rules are in operation. Jesus, in holding to the trance of Beauty, had no room for such distractions as an objectionable odor to crowd out the persisting sense of Beauty.

I speak only of the virtue of the trance rather than from any sense of self-praise in saying that although this trance dates back some thirty years, the resultant union with the principle of Beauty grows stronger each year rather than diminishing. Moreover one should know that these trances are actual experiences rather than something that one has heard at lectures or from reading of books. It is no exaggeration to state that, in the realm of Magick, one pound of experience is worth a ton of books! One thing is certain, I know more about Beauty per se than all of the books on the subject, lumped together, could ever reveal. Beauty, as with the other trance subjects, cannot be defined—not even divined; experience needs no definition, nor could tolerate it.

When experience is absorbed and is part of oneself it even becomes something that is communicative to others. Here is an exemplar of the communicative force. It was at that wonderful zoo in San Diego, California. I was looking at two fine specimens of the wild African dog. Two college girls stopped to have a look and one of them said, "How ugly they are." I spoke to her, "The appearance of this animal is strange to you and also you seem to have no empathy with the wild and all of this contributes to the sense of ugliness, but please look again and look for beauty." For a moment she seemed to be transfixed and then she exclaimed, "Why they are incredibly beautiful." Then she said, "Say, are you some kind of magician or wizard?" I left her in open-mouthed wonder when I replied, "It is you that is the magician. You have looked at those animals through the spectacles of your soul which understands more than you do."

The seriously interested person can easily see that there is good reason for not giving out the trance practices to a green beginner. Imagination, concentration, and willed direction of the mind and feelings make up the three abilities that are necessary for any worthwhile practice of the trances. The disciple has now had practice in these three disciplines through his previous Curriculum work. Both will and concentration must have been practiced in keeping the oath: I swear to regard every event as a particular dealing between myself and my soul. He has also vowed, "I swear to tell myself the Truth." Further, he has undertaken the practice of making everything that he does serve as some sort of magick ritual. Then also the weekly group ritual has required imagination, will, and directed emotions. And these three great disciplines are crowned by the great prince awareness. Surely one has seen the indispensable necessity for continual awareness in the trance practices. Awareness! Awareness! I would be tempted to say that "awareness" is the most important word in Magick were it not for the fact that there is a dangerous hazard in being "hung up" with one such category.

What are good subjects for the lunar trances? The G∴B∴G∴ favored the Trance of Beauty and the Trance of Joy because they cover such large segments of the sphere. Members of the Order, in practicing the Trance of Joy, would naturally be influenced by the verse in *The Book of the Law*, "Remember all ye that existence is pure joy." Then when one observes animals, domesticated or wild, very often what they see puts man to shame. Almost all of animals' actions show their joy in their existence—the mere fact of their existence.

This joy was of great importance to the Order. Existence is pure joy. Existence in the Order was infinite joy!

"Let the Rituals be rightly performed with Joy and Beauty."

"I am above you and in you. My ecstasy is in yours. My joy is to see your joy."

"Beauty and strength, leaping laughter and delicious languor, force and fire, are of us."

The members were permeated with the spirit of *The Book of the Law* and were fired by such as the foregoing quotations. It is easy to see that they would have a good headstart on such trances as Beauty and Joy— not to mention their previous disciplines of willed direction of the mind and feelings, imagination, concentration, and awareness.

Here is a different trance. It is for attaining the knowledge of one's totem (see previous chapter). In most cases the trance is for only a few hours—never more than one day. There is a very real correspondence between animals and facets of human individuality. The Technic is to think about some essential characteristic of oneself in relation to the "Great Work" and to identify with that animal of like basic character. Naturally this is progressive and as one advances in the Great Work one may be impelled to change the totem just as also one may change (progressively) one's magick name. To possibly aid one in this, the nature correspondence of the animals is given in the Table of Tree of Life Correspondences. There is great magickal value in having a totem and in being guided by it—precisely just what value is impossible to say because each individual is a different unique case. "Every man and every woman is a Star"—unique and travelling in one's own orbit and direction.

This is the end of the G∴B∴G∴ curriculum. No more work was issued from Headquarters. In a more significant way, however, there cannot be an end to magickal work. "Practice often, invoke often" and with unfailing regularity. This and inspiration continually opens up new horizons of Initiation. The magician will be able to find his own ways to greater heights.

The remaining material offered in this book supplements and augments the actual G∴B∴G∴ curriculum. There is, of course, no limit to the materials that can be studied as part of the Occult—but one must also, and first of all, work the Occult. This book has been written to give the reader the opportunity of undertaking a purposeful and efficient practice of a proven system of Occult training never before available outside of an Occult Order. If the reader undertakes this training—whether by himself or as part of a Group, there is no practical limit to the attainment that he can reach—except his own determination.

The G∴B∴G∴ curriculum is herewith closed with the same line that opened it. Every conscientious and aspiring member of the G∴B∴G∴ found by his own firsthand experience that the method of the G∴B∴G∴ was indeed a "shortcut to initiation."

An important reminder here repeated:

If one practices consistently, daily and regularly, then one should begin to see automatically why merely reading books about the theories and philosophy of magick and other phases of occultism is a sterile thing.

Those with a seven-year itch of the mind, who are preoccupied with books on the subject, will never, never, be magicians. The true magician's method is practice; not books and lectures. The magician's proof is results; the proof of the others is always beyond the rainbow's end

Here is the real proof—just practice the trance of Joy or Beauty for one week (every minute) and see what happens!

Commentary

There are three points to be considered:

One: *In giving the instructions for the practice of the Lunar Trances.* Culling defines the Lunar Trance as "a state of willed engrossment of the mind in being absorbed in some particular facet of the emotions and feelings—even though it might lead to a state of ecstasy."

The further point is made that this is not the more unconscious trance associated with hypnosis or the spiritualist or shamanic trance, but an attitude of particular state of awareness that is adopted to see and experience one specific emotional perspective or "quality" for a significant period of time—perhaps a week or more. It is imagination, concentration, and willed direction of the mind and feelings that make up the three abilities that are necessary for any worthwhile practice of the trances.

Among the suggested qualities are Joy, Laughter, and Beauty. Among others I can suggest are Optimism and Confidence, Happiness as distinct from Joy, Enthusiasm, Respect, Neighborliness, Scientific Wonderment, and Love. These all sound wonderful and desirable, but do we really need a "a state of willed engrossment of the mind in being absorbed in some particular facet of the emotions and feelings"?

Well, it really is more than that. When you are truly happy, you probably have a smile on your face. Now, practice saying "I AM happy" to yourself and smile. As you smile, you feel a difference for the very act of smiling causes some hormonal responses in the body to feel happy and let you see the world a bit differently. With a happy smile, you look at the trees outside your window and you feel their happiness, you talk to your pet cat and feel her happiness, you experience happiness in your work accomplishments and in your home life.

Because you are employing your imagination, concentration, and willed direction of the mind and feelings in determination to find and experience happiness, you will experience happiness within even in dire times but you will affect the world around you. You are a co-creator, and through your intention to have happiness you will make happiness.

Yes, it may seem like wishful thinking, but it is based both on experience and new understanding of the quantum universe. Remember these words from *The Book of the Law* and let them constantly inspire you:

"Remember all ye that existence is pure joy."

And feel the presence of the Goddess, for she says:

"I am above you and in you. My ecstasy is in yours.

My joy is to see your joy."

Two: *The selection and work with the animal totem. Who are you? Not what are you, but who among the animals are you? Are you a kingly lion, a soaring eagle, a loving cat, a loyal companion dog, a faithful horse? As any one of these, how has your relationship to others changed? How do you experience the world differently? What does it mean to express the character of this animal?*

With each of these, you have a new understanding of yourself, and a new way of magical acting in the world. As the high-flying eagle, you have broad perspective. As the companion dog, you add stability to relationships. As a faithful horse, people know you as dependable. And you are dependable, stable, and farseeing.

As you work with your animal totem you are also including more of the natural world in your human world. You are removing the unnatural barriers we have raised between the natural and human worlds. You realize and express Oneness with all there is.

As you grow and expand your universe, you may become yet another totem animal, and you may want to express this in your magickal name.

The process for attaining the knowledge of one's totem (see also chapter Eleven) is a different trance. In most cases the trance is for only a few hours—never more than one day. There is a very real correspondence between animals and facets of human individuality. You want to think about some essential characteristic of yourself in relation to the "Great Work" and to identify that with an animal of like basic character. This is progressive and as you advance in the Great Work you will want to change the totem just as you will change (progressively) your magickal name.

See the nature correspondence of the animals is given in the Table of Tree of Life Correspondences for further help.

Three: *The continuing program of the sincere student.* While the instruction includes the continuing practices of the Lunar Trances and work with the animal totem, the student is instructed to continue being a student and to select one of the natural sciences to learn more about the way our world functions.

While Culling singles out such subjects as botany, biology, zoology, zoography, and chemistry, I have to add quantum theory to your prospective study choices as it will give you a greater understanding of how "the real world" works and how magick works in making change happen. And even though his emphasis is on the natural sciences, I want to encourage the study of Jungian psychology for we certainly have as great need to understand our inner world as the outer world.

And he encourages the study of one occult subject, such as Tarot or the Kabalistic Tree of Life. I have to suggest both of these for their reach into the worlds of mind and spirit is so deep and both add to our engagement with the truly real world.

But, as you continue your studies, you will gain knowledge of other subjects, including—most likely—astrology. But no subject is off limits so long as you maintain your objective of Initiation, the becoming a Whole Person.

Definitions and Discussion Points

Awareness. In this last chapter, Culling makes a number of points well worth repeating.

"Surely one has seen the indispensable necessity for continual awareness in the trance practices. Awareness! Awareness! I would be tempted to say that 'awareness' is the most important word in magick were it not for the fact that there is a dangerous hazard in being 'hung up' with one such category."

Co-creators. "Let the cynic or quibbler, who would think that this is an avoidance of realism, a kidding of one's self, practice the opposite of these trances! He would then get a well-deserved dose of his own medicine." What we build in our consciousness shapes outer reality.

End of the G.˙.B.˙.G.˙. curriculum. "In a more significant way, however, there cannot be an end to magickal work. 'Practice often, invoke often' and with unfailing regularity. This, and inspiration continually open up new horizons of Initiation. The magician will be able to find his own ways to greater heights."

"This book has been written to give the reader the opportunity of undertaking a purposeful and efficient practice of a proven system of Occult training never before available outside of an Occult Order. If the reader undertakes this training—whether by himself or as part of a group, there is no practical limit to the attainment that he can reach—except his own determination."

Trance. "a state of willed engrossment of the mind in being absorbed in some particular facet of the emotions and feelings—even though it might lead to a state of ecstasy."

"Imagination, concentration and willed direction of the mind and feelings make up the three abilities that are necessary for any worthwhile practice of the trances. The disciple has now had practice in these three disciplines through his previous curriculum work. Both will and concentration must have been practiced in keeping the oath: I swear to regard every event as a particular dealing between myself and my soul. He has also vowed: I swear to tell myself the Truth. Further, he has undertaken the practice of making everything that he does serve as some sort of magick ritual."

"When experience is absorbed and is part of oneself it even becomes something that is communicative to others."

The Tree of Life

In Correspondence with the Tarot Trumps and the Kaballah of Numbers, etc.

This is actually a condensed diagram of the symbology that originated in the secret magick orders.

No small part of magick is replete with symbology. A symbol is something like a mental "shorthand" in that a symbol (if a good one) contains a number of ideas magically related to each other—called "correspondences." All good magickal rituals contain correspondences, which are magickal stimulants to the ritualist. Thus, for instance, the mere symbol of the number 93, the True Higher Will, is, at once, a mnemonic of a number of verses in *The Book of the Law.*

One need not be a deep student to get much of magick utility from the twenty-two Major Tarot cards. Merely studying the designs of these cards (and in relation to their order sequence) should be sufficient in most cases. If one desires to take some notes from a book on the subject, the one which the author recommends is *The Tarot* by Paul Foster Case. Case had been a member of the Hermetic Order of the Golden Dawn, and he has given the Tarot cards in the proper sequential order (for this age)—and particularly from the magickal standpoint. Only one change has been added to the Golden Dawn order: it is that card number 4, The Emperor, changes places with card Number 17, The Star. This is because, in the New Aeon (now trying to manifest) we recognize the God of all living nature to take precedence over the regimenting patriarchal ruler and lawgiver, the Emperor. It may puzzle some that the Star pictures a woman instead of the masculine God Pan of all living nature. The woman is Babalon, the feminine aspect of Pan (note—the "aspect," not the counterpart).

(Note—It is not the fault of the Magi that John of Patmos had a hang-up against nature, which he pictured as Babalon the Great Harlot. After all, even in modern times, William James wrote, "Nature is a harlot with whom we can hold no decent communion." Since William James is a part of nature and perforce consorts with her, he is, by his own words, a whore-monger!)

And now a few remarks on the Tree of Life Correspondences must be given.

The ten spheres of the Tree of Life represent the stages of man from that of the animal to the highest possible spiritual. The bottom sphere (Malkuth), called the Universe, represents the physical world containing unregenerate materialistic man. Sphere number 1, Kether, which means "the Crown," represents the few highest men of such as have traditionally been known as Christ, Buddha, etc.—Men of an Aeon.

Take particular note that the grades of attainment have the grade number followed by a zero and the sphere number by a square. For example, the beginning "Zelator" is $1° 10°$, which refers to Malkuth, Number 10. Adeptus Minor is designated as $5° 6°$, which means that he has now reached Tiphareth and that his direct work is to consolidate and maintain his attainment of the "Knowledge and Conversation of the Holy Guardian Angel" (not, however, actual union).

A caution! Each Tarot trump has a letter and a number. Do not confuse these numbers with the numbers of the letters per se. Example: The number of the card, The Fool, is 0 (zero) and the letter is A, but the number of A is 1. The letter for the Wheel of Fortune card is K and the number is 10, but the number of the letter K is 20.

Originally the letters on the Tree of Life were Hebrew letters. Long since then, these letters have been translated into English letters. The result has been that there are two instances where one Hebrew letter has had to serve for more than one English letter. This is to be noted under the letter *H* and the letter *V*. Also there are two letters, which are compound. There is a *T* and also a *Th*, and a letter *S* and also *Sh*.

One last remark—one of the Tarot cards is called "The Devil." This card represents the sex drive and procreation. It seems that even the most enlightened of the ancients had religious inhibitions about sex—so it was called "The Devil (or Satan) and his works." Just why and how the fallen angel Satan was able to outwit the Omniscient God and to gull even his most favored saints to be tempted by sex leaves one wondering—the "injustice of it all!" Even poor Babalon, "The Great Harlot," is "drunken upon the Blood of the Saints" (see Book of Revelation). But those of the Golden Dawn, the O∴T∴O∴, A∴A∴, and G∴B∴G∴ still look with reverence upon the sublime creation of God, Nature—Nature with a capital *N*.

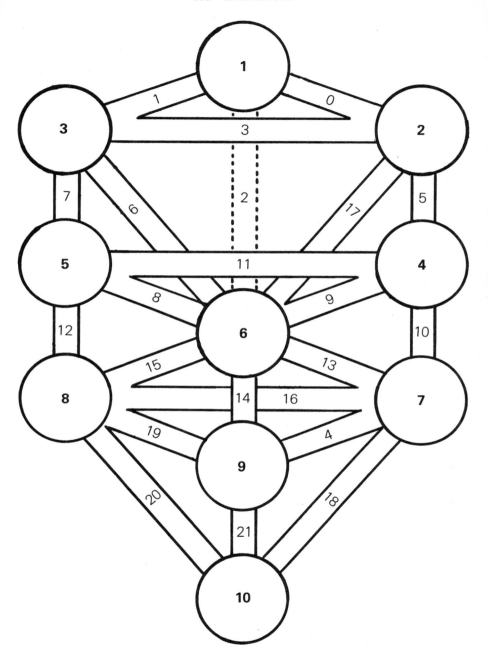

Tree of Life Correspondences
The Ten Spheres

Sphere Numbers	Sphere Names	Sphere Characteristics	The Grades
1	Kether	The "Crown"—highest possible attainment	$10° = 1°$
2	Chokmah	Masculine "Wisdom" Father	$9° = 2°$
3	Binah	Feminine "Understanding" Mother	Magister Templii $8° = 3°$
4	Chesed	"Mercy" Sustainment	Exemptus $7° = 4°$
5	Geburah	"Severity" Discipline	Adeptus Major $6° = 5°$
6	Tiphareth	"Brilliance"—The Sun K. & C. of H.·.G.·.A.·.	Adeptus Minor $5° = 6°$
7	Netzach	"Victory" Venus	Philosophus $4° = 7°$
8	Hod	"Splendour" Mercury	Practicus $3° = 8°$
9	Yesod	"The Moon" Feelings, Emotions	Theoricus $2° = 9°$
10	Malkuth	"The Universe" Man of Earth	Zelator $1° = 10°$

Note: The Grade number and name of any particular sphere does not mean that the person has mastered that sphere. One has advanced to that sphere and is taking on the task of fully attaining realization of that sphere.

Note: The old Hebrew names of the spheres are unimportant. What is important is the advancing implications of each sphere. Actually, the old traditional meaning of Number 8, Hod, as "Splendour" had better be described as the high intelligence of Mercury; Number 7, Netzach, better as beauty and love of Venus. The description of Number 6, Tiphareth, as here given is identical with the meaning of the Chinese trigram of the Pa Kua, "Brilliant Realization of the Sun," in the sense of the Attained Knowledge and Conversation of the "Great One."

Tree of Life Correspondences
The Twenty-two Paths

Kabbalah, Tarot, Animals, and Gods

Kabbalah	Tarot Trumps	Number	Animals & Gods
A–1	The Fool	0–A	Eagle—Jupiter
B–2	Juggler	1–B	Swallow, Ibis—Mercury
G–3	High Priestess	2–G	Dog—Diana
D–4	Empress	3–D	Sparrow, Swan—Venus
H–5	The Star	17–H	Peacock—Juno
V–6	Hierophant	5–V	Bull—Venus
Z–7	The Lovers	6–Z	Magpie—Janus
C–8	The Chariot	7–C	Turtle—Mercury
T–9	Strength	11–T	Lion, Cat—Whale
I–10	Hermit	9–I	Bear—Adonis
K–20	Wheel of Fortune	10–K	Hawk—Pluto
L–30	Justice	8–L	Elephant—Vulcan
M–40	Hanged Man	12–M	Snake, Scorpion—Neptune
N–50	Death, Reaper	13–N	Beetle, Wolf—Mars
S—60	Temperance	14–S	Centaur, Horse—Diana
O–70	The Devil	15–O	Goat, Ass—Pan
P–80	House of God	16–P	Rhinoceros—Mars
X–90	Emperor	4–X	Ram, Owl—Minerva
Q–100	The Moon	18–Q	Dolphin, Seal—Neptune
R–200	Sun	19–R	Lion, Tiger, Hawk—Apollo
Sh–300	Last Judgement	20–Sh	Hippopotamus—Vulcan, Pluto
Thau–400	Universe	21–Thau	Crocodile—Saturn

In the first column of letters is the number value (Kabbalah) of each letter.

Following the Tarot Trump names are the corresponding letters of these cards and the proper initiated numerical order of these cards—but retaining the old numbers.

In the last column are a few listed animals related to the various Tarot cards and also some corresponding "Gods."

Note: When Culling and the G∴B∴G∴, and other magical groups worked with the Tarot in the 1930s and up through the 1960s, the standard deck was the Rider-Waite as illustrated by artist Pamela Colman Smith. Today, of course, there are thousands of decks and perhaps nothing is "standard." In many cases, the new decks have followed much of the "formula" of the Smith-Waite model so most of the above references to the Trump names and the animal and God correspondences remain valid.

appendix two

Liber Yi King

The Oracular Meanings of the 64 Hexagrams

(It must be noted that at the time Culling wrote in 1969, the Legge and Wilhelm text were practically the only translations available. That is no longer true.)

The two best books available on the meanings of the Yi King, or I Ching, one by Legge and the other by Wilhelm, are founded on translations from the Chinese texts of King Wan and his son. These texts were written about 1100 BC. In the work of the G∴B∴G∴, however, it soon became apparent that the writings of King Wan and his son were, in many places, incorrect and contradictory. Legge, the translator, had already called attention to these errors.

King Wan and his son had written after the manner of fortunetellers, and had treated the hexagrams as one integral figure, even though they should have known better. The figure called a hexagram is actually two trigrams, the upper conditioning the lower and vice versa.

For example, Figure 18 has "Sun" for its upper trigram and "Air" for its lower trigram—Sun is thus conditioned by the Air trigram, and the entire hexagram should be considered as "Air of Sun." Analysis of this position is considerably different from, for instance, Number 22, which is "Moon of Sun."

King Wan had two good excuses for his inaccurate interpretations. He had been jailed by a rival king and, while in jail, King Wan wrote on the Yi much that was intended as a secret message to his followers. Also he used the Yi figures to preach to his followers and to give them advice. It is these meanings, used instead of the actual meanings of the hexagrams, which confuse the interpretations.

Now the Yi King is the greatest magick oracle ever given to man, and the G∴B∴G∴ felt that it was necessary to get the true essence of the Yi, that is to say, to bypass the Wan texts and reach back to the pristine Yi as given by the great sage, Fu Hsi, in 3300 BC. The pristine Yi is not Chinese in thought, but is universal, ageless, and as "modern" as today's English language.

The writer played a very considerable part in the reformulation of the Yi in its pristine meaning, for which reason the meanings of the sixty-four Yi figures are given in the writer's own words. It was in this form that the Yi King was used in the G∴B∴G∴ rituals. For further information, see Louis Culling's book *The Pristine Yi King*, Llewellyn Publications.

The trigrams which, doubled, compose the hexagrams are made up of combinations of Yang and Yin lines. The Yang is customarily represented by an unbroken line, and the Yin by a divided or broken line. One should become well acquainted with these elements of structure and commit to memory the eight original Pa Kua or trigrams with something of their basic meanings.

The following is a table of the basic correspondences of Yang and Yin:

YANG	YIN
Male	Female
Projective	Receptive
Startling	Sustaining
Initiating	Responding
Active	Passive
Beginning	Developing
Hard	Soft
Leading	Following
Extrovert	Introvert
Strength, energy	Nourishment, preservation
Sun	Moon
Brilliance	Reflected Light
Mid-day	Mid-night
Summer	Winter
Will	Emotion

Never are Yang and Yin to be regarded as antagonistic, or as a dualism. They are co-equal and co-operating partners in the basic concept. There can be no manifestation without the union of the two Great Principles, any more than there could be offspring without the union of male and female.

The worker in the Yi should know the meanings of the three positions of the lines of the trigram. The trigram and the hexagram are always constructed from the bottom line upward, the bottom line corresponding to the body, the second line to mind, and the top line to soul or spirit. To show this in more detail:

The Bottom Line Position

The physical body; the lower instinctive actions; the automatic or uncontrolled emotions. Also the drive to action.

Central Line Position

The mind, or Thinking Man; intelligence; the more or less consciously self-directing mind. Conscious will.

Top Line Position

Inspired direction, wisdom. The highest inspiration, thinking and action of man.

Now the line positions of the hexagram have added significance and correspondences, depending upon whether the lower or the upper trigram is being considered. The lower trigram is called "the Inferior," and the upper "the Superior," and this should be taken quite literally. The Superior trigram describes everything or every person that may be "superior" to the consultant, while the Inferior trigram relates to any "inferior" person or thing. For instance, any dealings with one's "boss" relate to the upper trigram. Also the Superior trigram often speaks of what the Chinese call "The Great One" or "The Great Man," that is, one's daemon or a reflection of it in wisdom and direction.

The line positions of the hexagram also correspond astonishingly with the chessmen on the chessboard. There is convincing evidence, in fact, that chess is derived from the Yi philosophy.

Bottom line, or Line 1, = Pawns, the many, foot soldiers.

Line 2 = Knights, more independent and self-directive.

Line 3 = Bishops, high thinking and intelligence.

Line 4 = Castle. The Yi texts call this the "Prime Minister."

Line 5 = The King, called "The King" in the Yi texts.

Line 6 = The Queen, Great Mother, or the Womb.

There is one Great Key, and only one (almost secret), to the interpretation of each of the sixty-four hexagrams in relation to any question or to any consultant. This Key is the right comprehension of the meaning of each of the eight trigrams, plus the special implications of the trigram's position in the hexagram, upper or lower. The worker in the Yi should be able to deduce the meanings of the hexagrams as applied to the hundreds of questions that may be asked, simply by considering the nature of each trigram and the special meanings of its position in the hexagram. He would not, then, have to depend entirely on the list of meanings, which will presently be given.

Try to memorize the following short exposition of the natures of the eight trigrams, or Pa Kua as they are named in Chinese.

NUMBER I KHIEN	Great. Originating. Penetrating. (Note: There is no Yin, or female, line in this trigram. It represents the pure initiating energy, force, and intent, but it must be nourished and developed by some Yin response before it can manifest.)
NUMBER 2 AIR	Penetration. Also easily penetrated. Rules the mind. Ease of operating but not solidly substantial or long lasting.
NUMBER 3 SUN	Realization, great brilliance. Realized manifestation. Union.
NUMBER 4 EARTH	Solid and fixed. Not easily moved or changed. Materialistic. Consolidation.

NUMBER 5 WATER	▬ ▬ ▬▬▬	Pleased satisfaction. Passive, receptive, and without initiative. Can be too easy going, or can carry too much sensual desire; but in general it is "pleased satisfaction."
NUMBER 6 MOON	▬ ▬ ▬ ▬	Called "Peril"—not an easy situation or condition. Inclined more to ambition than to ability or favorable conditions.
NUMBER 7 FIRE	▬ ▬ ▬▬▬	Exciting energy and action. May be too rash in action. The exciting will of the desires.
NUMBER 8 KHWAN	▬ ▬ ▬ ▬	Fully receptive, nourishing and developing. Infinite response. Infinite desire. Seeks to be filled up. Totally feminine (no Yang line), and dependent on outside initiative and strength—hence it is said to be weak.

Each of the meanings given in the following pages for the sixty-four hexagrams has two parts, (1) the Man-Woman relationship, and (2) the Superior-Inferior relationship.

The Man-Woman relationship is often indicated to be poor because of bad polarity. However, if the woman in the case is strongly masculine while the man is strongly feminine, then the augury would be read as a good Hexagram (see hexagram number 57).

The Superior-Inferior relationship is treated here as applying strictly to human beings. However, when the question of the querent applies to himself alone and does not involve another person, the reader should pay particular attention to the other aspect of the Superior-Inferior relationship. For there is a higher meaning to the Superior-Inferior relationship in which the Superior represents the daemon, the Higher Self, the Holy Guardian Angel.

Let the student pay particular attention to those hexagrams that have as the Superior trigram either Water Trigrams (5), or Khwan Trigrams (8). These are hexagrams 33 to 40 inclusive, and 57 to 64 inclusive. The interpretation in these cases should be that the daemon is fully complacent (if not interfered with) and will allow the querent a full, free course in following the indications of the Inferior Trigram (again, see hexagram number 57).

The Wan texts, placed first in each analysis of a hexagram, are given in quotation marks. Since King Wan did not always write correctly, one should check his text carefully with the rest of the analysis. In only thirty-eight out of the sixty-four hexagrams has he provided a good analysis of the figure.

Meanings of the 64 Yi Hexagrams

The following initial abreviations are used, not for space saving but rather for emphasis:

S.T.—Superior, or upper, Trigram.

I.T.—Inferior, or lower, Trigram.

M.—Man.

W.—Woman.

In any question involving both Man and Woman, S.T. represents the man, and I.T. represents the woman, unless the W. holds a superior position to the M., such as being his boss.

S.—The Superior. Any person who holds the superior position involved in a question. Also, if the question does not involve other people, the S. may be one's own supersensual mind or genius, or one's own superior directing force (called the "daemon" by Dr. Carl Jung).

I.—The Inferior. The one who holds the inferior position in the involved question. May also represent the desires, emotions, and involuntary instincts rather than intelligent willed direction.

Take note that the sixty-four figures are divided in series of eight, i.e., in the first series of eight figures Khien is the S.T., in the next eight figures (9 to 16 inclusive) Air is the S.T. A magician may gain more insight in the implications of the various figures by keeping each series of eight figures in mind and making comparisons between them.

In the delineation of each of the sixty-four figures there is a short comment on the Man-Woman Relationship (abreviated M.W.R.). This is to describe the auspice of the social or sexual relationship that may be in question (or often should be).

The 64 Hexagrams

Upper Trigrams

Lower Trigrams

	KHIEN	AIR	SUN	EARTH	WATER	MOON	FIRE	KHWAN
	1	2	3	4	5	6	7	8
1	1	9	17	25	33	41	49	57
2	2	10	18	26	34	42	50	58
3	3	11	19	27	35	43	51	59
4	4	12	20	28	36	44	52	60
5	5	13	21	29	37	45	53	61
6	6	14	22	30	38	46	54	62
7	7	15	23	31	39	47	55	63
8	8	16	24	32	40	48	56	64

The 64 Hexagrams

Upper Trigrams

Hexagrams 1 to 8, Khien is the S. T.

1. Great originating or initiating force, but there is no Yin line to give response, nourishment, and sustainment—therefore it requires vigilance and restraint to keep the force within bounds. The oracle for the outcome must wait until there is a Yin response. Time to meet the "Great Man" (one's Divine Genius).

2. The Yin response is confined to the lowest line, which is the materialistic desires and instincts. Ideally, the I. should be desirous and responsive to the direction of the S., and the S. should not squander the forces on the unworthy. M.W.R., at best (as the figure indicates in all ways), is good for only a short time and not of long duration because it is pleasant but superficial.

3. "Union of Men"—"Cross the Stream"—"Progress." Brilliant Realization (Sun 3) of the Great (Khien). M.W.R. is too masculine. Responsive only mentally. S. to I. relationship is very good if of the same interest and aspiration.

4. There is a growth and increase in power of small people before the superior. Earth 4 is fixedness and consolidation and is good if not restrictive to Khien, the Great. The fixedness is not conducive to the new and progressive. Let it be "consolidating" rather than restrictive fixedness, and then all goes well. The same applies to the M.W.R.

5. Complacence and even laziness brings some pleased satisfaction. In the Man-Woman Relationship, let the S. give "pleased satisfaction" only if the W. (or I.) is aspirationally receptive rather than sensually demanding. Even the daemon is willing to grant pleased satisfaction to the desires. Restraint may be only a matter of exigency.

6. Moon 6 is restrictive to the best correct force of Khien. It is a good time to "meet the Great Man" but not to try to "cross the Great Stream" because there is more ambition than developed ability. M.W.R. is exciting but requires caution. At best, it is good for the I. if not too emotionally ambitious and if the S. makes a willing sacrifice.

7. This is the Fire 7 of exciting energy of the physical will, desires, and instincts in conjunction with Khien 8, the Great Creative Will. Obviously, this requires intelligent regulation for the best outcome and is then best for starting rather than developing. The M.W.R. is conflicting, though could be good if confined to the highest aspiration and inspiration.

8. Khwan 8 is absorbing and developing the Khien 1 superior projection. M.W.R. is very good if the Yin supplication is not too selfish and sensuous. The Great Yang is a drive to "fill up" a worthy Yin, therefore let Yin invoke the highest and then this hexagram is of Great Augury—otherwise, not.

Hexagrams 9 to 16, Air is the S.T.

9. Easy penetration and easily penetrated. There is a small restraint, free movement, good fortune, and quick success, but not in the great things unless it be the creation of great mental concepts.

M.W.R.—there is strong superficial mutual response. Let the I. submit to the higher direction of the S. for the best outcome, otherwise no development of great value and duration is indicated.

10. Easy movement, but only small attainment. Flexibility, line of least resistance. M.W.R.—easy small attainments full of superficial desires, but not bad. Time to see the "Great Man"—for the substantial.

11. Sun 3 gives realization and integration of Air 2, the mental image or plan. This requires due exercise of consistency, regulation and cooperation. Here we see that the "Inferior" is truly Superior to the "Superior" in the subject matter, but the S. grants free course to the I. M.W.R.—not a good polarity response.

12. Good for maintaining anything in a fixed or stable way in conformity with certain fixed patterns or conditions. Not very promising for starting something new. M.W.R.—though the man is pliant, yet he has some capability in penetrating the fixed solidity of the woman, if correct.

13. This is the real imagination in its true sense, but studied self-honesty and due deliberation is advised because of the possible lack of stability in both of the trigrams, Air and Water. The S. should condescend and the I. should intelligently respond—i.e., mutual response. M.W.R.—very good, particularly if in sincerity with aspiration and inspiration; there is mutual satisfaction.

14. Good for meditation or concentration, but emotional impressions or obtrusions may interfere. The wise man should "retire to the ancestral temple." There is a dissipation or scattering of values with the average run of people and of good augury to superior people if not venturing beyond good judgment. M.W.R.—not recommended.

15. The Wan text says, "Adding or increasing; advantage in every movement even to crossing the stream." Actually, this can apply only to superior people, and if one does not move by intelligent restraint and well-planned objective it can be a poor augury. The same goes for the M.W.R.

16. The upper, Air 2, manifests to the lower, Khwan 8, and the lower receives and contemplates the higher. This is one of the rare times that the Wan text is so very correct in saying, "Showing, contemplating, manifesting." M.W.R.—good; woman is fully responsive to the man.

Hexagrams 17 to 24, Sun is the S.T.

This trigram implies understanding (and inspiration), brilliance, and realization—self-realization.

17. The I.T., Khein—creative impulse and forceful drive—applies to the S.T., Sun—realization of self. This hexagram has been called "Great Havings"—but it is not particularly promising for further acquisition. S. and I.—good if there is a mutual aspiration for realization (involving real individuality) rather than for overambitious energy.

18. This is well named "The Cauldron" because it is the great transformer. This is the mental concept of brilliant realization (including the nourishment of talent and virtue); hence progress and success. S. and I.—mutually excellent if held to the general meaning of the Hexagram M.W.R.—none better for inspired "Sex Magick," real magick transmutation. A magickal transmutation.

19. This is the Sun trigram doubled. It is brilliance, intelligence, inward adherence. No advance promised. W.R.—good only as platonic.

20. This is a fixation or consolidation (sometimes restriction) of realization or the realized self. S. and I.—should not try to contend with each other, just consolidate. M.W.R.—the Woman gives solid substantial support to the Man or S. Also materialism, stubborness, restriction, and constriction—not for good results.

21. The I. is the Water trigram, which indicates a strong desire for pleasure and pleased satisfaction and therefore some pleased diversity is indicated even though in general agreement. It is a very good union or agreement of Yang to Yin. Should rest in satisfaction of some realization rather than a drive for further advancement. M.W.R.—is the same as implied in the foregoing.

22. Here the I., the Moon, generally indicates more drive and ambition than is possessed in the subject matter and hence there is some peril in the situation. However, if the S. is of great potential (or there is enough resourcefulness) to relate with the I., it can be a good outcome. M.W.R.—good only if both have self-integration and they are both sincerely aspiring. Can be very bad and also very good.

23. The exciting moving energy of the Fire trigram can lead to realization if there is enough discipline and enough sustained action, rather than a mere flash. Emotional or instinctive action without intelligent direction is to be avoided. M.W.R.—not auspicious except for exciting, driving energy.

24. The S. advances in whatever direction while Inferiors give support is the best interpretation of this Hexagram Let the integrity, intelligence, and nobility of the S. evoke the responding support and development of the I.

Hexagrams 25 to 32, Earth—or Mountain—is the S. T. (The good phase is desired stability and solidity, fixation and consolidation. The unfavorable phase is stubborn fixedness and immobility up to the point of restriction or constriction.)

25. The I.T., Khien, gives strength and volumes of virtue and force and energy that is accumulated and fixed and consolidated in the S.T.—therefore this Hexagram is called "the Great Accumulation" as what is being accumulated is not spent or dissipated. It obviously requires intelligence and planning to avoid the stubborn restriction of the Earth trigram. This is good for the conservation of energy and force, but not very propitious for advancing or growing. M.W.R.—can be good if there is mutual agreeable response between "forceful energy" and disciplined restraint.

26. Some painful requirements must be met if there is no mutual good response between the hard and restrictive S. with the I.T. of easy motion and easy penetration. The best augury is for both the S. and I. to look to the "higher self," the daemon, the Real and True Superior. M.W.R.— only for "accumulation" for later expression or use.

27. The Earth trigram puts a limit upon the "brilliance" of the Sun. The brilliance is not of a high order and is materialistic. Therefore it is called "Ornament," which is, at least to some extent, superficial or materialistic. This is more outward show than inner greatness but it has its useful and desirable aspect. Beauty can mitigate binding conditions. M.W.R.—best only for planning and preparing rather than advancing activity.

28. This hexagram is called "resting and arresting" for it is the Earth trigram doubled. Body rest—thoughts do not go beyond the position. Absolute fixed concentration is possible—or impregnable immobility and fixedness.

Not an augury for new action or advance. Good for status quo. M.W.R. and S. and I.—generally to be stolid, fixed, uninspired, and unmovable—and stubborn.

29. Water under Earth. The stolid fixedness of the S.T., Earth, is softened somewhat by the easygoing pleasant I.T. of Water, unless, under some conditions the fixedness of Earth and the pleasure-seeking satisfaction become irreconcilable. M.W.R.—can be excellent as a fixation of pleasurable desires in "matter," i.e., leading to realization.

30. Moon under Earth. The S.T., with patience, and involving practical skill might influence the I.T. to be also practical and to subdue an overly ambitious drive that is beyond good ability and good judgment. Simple sincerity with no combativeness is necessary for any good augury. M.W.R.—good for the woman.

31. The S. is fixed and not easily moved and yet the I. has much exciting and energetic drive to advance or move. Obviously this requires much to be reconciled, though this can be done if there is a cherishing of real values and is carried out with temperate regulation. Conflicting unless there is plenty of "give and take." M.W.R.—not a propitious augury.

32. The I.T., Khwan, indicates nourishment and development of the already established S.T. However, this will bring fresh conditions and expansions for a future time. At present, any advancing move in any direction is not well advised. At best, it is good only for very stable and materialistic conditions. M.W.R.—good only if in accord with this hexagram, which is nourishing, supporting, sustaining, and consolidating—for a later time.

Hexagrams 33 to 40, Water is the S.T.
(The S.T. of Water always indicates a dominance of pleasure; easy-going, and pleased acquiescence.)

33. Khien, the forceful will, is in the process of challenging the easygoing Water. Also, on the other hand, the S.T., Water, can indicate pleased acquiescence to the initiating strength and vigor of Khien, and, in this case, complacency brings emoluments. This hexagram generally indicates free course for and to starting energy. M.W.R.—the polarity of the two trigrams are in reverse.

34. Water in combination with Air—the person may not act out the requirements even though he or she may have them, and also we note that the I. can outwit the S. The ancient text says that this hexagram indicates extraordinary methods (even wits and trickiness). There is much adaptability indicated, which if applied can lead to good results, though the results are inclined to be superficial with no great depth or solidity. M.W.R.—as indicated above.

35. There is a realization of the superficial Water images and thereby a welcome for change for the better—otherwise it may bring surfeit. S. is inclined to be complacent and tolerant, and even pleased with the brilliant character of the I. M.W.R.—the polarity is opposite of what is called "correct"—it is auspicious only if the W. (or I.) is of high character and potential brilliance and the M. (or S.) recognizes it.

36. Means Jointly—all together, mutual influence. This is the best potential which is mutual agreement between S. and I. (or understanding of the conditions which is then the free movement bringing about stability and consolidation), but there is no advantage in pushing forward. M.W.R.—is good only if there can be mutual agreement, understanding, and a desire and willingness to be mutually influencing.

37. Both trigrams are Water.
Appease thyself, harmonious in thy sphere.
Single thy desire, most utterly sincere.
Turn not aside when siren pleasures woo,
But search well thyself to make thy purpose clear,
Swim the placid waters for thy pleasure,
But let not the sensuous be the total measure.
Not a promise of long-time stability and sound foundation.

38. The augury is much difficulty and even peril in the contemplated subject. The best way to cope with this is to have a full comprehension of the difficulty and to gird oneself and make only necessary moves. There is a complacent Superior with an incapable or overdemanding Inferior. Wait! Wait!

39. For any good there must be reconciliation between the exciting energy of Fire and the easygoing complacency of Water. There is a rare possibility that a complacent Man might gain the adherence of a highly energetic and fiery Woman, to bring some "fire." In the same way, might that indicated by the Superior trigram profit by that indicated in the energetic drive of the Inferior.

40. Khwan indicates great capacity and sustainment of the upper Water trigram, pleased satisfaction. Therefore, there is no dispersion or separation for ill. M.W.R.—on the one hand, is inordinate desire for sensuous fulfillment. On the other hand, it can be one of the best hexagrams for even high "Sex Magick." Mutual desire of the nourishment and development of "pleased satisfaction." Very auspicious to "repair to the ancestral temple" and to "meet the Great Man"—in preparation for a new progressive cycle.

Hexagrams 41 to 48, Moon is the S.T.

(In this series that which is indicated by the S. T. is inept and over-ambitious and generally inferior to the I.T.)

41. Moon over Khien. In any question, the great originating energy of the I.T. is far superior to the inept, undeveloped, and overdemanding S.T. This indicates strain and constriction and it is better to "walk the due mean" until more propitious for action. If the querent is indicated as the Inferior (lower trigram), he or she can successfully cope with the "Superior" if anger or stubborn resistance is not aroused.

42. Generally unstable or upset conditions—at best of easy but small worth and not long lasting. A fair time to try to get ideas or make plans, all of which must later be improved or modified. Superior is inclined to need experience but is willful. The Inferior can grasp good mental concepts, but of no great depth. M.W.R.—No.

43. Incompetent Superior; very good Inferior. I.T., the Sun, ameliorates the unauspicious to the extent that, while advising to do nothing new, nevertheless is good to complete and consolidate the past up to the present. M.W.R.—polarity is reversed.

44. Good only for completing what has been started—to make stable and to consolidate everything in relation to the prevailing conditions. Let discreet small movement alternate with discreet inactivity—be very cautious. Difficulty in advancing. One must be continually on guard to be correct: a time not to challenge the status quo. M.W.R.—not promising.

45. The trigrams (both S. and I.) indicate some small satisfaction, but one that is restricted. Advises suppression of too much desire for pleasure or satisfaction—but some good. M.W.R. and S. and I.—some good can be extracted, but only under disciplined desires, necessary restraint.

46. Both trigrams are the Moon—double difficulty. It is best to be reconciled to just maintaining one's position (or status quo) and to make no unnecessary moves. M.W.R. and S. and I.—this hexagram is the runner-up for the worst of possible auguries.

47. One should struggle under the difficulty but not to attempt great things. This is the striving of the first stages of growth—movement amid hazards—no static security. Let there be prudence in action. M.W.R.—No.

48. Difficult conditions but good adherents and help can be secured if one lives up to the requirements. Let the S.T. sincerely invoke all help and support possible from the I.T. M.W.R.—from the foregoing it can be seen that the relationship is good, if mutually aspiring.

Hexagrams 49 to 56, Fire is the S.T.

(Whether it be superior conditions, superior person or persons, one's superior self, even the daemon or superior "destiny," there is always great exciting energy indicated—energetic instinctive drive to do or to advance.)

49. The lower trigram, Khien, is also great strength and initiating energy, which in most cases is too strong to handle unless held in subordination to intelligent direction and "correctness." Be warned against violent action and contention. Good for startingbut must await the future for a "place to go" and for development. A third factor or person is required. M.W.R.—polarity is in reverse and not good.

50. Air is the I.T.—the mind assisting the fiery will of the S.T. This is very good for movement and easy penetration, and in any direction is advantageous—but it is also either superficial or unsubstantial. M.W.R.—fiery and sensual.

51. The ancient text calls this "large and abundant" because it is best to receive, manifest, and maintain the "large and abundant" in manifestation rather than to be overconcerned with forward movement. The I.T. is superior to the S.T. M.W.R.—in the G∴B∴G∴ tradition it is stated to be "excellent for Sex Magick."

52. I.T. is Earth. S.I.—the S. gives some needed stimulus to the stolidness and fixedness of the I., while the I. gives some fixing stable focus for the energy stimulus of the S. Some success is indicated but it is limited and no advance is promised. M.W.R.—good for what the hexagram indicates only, which is good for formulating the "magick link" for future action.

53. The Water trigram is under Fire, and this is one of the rare occasions when the ancient text is right, calling

this "Disparity of conditions or things." The easygoing pleasure-seeking Water is not in much agreement with the exciting energy of the upper Fire trigram. However, intelligent worthy people will see and apply a mutual amelioration between the two trigrams—Water dampening the undirected Fire exciting energy, and the exciting Fire giving stimulus to the pleased satisfaction of Water. S. and I. and M.W.R.—is very good if completely taking advantage of the conditions just described.

54. The complication of Moon under Fire is difficult to resolve or unravel, but must be done to extract any good from the augury of this hexagram. In this hexagram the so-called "Inferior" is inferior in that there is more ambition than good judgment or ability. Just fully recognize the hazards and proceed intelligently.

55. This is the trigram of exciting Fire doubled. One should not meet this great exciting movement recklessly nor head-on. There are no responding compliments of polarity that give reception and development. Even one's judgment may be adversely influenced by the exciting Fire. Be very cautious—even to waiting.

56. A great deal of what was written for hexagram number 53 also applies to this hexagram. However, there is more harmony and contentment. The Inferior gives cooperation and nourishment, support and development to the energetic drive of the Superior trigram. However, for the best, it should be expansion and development of the status quo rather than advancing across the stream." M.W.R.—excellent—even for magick. Contrary to some indications of number 53 about "disparity," this hexagram indicates great potential for harmony and contentment—and development.

Hexagrams 57 to 64, Khwan is the S.T.
(The upper trigram, Khwan, is totally female and hence out of the correct polarity position. In some questions this indicates too much passivity, or a desire to be filled up. However, in many cases it serves the I.T. very well in being not only passive or permissive, but also in giving "nourishment" and full development of the subject matter.)

57. Khwan over Khien. The great originating force of Khien is given full acceptance and support by the Khwan, the S.T. This is a great beginning where even the "daemon" gives complete acquiescence and support to that which is initiated, but it must await a later time for full realization. M.W.R. and S. and I.—relationships, containing reversed polarities in trigram positions, can be good only under the foregoing described conditions, i.e., dominant I. and passive S.

58. Khwan over Air. Everything in "high position" is in accord with the easy penetration of Air (the I.), but it is not promising for a great or extended advancement because this is mostly a mental initiation starting or a very good plan that must await realization. All relationships can be very good if there is mutual understanding and sincerity above blind desire.

59. The lower trigram, Sun, gets no opposition from the S.T. and gets great support. In its best phase, the S. gives great free course to manifested intelligence and brilliance; therefore, let the S. depend upon and cooperate and develop that brilliance of the I. M.W.R.—Woman must be of a high type for any good.

60. The I.T. is Earth, which is fixedness, stability, and consolidation (at its best) and therefore the I. (for the best) should be humble and honorable within one's own sphere. The I. must not restrict the S., but should seek support.

This is (from the Occult view) the consolidation in matter of infinite desire. It is good for diminishing excesses and for accumulation rather than for advancing. Danger is grossly materialistic and selfish desires and stubbornness in maintaining status quo.

61. The "Higher authority" of the "Superior" submits to (and even supports) the expansion of gratification and pleased satisfaction of the I.T., Water—the infinite expansion of pleasure and desires. Both trigrams are "easygoing," except there may be great sensual desires for pleasure and satisfaction. There can be contentment in submitting to the S., whether benevolent or not. M.W.R. and S. and I.—good for the expansion of pleased satisfaction.

62. Full sway is given to even immaturity, rashness, and incompetence. Inclined to excessive optimism, but it is better to seek the blessing of the "Great One"—and wait.

63. Fire is the Inferior trigram. There is no deterring obstacle except what might be unfavorable in a blind drive for action, misdirected energy plus a too-ready acquiescence. Only with intelligent direction and due restraint against bad moves can this be a good augury and very good on the materialistic level.

64. This is the doubled trigram of Khwan. It is totally feminine, just as hexagram number 1 is totally masculine. What can the feminine polarity be without the masculine polarity, and vice versa? This hexagram indicates great capacity and development of what has been started beforehand; if not, then resting in the womb of potentiality for an initiating start.

appendix three

Magickal Postures, Movements, and Gestures

When you look at the posed photographs accompanying this appendix, you might be inclined to think of them portraying merely dramatic actions intended to accompany dramatic dialogue in a theatrical play.

Not really!

The best analogy I can offer is to consider actual martial arts postures and movements. You know that these movements—no matter the particular style—generate and deliver amazing power. And when you study any of the martial arts you will often find illustrations showing the many subtle body energy channels, meridians, and psychic centers involved.

Now, think of your own body. Earlier in this book I suggested you to smile, and then feel how your body and emotions respond to that simple "posture." "When you smile, the whole world smiles with you" is more than a pretty phrase because that gesture is infectious and brings smiles to other people as well. But, what happened to you when you smiled? You felt better! The small act triggered not only an emotional response but through the nerves and muscles involved switched on many electrical and chemical transfers in your body. And then projected energy into your aura and broadcast it to these other people who "smiled with you."

Pretty amazing, isn't it?

Energy at Work

Every posture, movement, and gesture involves muscles and nerves, electrical currents and chemicals, energy flows and hormones along with emotional and spiritual responses, and changes in the aura.

Yes, every movement of the physical body triggers a complex of responses, but some are very specific in what they do. Some of the accompanying photographs have accompanying text describing the position and gesture as a "sign." Yes, they are that, too, but the important point is to understand the psychic and magickal side of all these positions, postures, movements, signs, and gestures.

While recognition of this inner body psychic dimension has not been common in the Western Tradition, it is a reality nevertheless.

When you assume any of these positions and make the movements, you should learn to be sensitive to the energy flow, and with that learn to adjust your stance and movements until the energy flow feels just right. It will help to allow yourself to "imagine" seeing those energies from outside your body, seeing them just as if viewing a schematic diagram of channels and centers.

I think it is unfortunate that Western magicians do not, as a matter of course and practice, study the oriental martial arts, and incorporate them into their magickal work.

Note: The movements and postures are accompanied by gestures that must all function in unity with the voiced expressions, chants, invocations, evocations, and mental visualization and astral extensions. Everything works together, just as must all the ritualists in a group working. No one is idle—psychically.

Let's consider each of the illustrations in turn.

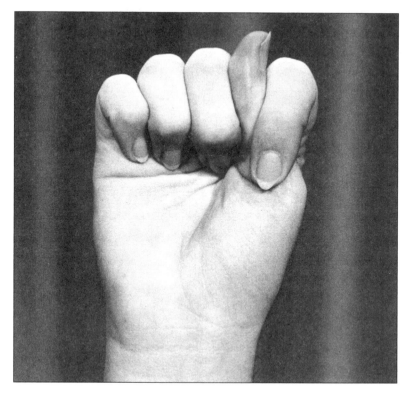

Clenched Thumb

The "opposing" thumb has long been recognized as a distinguishing and enabling human characteristic. It's the most powerful of the five fingers and enables the hand to grasp things, and hence to do work.

Now, clench your thumb as shown (whichever hand is your power hand), close your eyes, and sense the energy flow. Then, instead, point your index finger, and note the difference in energy flow. It's subtle, the clenched thumb allows the energies to circulate and build in strength. The pointed finger works to strongly project energy, but requires energy to be drawn up from the feet, and earth, and through the body.

Each "wand" functions, but differently. With the clenched thumb you are working within a circle; with the pointed index finger you are projecting beyond the circle.

Prayer and Inspiration

This, of course, is very familiar to many religious traditions, East and West. It is a gesture suited to both prayer and peaceful greetings. Try it yourself, eyes closed, and sense the energies. With the palms flat against each other, the energy circuits are in repose, neither blocking nor inviting energies from outside the body and its circle.

It's a natural position for meditation and "passive" prayer. See chapter Three.

The Opening

Whether with bell, rattle, or gong, or a simple gesture, the intention
is to announce the opening. The position is masculine and authorita-
tive. It could as easily announce a store opening, and that too would be
magickal. Magick is not reserved to a private room, but is part of life.
The priest here is Louis Culling.

Isis in Welcome

Culling describes this as "the sign of complete feminine Reception, Nourishment and the Spiritual Objective." The legs are spread apart as shown in "Pan Triumphant." There are variations of the arm and hand positions, but you can readily perceive that this is both receptive and retentive within a semiclosed circle. Eyes are focused on the circled arms. See chapter Nine.

Sign of Aspiration (Fire)

The Element of Fire is signified by creating an upright triangle with the two thumbs and two index fingers. The arms are elevated and the feet should be spread. Eyes are focused on the sign of the element formed by the enclosing hands.

The Enterer

Invoking the aid of the elements. The left foot in thrust forward and the arms are thrust straight out from the shoulders—not quite as high as shown in the photograph. The palms should be only slightly elevated. Eyes are focused straightforward.

Prayer and Inspiration

This is the Sign of the Initiating of the Magickal "Offspring" in Sex Magick. Note how the arms are positioned in an almost diamond pattern, and the palms nearly so. The hands are retaining that which has been borne. The eyes adore. See chapter Ten.

"Abrahadabra"

The Great Work has been performed, finished, and consecrated. The sign is of the feminine aspects of containment and nourishment following the Sex Magick Creation. See chapter Ten. The eyes are contemplating.

Pan Triumphant

"Hail! It is accomplished!" Notice the finger is a "victory" sign. Arms are straightly elevated and feet spread. This is an announcement of the job well done. The feeling is "controlled" elation. The eyes should be centered and only partially upward.

Countenance beholds Countenance

The priestess, still in light trance, has performed the Invocation of Pan eight times during a period of eight hours and received a great illumination and transforming initiation. She was aided by the three ritualists.

Egyptian God Posture

The priestess is shown seated in the traditional Egyptian God form of magickal attention and concentration. Note the interlocked thumbs of the priest. The Western Esoteric Tradition has adopted the Egyptian God postures as seen in paintings on tomb and temple walls. Whether standing, moving, or seated, these show positions of dignity and energy restraint. You can sense power that would be released in a simple gesture.

All postures involve intentional movement—even if just sitting with grace and awareness of energy flow. There are, of course, other postures: those of the martial arts in China and Japan, belly and dervish dances in the Middle East, hula from Hawaii, and much more. Any movement and posture that involves energy probably have an associated shamanic or sacred tradition.

In the world of magick, the motto is "Energy at work!"

Eye Positions

Note the eye focus in the different photographs. The eyes are powerful magickal "tools"—both receiving and projecting energy. While their positioning is often spontaneous with any of the body postures, the more aware you are of the energy flow, the more expressive will be the eyes. Learn to sense and control the energy flow.

The Ritual Positions

Sign of Opening of the Temple—Palms open, fingers extended, arms held overhead in the form of an inverted triangle. Then drop the palms and fingers before the eyes; then raise them back up in the original position.

Sign of Closing of the Temple—The same sign, except that the three-part motion begins with palms and fingers before the eyes, then overhead, then back to the original position.

Sign of Veneration or Eagle Sign—Arms crossed over chest, left palm over right shoulder and right palm over left shoulder, with the two thumbs interlocked. This is the "Eagle" sign, which means "Countenance beholds countenance."

Sign of the Enterer—Lunge forward on the left foot and extend the arms straight forward, fingers extended. Hold this position while speaking the "Enochian Words."

Receiving or Welcoming Sign—Straddle the legs widely apart, sideways; extend the arms above the head in a half circle.

The Elemental Invocations

The described signs are to be traced by the Thumb-Wand. Make them about three feet in diameter. The pentagrams and hexagram are to be made in one continuous line. In the Rose Cross Sign the outer circle is drawn first, then the inner cross.

Of course, you visualize the signs as they are drawn, but be aware of the energy being projected from the wand and from the eyes. What you see is what you will get!

Operation of the Retirement Ritual

See chapter Four.

1. Make the Sign of the Opening of the Temple.

2. Pace slowly three times around the circle while holding the concentrated thought that the circle is encompassing all good magick forces and is excluding all distractions and whatever alien forces. See the circle formed in pulsating bluish light floating above the floor.

3. Go to the center and say: "Let the rituals be rightly performed with joy and beauty." Feel joy and see beauty. Never let your words be "empty," but accompany them in your imagination to make them real.

4. Go to the East corner and trace with the "wand" the trigram of Air, visualized as glowing yellow.

5. Make the Sign of the Enterer, saying: "Great Elemental of Air, I unite with Thee."

6. Make the Sign of Welcome, saying: "Great Yellow Powers of Air, come thou forth and aid and guard me in this work of art."

    Go to the South corner and repeat steps Four through Six above, except that the sign is the trigram of Fire seen in red, and the name is changed to Great Red Fire.

    Go to the West corner and repeat as above, except the sign is the Blue trigram of Water.

    Go to the North corner and repeat as above, except the sign is the Green Earth.

7. Go to the center, clap hands together in a rhythm of 1—3—3—3—1, a total of eleven claps.

8. Make a circle (with wand) above the head, crying: "Nuit."

9. Touch the wand (thumb) to the Muladhara (sex chakra), crying: "Hadit."

10. Touch the wand to the center of the Breast, crying: "Ra—Hoor—Khuit."

11. Now visualize yourself as being enclosed in a great silver cone that extends in great height above you. Project your consciousness higher and higher in the cone, saying: "Great Goddess Babalon, carry me safely and closer to my divine genius, my immortal daemon, my Holy Guardian Angel." Let this be done slowly and also lasting long enough that you do not feel like enduring the aspiration any longer.

12. Make the Eagle Veneration sign and hold it while saying: "I hear and heed the words of mine Angel. My Angel tells me: I am above you and in you. My ecstasy is in yours. My joy is to see your joy. To me! To me!"

13. Go to the edge of the circle and say: "Now let there be a veiling of this shrine." Make the Sign of the Closing the Temple and say: "Abrahadabra."

Final Notes

"Let the rituals be rightly performed with joy and beauty." Spoken as the opening of your ritual from the center of the Circle, it has the power of similar phrases like "Man your stations" and "Let the games begin!" Note there are three admonitions—that the rituals are to be performed rightly, and with joy and beauty.

This is not an idle statement; indeed, nothing said or done in your magickal circle, or temple, should be done without full awareness and intention to do anything less than your best and that is not only right action, but the feeling of joy and happiness in your heart, and the intention that all your movements, gestures, words, and thoughts will be done with the purpose of grace and beauty.

How you think when doing magick will affect how it works, and you want joy in your heart and beauty in our world.

Silver Cone. Also known as a "cone of power." A cone is commonly visualized as an extension of the magick circle to function as a container of inner strength and purpose and as a barrier against external disturbance.

Crying. In steps 8, 9, and 10 above, and elsewhere, the instruction calls for the words to be "cried" out. "Crying" is not the same as shouting, or speaking, or "vibrating." It comes closer to "calling out," yet is a little softer and less demanding. Like many other things, when you do it right, it will feel right. True enough, so long as you really stay consciously aware and pay attention to the feeling.

Glossary
and Suggested Readings

A glossary is not a dictionary but a list and description of words, phrases, and concepts as used within the particular book.

The descriptions used, however, are not arbitrary. They are "standard" but do have explanation of their meaning and particular application to their usage as related in the book. In this glossary I have tried to do so in particular regard to ceremonial magick and to how they were used and applied by the secret magickal Order of the Great Brotherhood of God.

In doing so, the glossary becomes a quick alphabetical reference to the curriculum of the G∴B∴G∴.

I've also included some material from outside the curriculum to better enable the reader to place it in perspective within the magickal community and the spiritual community of which it is part.

Ceremonial magick and the "secret" orders that developed particular methodologies should no longer be perceived as isolated and elitist but as simple variations on a common theme—that of integrating the disparate elements of the human psyche and to provide a roadmap to the development of the as yet unrealized potentials of the Whole Person. Their graded curriculums are like those structured for any serious study and our eclectic study of them provides an expanded understanding coincident with our broader knowledge and understanding of both inner and outer worlds.

The goal of all programs of self-development, whether set in a framework of ceremonial (or "high") magick, self-help, psychological therapies, the various yogas, the martial arts, Qabalistic path-working, shamanic practices, or any of the many spiritual paths, is summed up in my favorite phrase: *To Become More Than You Are.* In other words, to grow, to develop your innate powers into skills, and to fulfill the biblical promise (shared by most traditions) that we are all created in the image of the Creator and hence must have all the attributes of deity albeit we are in the process of making that image reality.

The premise is that we can and should accelerate the natural evolutionary process that brought us where we are today by taking individual responsibility for what the esoteric traditions name the "Great Work" and which I also call the "Great Adventure."

But it does mean work—work on self through a serious and structured developmental program whether that of a magickal order or that found in books and online courses, or as self-developed to fit your own particular needs and circumstance. Your opportunities are no longer geographically limited to the lodge system or to membership in organizations that may have particular agendas beyond facilitating the Great Work.

The Great Adventure is a journey we must all travel. The more you know about the territory ahead, the better can you map out your own road from your particular starting point and adjust to circumstantial detours and short-cuts, taking opportunities for side trips to visit subjects of interest, but always looking ahead to the goal of *Becoming More Than You Are.*

∴ Many readers may wonder what the three dots ∴ used in magickal books signify. This usage derives from the very old Masonic connections of the early Occult orders. The meaning varies according to the way in which it is used. Thus, at one time, it means "Honorable Initiate," at another time "sacred" or "Illuminated." It always signifies something "holy" or that an esoteric meaning is involved.

A∴A∴ (Argenteum Astrum or Order of the Silver Star) A magical order founded in 1907 by Crowley after leaving the Golden Dawn. It was reputed to reflect Crowley's bisexuality. See the website www.ordoaa .org/ for information and essential instructions for aspirants of the A∴A∴

Abracadabra. The spelling of the word was changed by Aleister Crowley to "Abrahadabra" to place the name *Had,* the second person of Crowley's Thelemite trinity, at the center. Abracadabra is traditional outside the Thelemite community.

Abrahadabra. Not to be confused with "Abracadabra." Crowley declared *Abrahadabra* to be the "Word of the New Aeon" that would unite microcosm with macrocosm in the new phase of human evolution. In itself, the word is understood as a formula of sex magick performed within the Great Work.

Abyss. (Kabbalah—Tree of Life) A division on the Tree of Life separating the top three Sephiroth from the rest of the Tree. A separation of the noumenal from the phenomenal, and the perceived separation between the upper, *unmanifest* trinity of Kether, Chokmah and Binah, and the lower seven Sephiroth that are manifest. It is believed that only adepts can access those higher levels.

Adept. Unfortunately, the term is used loosely and variously to mean: One who has reached a recognized higher grade in one of the initiatory orders; One who has made contact with their Holy Guardian Angel; One who has 'crossed the Abyss'; or for an advanced student.

Aeon of Horus. Following the channeling of *Liber Legis—(which see)—* The Book of the Law—in 1904, Crowley believed he was to lead a new age, the *Aeon of Horus* replacing the older matriarchal *Aeon of Isis* and the patriarchal *Aeon of Osiris.* The *Aeon of Horus* is based on the magical union of male and female polarities, and replaces all repressive religious traditions. According to Kenneth Grant, the *Aeon of Horus* will be followed by that of *Maat,* the Egyptian goddess of truth and justice.

Alchemy. The alchemy of the occultist and of sex magick is the transformation of the 'baser' self into the 'gold' of the higher self. The procedures, tools, and materials of the *physical* alchemist become symbols for the psychological and magickal operations of the occult alchemist.

Alien Forces. Are there such things? Are not all forces and beings part of a single and Divine Cosmos? Presumably, we have to say *yes* to that, but we also recognize that at different circumstances and times there are negative options. A snake bite can be poisonous. Even your pet cat can bite you and cause a severe, life-threatening infection.

In the context of magick, we are excluding from the Circle anything alien or unfriendly to the intent of the operation. Note the instructions in the GBG Curriculum that the magician is to pace three times around the Circle while holding the concentrated thought that the circle is encompassing all good magick forces and is excluding all distractions and whatever alien forces.

Circumscribing the Circle three times is traditional. Holding a "concentrated thought" is another way to state our "intention" to exclude unwanted influences. Important to this concept is to believe in the effect, and to have no fears or visions of frightful spirits or nasty forces trying to enter the Circle. In magick, as in any psychological practice, always keep the emphasis on the positive as already reality and avoid any thought of the negative while doing the operation.

This practice of exclusion also applies to thoughts and fantasies and day dreams that are common indulgences. Especially in group working, members not active at a given moment sometimes do 'drift off' and that interferes with the purity of the magickal atmosphere inside the Circle.

Alphaism. *Alphaism* means first or beginning because *alpha* is the first letter of the Greek alphabet. Alphaism was the beginning of the GBG instruction Sex Magick. Alphaism simply means no sexual intercourse. Erotic thoughts of imaginations should not even be entertained in the mind during the one or two months that the practice was required.

Instead of sex, the Alphaist member was to begin with the first verse of the first chapter of The Book of the Law, and take one sentence every day, in sequence, and meditate/concentrate on that sentence for at least an uninterrupted fifteen minutes one or more times daily. "Beware against making an intellectual study of this book. This is a very cryptic book, and is beyond intellectual rationalization. Get what you are capable of getting by inspired meditation."

Concentration is defined as: "Close mental application or exclusive attention." The mental activity is confined to a definite point. When one visualizes tracing a pentagram in green light, one must really concentrate in order to make it subjectively real.

Altar. An altar is really a work bench holding your magickal tools. Usually it is placed at the center of the circle or working area. Sometimes it may be moved to face any of the four corners. Traditionally it is composed of two equal size cubes, one on top of the other.

Ancient Wisdom. "The Ancient Wisdom" remains a mystery, perhaps a myth, perhaps lost history of a time when "Men were Gods." Or, was it when "The Gods walked on Earth"? or when "Space Visitors seeded the Earth"?

However we treat it, the Ancient Wisdom purportedly included knowledge of great powers and energies, of technologies still surpassing those of the modern world, and of wisdom that would transform our present world into one of Peace, Prosperity, and Progress.

It's the real concept underlying the belief in the *New Age*, and in *Novus Ordo Seclorum*—a "New Order of the Ages."

Real or not, we are pushing back the edge of known history and finding that the artifacts we see—the Great Pyramid, the Great Sphinx, the mountain monuments in Peru, and much more—are much older than previously believed and indicative of technologies still to be "rediscovered" today.

Was that Ancient Wisdom hidden away in the Tarot? Are whispers of it contained in the symbols and signs of Freemasonry? Is it waiting for us in the practices of Magick, Yoga, and the Martial Arts? Can it be glimpsed in the ecstasies of Sex Magick?

The mystery remains and all our esoteric practices are founded in the belief that we can each solve the mystery and move beyond the still luminescence of the Ancients.

Aquarian Age. The zodiacal age of approximately 2,150 years' length following the Piscean Age. The spirit of these Ages is believed to be characterized by symbolism and general astrological characteristics of the zodiacal sign. As the Piscean Age is identified as the age of Christianity (and its authoritarian offshoots), the Aquarian Age is associated with the "New Age" which Carl Jung believed to have begun in 1940. The general association ascribed to Aquarius is that this will be the Age of Man, of Intellect rather than Emotion, and of self-responsibility rather than the shepherd's crook of patriarchal (and patronizing) religion.

While the ending of an age and the beginning of another is theoretically well determined by the astronomical position of the Sun at the Spring Equinox, even that is debated as occurring in a range from 2012 to 2374. As a practical matter, like "morning" or "evening," the transition between zodiacal ages is indefinite.

The Aquarian Age demands that Knowledge be applied to Man's Spiritual Needs, and that schools as "places of knowledge" become the temples (not that temples become schools!).

There is no real secrecy in the Age of Aquarius—no magical secrets that only the initiate can attain. Esoteric Knowledge is coming out into the open to provide the opportunity to everyone who can to "walk with the Gods." The World of the Mind is the new dimension for exploration—it is Inner Space through which we travel now. Our scientific and technological thrust must direct itself to saving the planet and opening the inner doors of consciousness as well.

There are today opportunities for people to come together in learning Esoteric Knowledge, in research and the sharing of discovery, in participation in the reviving Nature Religion, and in learning how it is that Man and Woman can liberate each other.

The new *Aeon of Horus*, the demands of world crisis, requires us to make of our spiritual knowledge a living and growing knowledge, not a static faith. That is why we make our celebrations renewals and conventions of discovery and teaching as well as festivals. We take joy in the responsibility that the Age thrusts upon us, for with it is the opportunity for a tremendous leap forward in spiritual evolution.

Man is balanced upon a precipice—but he has the opportunity to ascend to the Gods if he chooses not to fall. He must, like Icarus, make his own wings if he is to fly—but he must turn to the guidance of proven Knowledge and Technique if, unlike Icarus, his wings are to carry him through to his victory.

Arcane School. An occult organization founded in 1923 by Theosophist Alice A. Bailey and her husband, Foster Bailey, was designed to bring in the New Age by the Great White Brotherhood, the spiritual hierarchy of masters who are believed to guide human destiny.

Over the next years Bailey dictated a series of books laying out a program for bringing in the New Age. In addition, there is a correspondence course. International headquarters at 113 University Pl., 11th Fl., Box 722, Cooper Sta., New York, NY 10276. More information at their website www.lucistrust.org/en/arcane_school.

As Above, so Below! The key phrase found in the Emerald Tablet that recognizes the dynamic formula established when "God created Man in his own image." Simply stated, the human person is the Microcosm and the Universe is the Macrocosm. Not only is there identity between Man and Cosmos but there is a continuous correspondence of action between the two.

Each human being is a miniature cosmos, complete in every detail even though those details may exist in more potential than current fulfillment. In our new perspective, this means two things:

First: Each person functions through the same laws, principles, formulae, etc., as does the Universe as a whole. It means that the "Laws of the Universe"—the systems by which it functions—are also the "Laws of Magick."

Second: Each person has the potential to become successively a greater representation of the Universe in all its glory. We are "gods in the making!"

Each of us is in process of *becoming more than we are*. The life purpose of each person is to grow in our wholeness, developing innate powers into actual skills. Through the study and practice of Magick we grow into the whole person we are intended to be, uniting the Lower Self with the Upper Self. In magick this is called "Initiation." *It is also known as* Self-Empowerment *because the process heals the divisions of Self enabling the Whole Person to draw upon all the Knowledge, Powers, and Skills of the entire Consciousness.*

Aspiration. The aspiration of the student (we are all students) towards growth and the attainment of Initiation should be a burning flame like a lover's desire for his beloved.

Aurum Solis. (*Gold of the Sun*) A magical order founded in England in 1897 by George Stanton and Charles Kingold which claims descent from the *Ogdoadic Tradition* of the Western Mysteries. It is best known through the published works of two of its leaders, Melita Denning and Osborne Phillips, pseudonyms of Vivian Godfrey and Leon Barcynski. Together, they authored many books on magical practice, such as *Astral Projection, Creative Visualization*, and *The Magical Philosophy*. More information is available on Google.

Awareness. Awareness is the focus of consciousness onto things, images, ideas, and sensations. Awareness is more than what we physically sense. We do have psychic impressions independent of the physical apparatus. And we can focus our awareness on memories dredged up from the subconscious; we can focus on symbols and images and all the ideas, and memories, associated with them. We can turn our awareness to impressions from the astral and mental planes, and open ourselves to receiving information from other sources, from other planets, other dimensions, and from other minds.

Awareness is how we use our consciousness. It is just as infinite as is consciousness, just as infinite as is the universe in all its dimensions and planes. When we speak of expanding or broadening our awareness we are talking about paying attention to new impressions from new sources, and from other ways we can use our consciousness. Awareness is like the "Operating System" that filters incoming information, sometimes blocking "what we don't believe in."

Awareness is something of a corollary to Concentration. We are used to thinking of it as passive in sensory perception but it changes dramatically when used actively. Your perceptions can be extended with expanded awareness, and what was invisible can become visible, or heard, or tasted, or sensed. To become more aware is to become enriched. And becoming aware is not limited to objects and people, but includes energies pulsing through and around objects, persons, and their environment.

Through extended awareness, we grow and develop our latent psychic powers into reliable skills.

Babalon. Mother Earth. Also the *Scarlet Woman* as the ruling spirit of Earth. Crowley said Babalon was the goddess of the New Aeon as found in Thelema, the religion he founded in 1904. She represents the female sexual impulse and the most fertile Great Mother, the womb of all life and the mother of each of us. She can be invoked into an actual woman as priestess in working Sex Magick to manifest the energies of the *Aeon of Horus*. She is the Liberated Woman.

In Sex Magick she becomes the "Scarlet Woman" and the mixture of semen with menstrual blood is called the "menstruum of the lunar current." It is Babalon who gives birth to Life and Beauty, and who transforms men into Masters of the Universe by freeing them of fears and inhibitions.

Barbarous Words. These are really "words of power," whether intelligible or not. Originally, the name comes from the languages spoken by the *barbarians*, those who did not speak Greek when the Greeks thought they had invented civilization.

In ritual, barbarous words and names don't have to make sense or be understood by the ritualist. Many are derived from Hebrew, ancient Egyptian and Persian; some are based on the Enochian language given us by Dr. John Dee. Rather than rational sense, they make emotional sense with the drama.

There is some evidence—see Patrick Dunn's book, *Magic, Power, Language, Symbol: A Magician's Exploration of Linguistics*—that experienced magicians created certain barbarous words without regard to proper language but entirely to have a magical effect. Or, rather, the magician spontaneously speaks these words without plan as if derived from or through the sub-conscious mind. It is, perhaps, related to *speaking in tongues* where a person speaks with no awareness of what she is saying.

Suggested Reading:

Dunn, Patrick: *Magic, Power, Language, Symbol: A Magician's Exploration of Linguistics*, Llewellyn, 2008.

Black Magic. Magic performed to cause harm. Louis Culling's point about "it is prevailing mental aberration of the ignorant to label as *Black Magic* the pentagram with two points upward" is that it is not the tools of magic that are evil but only the intentions of the magician. A pentagram is a pentagram no matter which end is up; a knife is a knife no matter how it is used, and a gun is a gun no matter it held by a policeman or a murderer.

Book M.N. Obviously, "M.N." is to be replaced with your Magickal Name. I make this point simply because I have found some people so literal that they use such abbreviations in their rituals, so—if the instructions say "Call the Angel 'N'" that is exactly what they do rather than calling the Angel by its name.

Borderland consciousness. I will quote Louis T. Culling for emphasis: "the dream state is the Borderland consciousness state. *The importance of the ability to function in a quasi borderland-state may well be more than half of the technic of Magick.* It is involved in making the IMAGINA-TION to be SUBJECTIVELY REAL. Without this, a large part of Magick is a futile thing."

He describes the Borderland Consciousness as approximately 15% awake and 85 percent asleep. Regardless of the actual percentage, these states are also called the hypnagogic and hypnopompic states of being awake and falling asleep and being asleep and waking up. It is also called the *Borderland State*. It is during this state of consciousness when we are most receptive to images, symbols, impressions, sounds, ideas, and feelings. It is also a state very receptive to intuition.

Borderland State. An alternative state of consciousness in which the demarcation between ordinary reality and subjective reality disappears, and that which is built in the imagination becomes magickally and psychologically real. The woman partner in Sex Magick becomes the Goddess incarnate.

The aim of the GBG practice of Dianism is to continue sexual union until trance occurs. This not the trance of hypnosis, or of spiritual or shamanic practices, but rather a state characterized by poise and non-movement. The sexual stimulation is felt, but controlled and the focus is on consciousness and not the body. Louis Culling wrote: "A hallucinatory meditation may be achieved, in which one is submerged in spiritual inspiration and aspiration."

It requires two hours or more "to build up the energized enthusiasm of the Magickal Imagination which gives one's thoughts subjective reality." It should be felt as a *force field* about the couple. Some may even see it as a glowing aura.

Calypso Moon Language. I am rather at a loss to give definition to this. Culling calls it a quasi-Enochian Language. Researching, I find that Calypso is a West Indian musical style influenced by jazz; it's also a small species of orchid (*Calypso borealis*), having a flower variegated with purple, pink, and yellow that grows in cold, bog-like localities in the northern part of the United States. It is also the name of a tiny moon of the planet Saturn, discovered in 1980, and in 1983 named for the goddess Calypso who detained Odysseus for seven years in Homer's *Odyssey*. And, finally, it is a fashion in which women tie a knot in their shirt and expose their waist. There is some indication that it closely resembles Modern Greek.

Ceremonial Magick. The object of ceremonial magick is to stimulate the senses, to power-up the emotions, and to firmly conceptualize the purpose of the operation—which is to create a transcending experience to unite Personality with the Divine Self.

To this end, rituals, symbols, clothing, colors, incenses, sound, dramatic invocations and sacraments are selected in accordance with established *correspondences* of one thing to another to transport the magician towards a mystical reality.

Choronzon. The number is 9, also the number of Man. But Choronzon is also a *demon* within the Enochian writings of Dr. John Dee, likewise within Crowley's system where Choronzon is *the Dweller in the Abyss*, believed to be the obstacle between the adept and enlightenment. But Choronzon is also the name of the demon that guards the Abyss on the Tree of Life—separating the lower from the higher. It's that Abyss that we must cross to fulfill our spiritual destiny. That demon is no longer an obstacle if met with proper preparation by the magician, for his function is to destroy the ego, allowing the magician to cross the Abyss. We all must confront our demon.

The demon is also our Shadow, the lower self of the subconscious-ness with our fears and repressions.

Choronzon Club, or C.∴C.∴., appears to have been a magical group active in Chicago as early as 1931 and at least as recently as 1979. Exactly what it was or is is confusing and probably of no pertinence to our study here. According to the occult scholar, P. R. Koenig, in 1933 a small group of homosexual men split off from Russell's original group in order to practice Crowley's XI° It was led in recent history by Michael P. Bretiaux teaching Haitian Voodoo and O.∴T.∴O.∴. magic.

Unfortunately, the study of Western magical philosophy is often obscured by the number of *secret orders* cast on Masonic models that claim to teach true magic. At least in some instances these are success-ful business operations and in some other cases provide opportunities to indulge the vanities of members who adore dressing in expensive robes and addressing each other by their secret names. Most of their magical teachings of value were derived from the serious work of the Hermetic Order of the Golden Dawn and the Aurum Solis. These teachings were long ago made available in book form. Experience demonstrates that the study and practice of magic is as suitable to the solitary person as to group membership.

Circle. A temporary boundary within which a séance or magical opera-tion may take place. The theory is that it becomes a kind of psychic con-tainer for the energies used in the operation and a barrier to unwanted energies from outside. See the earlier reference to "Alien Forces."

The Magick Circle—whether drawn physically or in the imagi-nation—is the "container" of magickal operations. The "Opening" and the "Closing" of the Temple—or of the Circle—is an operation that is both magickal and psychological. The rituals of Opening and Closing are various but all are simply projections of energy guided by will power with the express intent to provide a barrier against exte-rior forces while establishing the Circle (or Lodge) as container of the magickal energies.

Clothing for rituals. The GBG calls for simplicity. The requirement is only that the ritual clothing be different from one's customary clothing. While fancy ceremonial robes would fulfill this requirement, they would be contradictory to the emphasis on the Great Work. A simple garment cut from cloth with holes for neck and arms could be sufficient, as could an inexpensive bath robe or night shirt. Any symbolic distinctions among the participants can be accomplished with simple accessories.

In some Wiccan circles the choice is "skyclad"—nakedness so that all are equal before the gods and nothing is in the way of the body's natural energy. The observation can be made that nakedness does not make us equal since we are very conscious of our physical appearance—slim, fat, tall, sort, hairy, etc.—a distraction from the Magick.

Communicating with your Higher Self. *I swear to tell myself the truth. I swear to regard every event (or condition) as a particular dealing between myself and the Holy Guardian Angel.* These were the two primary oaths in the work of the GBG (which see).

What we're doing, of course, is building more lines of communication between the middle (everyday) consciousness and the super consciousness, or between the personality and the Holy Guardian Angel. And, we are doing one more important thing: in promising to tell the truth we are building trust between the selves that often act as if separate entities. Therein lays a mystery and an important recognition.

On this basis of trust, the Higher Self knows that its messages will be respected and attended to.

But, there remains a problem to our communications, and that is that—in part—the Higher Self doesn't speak directly in the common language. Your Holy Guardian Angel doesn't just shout: "Hey, down there, listen up! I want you to stick with the GBG for six more months."

Instead, through the use of clues and symbols, you have to put effort into understanding the message, making communication a two-way street and a learning situation with direct application to your needs of the moment. In other words, despite the cautions against a pathological belief that everything is a message just for you, almost anything can be used to bridge the gap between meaningless and meaningful. A crystal ball is just a polished rock, but it can open your vision to another world. With intention, anything can become a key to unlock the doors of the Unconscious.

Before Integration there must be Communication. Divination and Meditation on the divinatory results and your dreams provide the basis for communication.

Congrex. Here's another of Lou Culling's fancy words he was so fond of using. It just means *intercourse, having sex, sleeping together.* But the use of an unfamiliar word, even when the meaning is obvious, does have a certain value of "stop, look, listen, pay attention."

Having Sex is more than a physical act. In the GBG's Alphaism you were instructed to avoid any sexual thoughts, feelings, and fantasies for an entire month. It was not so much denial as it was to emphasize their importance and the role they do play in whole and healthy sex whether within the context of Sex Magick or not. When you do have sex, all of these are present because sex is a *complex* of physical, emotional, energy, mental, and spiritual exchange between two people.

Even fantasy is part of real sex whether recognized as such or not. *Is your lover a 'big, strong, heroic man'? Is she 'beautiful, soft and loving'?* No matter the outer reality, the answer through emotional fantasy is 'yes' and that brings you into contact with the archetypal levels of the Subconscious and Collective Unconscious important to the program of Wholeness.

Openness with regard to emotion-level fantasies is important to release associated repression and fear and childish dependencies so the powerful fantasy *Imago* can become more inclusive of the 'real' lover, making the exchange between two people deeper and stronger, building a partnership at all levels.

In Dianism and Sex Magick, the fantasized *Imago* is not the personal fantasy but rather that of a god or goddess. The technique is similar and the imagined god or goddess can eventually impose and transform the personal fantasy.

Even if others tell you that your lover is nothing but a beer-drinking no-good lay-about, this transformative power of the *Imago* is one of the greatest things that we can give and receive within our intimate relationship with our partner. With the added empowerment of Sex Magick, the old reality can become a new reality.

Consciousness during Ritual. Within a ritual, you are in a state of light trance, and you do not want anything to startle or jar you back into full objective consciousness until the ritual is over. The Ritual must work up without interruption to an absorbed seeking of inspiration from the Holy Guardian Angel.

Conversation. Yes, it is possible to converse with your Higher Self. First you have to honestly believe in the Higher Self, and that the person you think of as your self is not it. At the same time, don't let the name "Holy Guardian Angel" deceive you into thinking of a separate being that is so *holy* as to be beyond your ability to deserve the attention of the HGA.

True, the HGA is normally distant from the personality that is the everyday 'you,' but the function of the Great Work is to build a relationship between the personality and the Higher Self leading towards *Integration*—when the two become as one.

"I swear to regard every event (or condition) as a particular dealing between myself and the H G A." Culling had done a beautiful job in explaining the practical issues around this magickal oath, and his examples demonstrate its value and effectiveness.

This practicality is rather unique among magickal oaths! Many are too grand for realization within a single lifetime. While their intention is to stimulate spiritual growth and attainment, it is usually not some grand event or rare or expensive artifact but very ordinary things that call to us for our deeper awareness. Their symbolism may be obscure—normally—but suddenly they glow with meaning or practically yell at your for attention. Or, it may seem like nothing, but still your attention has been re-directed to the event as if it has a special meaning for you, *and it does!*

But, note further: this oath directs your attention to everyday events of all kinds so that your awareness is alerted to the greater meaning and potential that each may represent. Magick and meaning may be found in the most mundane of events when there is that possibility of relationship between the inner you and the inner side of the event. The effect is to activate connections to your Higher Self, and that is the goal.

"I swear to tell myself the truth." This, of course, is very challenging. *What is truth?* Can we ever really know it? Again, Culling has given us a good but simple example. It is perhaps too simple. The real requirement is to be *honest* with yourself; to test your answers for their truth and honesty. This is more than "knowing yourself" for it is also a test of your truth and honesty in relation to others and to the world you live. We too easily deceive ourselves and once again the entire purpose of the oath is to prepare yourself to communicate with your Higher Self, the HGA.

Even though your communication with the HGA isn't always in *plain English*, it is not a game! The Great Work is serious business.

Correspondences. The Kabbalah, using the symbolic system of the Tree of Life and numerological associations provided through the Hebrew language, Astrology, and Natural Science identifies a wide range of *correspondences* between subjects, planets, herbs, plants, metals, crystals, colors, animals, angels, deities, etc., that allow substitutions of one thing for another, or that augment understanding about one thing by knowledge of another of corresponding value.

Mostly the applications of correspondences are divided into Magical, Medical, Numerical, and Tarot usages.

Suggested Reading:

Whitcomb: *The Magician's Companion,* Hulse: *Western Mysteries*

Crowley, Aleister (1875–1947) was one of the most controversial figures in recent Western occultism. He inherited a considerable fortune, and died a pauper. He had great intellectual genius and wasted a lot on shocking the world as he knew it with occasional bizarre antics and lifestyle. He was trained in the Hermetic Order of the Golden Dawn and later formed his own Order of the Silver Star and then took over the O.T.O (Ordo Templi Orientis). He was a prolific and capable writer of magic technology and is best known for his transcription of the *Book of the Law* received from a spirit named *Aiwass* proclaiming Crowley as the Beast 666 in the Book of Revelations and announcing a *New*

Aeon of terror and advancement for the world. His magical books and his Thoth Tarot Deck are worth study.

Daemon. Not a "demon," but a mythical being, part-human and part-god serving as an intermediary between God and humanity—an inspiring intelligence similar to if not identical to the Holy Guardian Angel.

Note the role of "an intermediary between God and humanity." Once attainment of the Knowledge and Conversation of the Holy Guardian Angel is achieved, the Great Work takes on added dimension. The role of a Co-Creator expands in service to all humanity, and to all life and consciousness of our planet as a whole.

The path to glory is endless to our still limited vision just as Love knows no bounds.

Dee, Sir John. (1527–1608) With Edward Kelley as clairvoyant, the source for the Enochian language and the eighteen Enochian Calls.

Dianism. The Second Degree of Sex Magick in the GBG, Dianism is sexual union without climax. It's further training, but unlike Alphaism with its emphasis on avoidance here the partners should be warm and ardent, but controlled. It's like a surfer riding the crest of the wave forever. There should be no feelings of frustration for it is without "lust for result." Rather than allowing oneself to be submerged in the full flow of pleasurable sensation, one should allow the ecstasy to feed the fires of aspiration and inspiration.

Dianism is not an end in itself but rather is the means to a greater end than orgasm, which is fleeting. One *comes*, and then it's gone. Here, Dianism uses the energy of sexual ecstasy to feed the fire of concentration—which we will learn to project in the attainment of our magickal goal.

Both concentration and meditation disciplines are involved in the practice of Dianism. The role of the male is the more challenging, and he should withhold from consciousness any awareness of a known earthly personality. Each partner regards the other as a god or goddess. While it is natural at first for the known personality to intrude, it should be as persistently suppressed, so that the partner is regarded, finally, *as a visible manifestation of one's own Holy Guardian Angel.*

The aim of Dianism and its highest magick lies in continuing the union until such time as one goes into the "Borderland" state. A hallucinatory meditation may be achieved, in which one is submerged in spiritual inspiration and aspiration.

All things require time, regularity, and persistence for results. Many experiments indicate that one or two hours, or even more, are required to attain to the Borderland state. And it takes time to build up the energized enthusiasm of the Magickal Imagination which gives one's thoughts subjective reality. It might take thirty minutes or it might take hours to build up a satisfactory force.

Individuals are different, and each must work out his individual technique. Dianism is not to be regarded as an end in itself, but as a great means to further very great ends. In time one will learn through practice to *concentrate* on a chosen point, while at the same time suffering the sexual ecstasy. The fire of concentration will replace the preoccupation with sexual sensation.

What seems difficult at first will become greater pleasure with accompanying spiritual awareness with experience.

Dispensation. A special empowerment to dispense and manage religious or spiritual instruction and practice. Within Christianity, it is the official granting of a license to organize a church. It is also a special time period designated by God for certain things to happen. For Esotericism, it is believed to be both a time period and a *licensing* to a particular group or groups to establish themselves and their message seemingly granted by spiritual *higher-ups*.

There are those of us who believe that we live in a special time when dispensation is universal for all who will open their mind and spirit to the influx of higher consciousness happening now. We are approaching a turning point when the "world as we know it" will end and a new world order will begin to replace the old. Few things happen overnight, but time is critical and changes will be rapid as global conditions require new world organizations and new worldwide solutions to problems arising from the past.

Divine Plan. Most Occultists believe that there is some kind of Divine Plan, or Great Plan, guiding the evolution of Humanity, and indeed of all life, all consciousness, and the Universe itself. *Is the Plan knowable by mere mortals?* Perhaps not, but some believe there are "Masters," "Inner Plane Adepts," or other "Great Ones" who know it, at least partially, and who themselves work under its guidance at high spiritual levels.

Do these Masters ever appear on Earth? In Physical Form?

Some say yes. And even that they have incarnated in such men as the Buddha, Christ, and others in order to bring about certain transitions in Humanity, in Consciousness, perhaps even in the genetic structure.

Can more be said? Is there really an Inner Plane Hierarchy guiding the affairs of men? An "inner government"?

The answer given, at least generally, is that we have to work things out for ourselves.

Dream ESP. A previously unpublished book by Louis T. Culling and Carl Llewellyn Weschcke to be released in 2011.

Ecstasy. Through prolonged intercourse and visualization of woman as the Goddess Incarnate, sexual ecstasy must be made to become psychic ecstasy, the fire that excites and powers the magickal imagination. Body, Mind & Spirit are united with a transfusion of energy to transform subjective reality into objective reality.

Effluvia. The mixed fluids of Male and Female in the vagina make up the "First Matter" which is to be transmuted by the magical imagination by their aspiration and inspiration, and by the Fire of their sexual/mystical ecstasy while engaged in Sex Magick.

Eidolon. Ghost.

Elemental. The elemental forces of this world and possibly for the whole Universe. They are variously ascribed to the inner side of natural forces, and also to the Spirits of the four Elements of Air, Fire, Water, and Earth, along with the fifth Element of Spirit from which the four are derived. The Elemental Spirits, or Forces, are the Guardians of the Four Directions of the Magickal Circle, thus transforming the Circle into a miniature of the Universe.

Elixer. The "Elixir" or "blood of the Red Lion" is the essence of the male orgasm.

Enochian Language. (Also known as the Language of the Angels, and the Secret Angelic Language) The words transcribed by Dr. John Dee (1527–1608) and Edward Kelly in their spiritual contacts, starting in 1582, were eventually seen to form a genuine language as well as a system of magic.

Enochian is pronounced Eh-no-kee-an, and is supposedly the same language spoken by the angel Ave to the prophet Enoch, whose name in Hebrew is spelled *Heh Nun Vav Kaph.*

Enochian Words. In the magickal workings of Dr. John Dee (1527-1608), astrologer to Queen Elizabeth I (and some also claim him to have been her spymaster), he made contact with certain angelic beings who used a language distinct from any other. Dee believed these beings to be the same angels that transported the Hebrew prophet, Enoch, to heaven, and hence the name for the language. Enochian words are sometimes called "barbarous" because their pronunciation is so evocative.

Exemplar. *An ideal example, worthy of being copied.* Lou Culling liked *words* and liked to get his listeners and readers to take note of his sometimes unusual terminology. I think I more than once caught him making up words to fit what he wanted to say. I believe "example" would have been a better choice than "exemplar" because he was not pointing to something worthy of being copied; but by using it he was saying, "Pay attention to this example."

Every man and every woman is a Star. This is from Crowley, and is one of the most important as well as poetic things he ever wrote. There is a dual meaning here: (1) that every one of us is Divine at our core and that our destiny is to make our Whole Person Divine; (2) that we are all evolving towards roles of greater responsibility. Some have interpreted this to mean that as we become greater can actually become "stars" in the astronomical sense for every planet, every star (sun), every solar system, every galaxy is a living system of similar to a person only on a macro scale. All is consciousness and our source is universal.

The *Book of the Law* spells out that the Great Work is to unite with and do the will of one's own True Self. Thus, "Every man and every woman is a star" moving in their own orbit, by their own unique nature, not to be diverted into a common mold of uniformity.

Familiar. The "Magickal Childe" created through Sex Magick.

First Matter. Together, the effluvia of the Lion and the Eagle is the "First Matter," the original Creation. This First Matter is to be transmuted by the magickal imagination, by aspiration and inspiration and by the "Fire" which is the ecstasy. Ecstasy is, as it were, the magickal fire for transforming all into inspiration and aspiration.

Forces. Physics recognizes four primary forces: Gravity, Electro-magnetism, and the Strong & Weak Nuclear Forces.

In occult theory, East and West, and in classical natural philosophy, there are the four elements: Earth, Fire, Air and Water. In magickal practices, the four elements are used as "forces" and often imbued with consciousness as when they are identified with particular archangels. *Might these really the same as the four forces of physics?*

In occult theory, East and West, Spirit is the fifth element from which the other four are derived. *If, as some of us speculate, Consciousness is the primary force, then are Spirit and Consciousness one and the same?*

If Consciousness is the primary Force from which the other four Forces are derived, is *this primary consciousness or Spirit the same as the Creator, we otherwise call God?*

G∴B∴G∴. The 'G∴B∴G∴' stands for *The Great Brotherhood of God.* The promise of the Order was "A Shortcut to Initiation." That was the headline of a 1931 announcement appearing over a Chicago box office number. The founder of the G∴B∴G∴ was C. F. Russell whose magical name was Frater Genesthai. Lou Culling described Russell ". . . as a teacher in Practicing Magick, was, without question, the greatest genius of this century, or of several past centuries that I have been able to trace." This was the man who had a tiff with Aleister Crowley about giving up his room at the Abbey in Cefalu, Italy and spent the next sixty hours in magical retirement sitting on 'The Rock' without food or water.

Unless you are both interested and a good historian in regard to the world of Crowley, this information won't mean much to you, and perhaps it really doesn't mean anything other than to tell you that Russell was a magician who studied with Crowley and was intimate enough to be part of Crowley's inner circle.

Following this event, Crowley gave Russell his blessing to found his own Order to be based on these three points:

1. Liber Legis. Crowley's "Book of the Law."

2. Thelema

3. The Aeon of Horus

Reading that 1931 announcement, Louis T. Culling wrote of his interest, and was the first to have responded. He was required to pay a fee of $5.00 and to secure at least eight "loyal and active" members to form a "Neighborhood Lodge." We have only limited information about the full size of the Order. In San Diego, there were 25 members, in Los Angeles 75, in San Francisco 50, and in Denver 125. Culling writes that there were other local lodges in all the large cities.

The GBG was not an exclusively male organization and had both men and women in equal status. A "Brotherhood of God" becomes an association of men and women *with God*. Perhaps this is not a claim to equality with God, but when we look to Biblical texts we see that *God created man in His own image, in the image of God created He him, male and female created He them* (Genesis 1:27). Elsewhere we read that Jesus—equated with God—promises that men will be able to perform miracles just He does. *Does this make us equal to God?* Perhaps, for we are all part of one creation, and quantum theory demonstrates that the process of creation is continuous and that with will and intention we can bring about change.

The G.B.G. closed its doors to new members in 1936, and then ceased entirely in 1938. In 1936 Russell, as Head of the Order, wrote to Lou Culling: *The closing of the doors of the G∴B∴G∴ does not mean that the Great Work must be lost to the ken of man. I appoint you to reveal the entire curriculum of our Magick Order. This is not to be before the year 1956, and furthermore, only when you are ready to assume the responsibility.*

Why was the Order closed? Apparently the closing was planned at the time of its beginning. Culling writes, "As early as 1932, I received official notice that the doors would be closed to new members after 1936, after which the existing members would continue operations until the final closing period of 1938." He also noted in an interview transcribed in 1971 that "Russell's prediction was that after the G∴B∴G∴ closed its doors, that all occult orders were losing their dispensation (amount to nothing) and there would not be another legitimate order of any kind with any real dispensation until the year 1972."

What the GBG claimed to have accomplished was to reduce all the extensive magickal material derived through the Golden Dawn and Aleister Crowley to an efficient and essential curriculum of personal or group study and practice as a true "Short Cut to Initiation."

The purpose of all magickal study is this Initiation, which culminates in the attainment of the Knowledge and Conversation of one's Holy Guardian Angel—one's true Inner, or Higher, Self. While Culling claimed that the practice of this curriculum would also lead to the attainment of magickal powers, these are considered here only as aids in the Great Work, described in psychological terms as "the integration of the subconscious with the conscious personality," and ultimately *union with the Highest Self.*

Gestures. The different positions and motions of the hands are as important as the Signs—or positions and movements of the body—in magickal and religious ritual, and in energy healing. They are also found in various ecstatic and shamanic dances. They are not "empty" gestures as a little experimentation will readily show. See Appendix Three for more guidance.

Gnosticon. These gatherings were originally called "The Gnostic-Aquarian Festival of Astrology, Magic and Witchcraft" but the name changed at the suggestion of Isaac Bonewits who moved to St. Paul to serve as editor of Llewellyn's house publication, *Gnostica News,* later to become *Gnostica* magazine. Both were named after Llewellyn's metaphysical bookstore just off the Minneapolis downtown district, a block away from the large *Basilica* Catholic cathedral. These festivals drew people from all over the United States, Great Britain, Canada, and Australia. They were the first of what later became psychic fairs and then conferences serving various interests of the larger New Age community around the world. Llewellyn discontinued the Gnosticons in 1976.

Goal of High Magick is Initiation. The goal of the rituals and training of High Magick (also called "Ceremonial Magick," but there are differences) is none other than the attainment of Knowledge and Conversation with your personal Holy Guardian Angel. It's the 'initiation' that marks your transition from a mostly unconscious human being to a mostly conscious Whole Person.

There are many Paths to the Center (becoming Whole), but this Magickal Operation has the advantages of being designed just for that purpose. Even the solitary Magick of Abramelin the Mage required six months for accomplishment of the Knowledge and Conversation of the Holy Guardian Angel.

The GBG was neither a 'social' club nor a traditional magical order in which other magical operations and celebrations might be practiced. The "Shortcut to Initiation" was the substance of the GBG's work. Each group met often and regularly, repeating the ritual again and again without loss of pertinence and interest.

Why? Because the program speaks to the soul of the aspirant. The Higher Self is gathering the strands of self-discovery as the Lower and Middle Selves work their way through daily life, weaving those strands into thicker skeins to become the Rainbow Bridge of conscious integration made possible through life-experience.

Note that it is both Knowledge and Conversation—the goal is two-way Communication but the realization of Union and Self-Knowledge is instantaneous.

Golden Dawn, the Hermetic Order. Founded in England in 1888, this magical order provided the impetus and source for magical study and practice within the Western Esoteric Tradition.

Israel Regardie's *The Golden Dawn* is an encyclopedic resource for the rituals and knowledge lectures of the GD, while his *The Tree of Life, The Middle Pillar,* and *A Garden of Pomegranates* provide in-depth exposition of the GD's magical system. See also books by Chic and Tabatha Cicero, including *Self-Initiation into the Golden Dawn Tradition.*

Great Work. The path of self-directed spiritual growth and development. This is the object of your incarnation and the meaning of your life. The Great Work is the program of growth to become all that you can be—which is the realization that you are a *god in the making*. Within your being there is the seed of Divinity, and your job is to grow that into the Whole Person that is a *Son of God*. It is a process that has continued from "the Beginning" and may have no ending but it is your purpose in life. It is that which gives meaning to your being.

In this new age, you are both teacher and student and you must accept responsibility for your own destiny. *Time is of the essence!* Older methods give way to new ones because the entire process of growth and self-development has to be accelerated. Humanity has created a *time bomb* that's ticking away, and only our own higher consciousness can save us from self-destruction. But—have faith and do the Great Work for it is all part of a Great Plan.

Suggested Reading:

Denning & Phillips: *Foundations of High Magick*

Hadit. The Chaldean aspect of the Egyptian god of evil or darkness. Crowley regarded Hadit as the master of magickal initiation and that is the understanding in this ritual. Hadit is the point in the center of the circle that is Nuit. He is "the flame that burns in every heart of man and the core of ever star."

Hebrew, Language and Alphabet. Hebrew is sometimes referred to as the "sacred" language of the West and compared with Sanskrit for the East. There are no vowels per se in Hebrew, only diacritical marks over the consonants performing that function. In addition, there are no numbers in Hebrew, but letters alone and in combination perform that function. The number basis provides a system in which words of comparable value have related meanings. It also provides the magical meanings of Hebrew names.

Hexagram. (1) A six-pointed star consisting of two superimposed triangles, one whose apex is up and the other apex down. The upward triangle is masculine, the downward is feminine—together they symbolize union of energies or sexual congress. In ritual magic they are used to invoke or to banish planetary forces. (2) One of sixty-four combinations of long and broken lines used in the I Ching (or Yi King) system of Chinese divination that are traditionally determined by throwing

Yarrow Sticks, or by means of coins (heads, tails), dice, dominoes, or other means. (3) As a symbol, it is the Hebrew "Star of David."

Suggested Reading:

Regardie, with the Ciceros: *The Tree of Life, An Illustrated Study in Magic*

Kraig: *Modern Magick, Eleven Lessons in the High Magickal Arts*

McElroy: *I Ching for Beginners, A Modern Interpretation of the Ancient Oracle*

Nishavdo: *I Ching of Love*—a boxed set of 64 illustrated cards with booklet.

Hierarchy. It is believed that those of a higher initiation compose a leadership that has the ability to transmit spiritual energy to those of lesser spiritual stature and thus "raise them up."

Nearly every kind of group is formally organized in ranks of power, authority, and seniority. Whether in government, business, social club, military group, non-profit organization, church or religious order, a hierarchical structure has generally proved to be more effective in accomplishing the group mission than an unstructured democracy.

What is important, however, to the health of any organization, is the basis of the ranking. In an esoteric group it should be by knowledge and expertise, and demonstrated merit in any degree or level of initiation. Nothing is worse than authority without demonstrated merit.

It is both unfortunate and passé that some esoteric groups, like the Catholic Church and some Masonic lodges, devote so much of their resources to the embellishments of office instead of effective teaching or service. A simple badge of office should normally be sufficient. Within a ritual drama, symbolic costuming may be important just as are other elements of ritual.

Higher Self. The third aspect of personal consciousness, also known as the Super-Conscious Mind. As the Middle Self, or Conscious Mind, takes conscious control of the Lower Self, or Sub-Conscious Mind, the Higher Self becomes more directly involved in functioning of the Personal Consciousness.

Even though the Higher Self is also known here as the Holy Guardian Angel, there is value in using a more easily comprehended psychological term. Words are words and there are often many names for the same thing. But each gives a particular shape or color or tone to the thing named to expand our understanding comprehension when we are relating to larger concepts.

Qabalistically, it is the Super-Conscious Mind in Tiphareth that mediates between the Divine Self and the Lower Personality.

Holy Guardian Angel. (Also the HGA) The transcendent spiritual self that mediates between the Divine Self and the Lower Personality and serves as guardian and guide. The term was used by Abramelin the Mage as the focus of the magical operation known as "the Knowledge and Conversation of the Holy Guardian Angel." The HGA is also called the Higher Self, the Augoeides, the All-Knower, the Divine Genius, the True Ruler, Adonai, the Indwelling Spirit, etc. Carl Jung calls it his Daemon (not demon!).

Contact between the Higher, Divine Self and the Lower Self/Personality has to be initiated by the Personality, and that contact is the first step in the Great Work that leads to integration, and thus to Initiation.

Hubbard, L. Ron. (1911–1986) A still controversial figure, Hubbard appears to have been largely self-educated despite having attended prestigious private schools and two years at George Washington University. As the son of a naval officer, he traveled twice to the Far East and claimed to have traveled to India and studied with holy men.

He wrote many pulp fiction stories and over a hundred adventure and science fiction novels, and was reputed to have written a million words yearly at a steady clip of seventy words a minute.

He served as a Lieutenant JG in the Navy during WWII.

In 1945 he met Jack Parsons, a researcher at CalTech and an associate of Crowley who said that Hubbard and Parsons practiced ritual magick including sex magick with Parsons' girl friend. Later Parsons claimed that Hubbard stole both the girl friend and money.

There are numerous reports in the late 1940s that Hubbard stated that he would found a new religion to make money, and in 1950 he published a self-help book, *Dianetics: The Modern Science of Mental Health,* which sold 150,000 copies the first year but received mostly negative reviews and in August 1951 *Consumer Reports* called it "the basis for a new cult."

In December 1953 he founded the Church of Scientology and opened various branches and offices around the world providing various self-help counseling services.

Whether religion or psychology, it was profitable and Hubbard left a $600 million estate.

I Ching. (Also Yi King) A Chinese divinatory system of 64 'hexagrams' that express the dynamic flow of energies into their physical manifestation. Like most divination, it is a manipulative system calling forth the practitioner's psychic abilities. The 64 hexagrams are all the possible combinations of pairs of eight trigrams—which are blocks of three parallel lines either broken in the center or unbroken.

In the ancient form, 50 yarrow stalks charged with 'magical' powers were used in a complicated system of spontaneous division and division again until a final number indicated either a broken or unbroken line. After six lines were obtained, a book was consulted for the meanings.

In contemporary practice, the system has been simplified to twelve sticks, half marked with a yang line and half with a yin line, all held in one hand as a prayer is made, and then six are drawn to reveal the hexagram of the moment in time. Some even use coins to determine the hexagram. By placing yourself in touch with the flow of universal energies through the random draw you will find your place in the scheme of things—at this moment. The I Ching is not so much predictive as revealing of your circumstance if you continue to follow the path you are on. The interpretation will suggest ways to realign yourself with the deeper harmony.

Suggested Reading:

McElroy: *I Ching for Beginners, A Modern Interpretation of the Ancient Oracle*

Brennan: *The Magical I Ching*

"I am above you and in you. My ecstasy is in yours. My joy is to see your joy. To me! To me!" This key part of the GBG Retirement Ritual is your Holy Guardian Angel speaking to you. Saying it with feelings of deep emotion and acceptance of the reality that your HGA is your Higher Self and is the dynamic partner of you as a Whole Person, and that your HGA loves you and all parts that make up the Whole Person, is an invocation of the deepest kind.

Imagination. The ability to form and visualize images and ideas in the mind, especially of things never seen or experienced directly. The imagination is an amazing and powerful part of our consciousness because it empowers our creativity—the actual ability to create. On the Tree of Life, imagination is found in Tiphareth as part of Ruach, the Conscious Self.

Imagination is the making of images, and magick is accomplished by making images and their movement real. Some of that reality comes in the process of charging those images with energy, but more comes by the acceptance of their reality on the astral plane. As images are charged in the astral world, they can be drawn into the physical world, or to have an effect on the physical plane.

Imprinting. A GBG practice of "imprinting" an imagined symbol by concentrated visualization and seeing the image on a body part—almost like an imaginary tattoo.

Initiation. The word has been given a variety of definitions over the years—everything from the pledging and hazing of college (and even high-school) students into fraternities and sororities to the admissions trials of secret societies, entry into occult and Masonic lodges and their grade or degrees, and to the more serious dramatic and transformative rituals of Wiccan and other esoteric groups. In some cases, the initiation rituals are truly effective in raising the consciousness of the "candidate," whereas in other cases the initiation is more a certification of the levels of study and practice the student has mastered.

In the true Occult (and psychological) sense, *Initiation* is more an inner experience than an outer one—even though a dramatic ritual may induce an inner transformation and flowering of the psychic potentials and powers of the person. Despite the promises of various teachers, gurus, priests, and adepts, it is less something done to the person and more something that happens "when the student is ready."

It has been called a "tearing away of the veil" so that the new initiate now sees with new eyes, and perceives a world of greater complexity—one of added dimensions, forces, and living beings. Progressive initiations mark further growth and development as the person becomes more of the Whole Person each of is intended to be. The potential is there from birth and before, and can be realized through knowledge, experience, and growth practices.

In the Theosophical concept, Initiation refers to a non-magical and more eastern process of expanding consciousness of which there are ten in number usually administered by an enlightened teacher. *And maybe there are not enough of them to go 'round.* Self-Initiation bypasses that shortage along with the high costs of travel and the possible dangers of international travel in troubled times.

Inner Relationship with the Holy Guardian Angel. This is the goal for the Retirement Ritual, and of the Great Work. Think what it is saying—that you can and will establish an actual relationship with your Higher Self. Through this relationship—the knowledge and conversation with your Holy Guardian Angel—you have the opportunity to bring together all the "parts" that are your sub-conscious mind, your personal consciousness (the personality that you think of as yourself) with the super-conscious mind, or Higher Self—into a unified, integrated, Whole Person.

Thus you become a fully conscious, fully awake, whole person in whom lost memories are restored, lost knowledge is regained, your psychic powers developed into usable skills, your magickal abilities energized, and your Divinity awakened.

Intention. Acting with a goal in mind. However, "Intention" has become a key word in applied Quantum Theory where it is demonstrated that directed thought and image can effect changes in the Universal Field at the foundation of physical reality.

Invocation. Invocation and Evocation are often, mistakenly, used interchangeably and with little appreciation of their vast difference. Invocation precisely means to actually bring a spirit or divine presence into the psyche and even the body of the magician.

Evocation, in contrast, calls a spirit or other entity into the presence, not the being, of the magician and usually into a magical triangle placed outside the magic circle of the magician.

Invocation requires psychological and spiritual strength as well as proper preparation. It's not just that there are dangers but that the opportunities are so great.

Kelley, Edward. (1555–1595) Dr. Dee's assistant. As a clairvoyant he could see the angels and what they were doing.

Khabs is in the Khu, The. Khabs is Consciousness of one's real Individuality, while Khu is the active conscious Personality. "The Khabs is in the Khu, not the Khu in the Khabs." This very clearly states that the Divine is not outside of man but is part of the Personality. Awakening to this is the beginning of Knowledge of the Higher Self. The Divinity is not distant and separate but right in the heart of the matter—in fact, it's the Soul of the Matter. The Khabs is the soul and the personality is function of the soul.

Knowledge and Conversation . . . This is an important concept for you are to recognize in your Holy Guardian Angel your own teacher with whom you, the present personality or (small 's') self, must actually converse, recognizing the HGA as your (big 'S') Self.

. . . Of One's Holy Guardian Angel. Yes, *the Big 'S' Self, the Higher Self, the Augoeides, the All-Knower, the Divine Genius, the True Ruler, Adonai, the Indwelling Spirit, your Daemon (not demon!), your Spirit Guide.* It's the BIG SHOT, the God Father, of your personal family of psychological parts you will integrate.

This *conversation* between personality and higher self is an art as well as an "act of faith" that you must believe in. There are practices that will establish the reality of this Indwelling Spirit as well as that of your communications. For the moment, accept as fact that you are a *fractured* being consisting of sub-conscious and conscious-mind and of higher-consciousness which will eventually unite in a Whole Person as you *become more than you are.*

"Let the rituals be rightly performed with joy and beauty." Spoken as the opening of your ritual from the center of the Circle, it has the power of similar phrases like "Man your Stations" and "Let the Games Begin!" Note there are three admonitions—that the rituals are to be performed *rightly,* and with *joy* and *beauty.*

This is not a idle statement; indeed, nothing said or done in your magickal circle, or temple, is done without full awareness and intention to do anything less than your best and that is not only *right action,* but the feeling of *joy and happiness* in your heart, and the intention that all your movements, gestures, words, and thoughts will be done with the intention of grace and beauty.

How you think when doing Magick will affect how it works, and you want joy in your heart and beauty in our world.

Liber Al vel Legis. Crowley's "Book of the Law," channeled to Crowley by an entity known as Aiwaz, and considered the holy book of the Aeon of Horus and the foundation of Crowley's spiritual tradition, Thelema.

Liber Hexagram Aton. Liber Yi King. See Appendix Two, The Oracular Meanings of the 64 Hexagrams. While not available when the GBG was first published, today the choice would be Culling's own *The Pristine Yi King.*

Love under will. It's the second part of the phrase that begins with 'Love is the Law.' "Love magickally directed, and used as a spiritual formula," says Crowley. This is an important clarification for what otherwise has commonly been interpreted as justification for a kind of 'free love' movement. As a 'spiritual formula' it is a concise instruction for Sex Magick as practiced by the GBG.

"Will," of course, is the True Will of the Higher Self, while Sex is the engine of energy to be directed by the True Will in fulfillment of our goal.

Lunar Trance. This was part of the curriculum of the GBG, and could be said to be more of a deliberate attitude than a traditional trance.

The word "trance" is not used in the sense of a condition where a person is in a near complete abstraction of the normal mind. Rather it is a state of willed engrossment of the mind in being absorbed in some particular facet of the emotions and feelings—even though it might lead to a state of ecstasy.

The first rule of the trance practice is that it is not a thing of a few minutes practice daily. It is an ATTITUDE to be maintained for at least a week. This may be partly imagination but it must be a willed imagination. Let us suppose that the chosen trance is JOY. Then one must apply the act of concentration, fortified by imagination, which becomes a close mental application or exclusive attention to that emotion and feeling called 'joy.' If and when this is done there remains small room for feelings of sadness. There is just plenty of room in one's living, and attention for engrossment of the feelings in joy, so that the melancholy and sad have small chance of crowding out the willed concentration upon the manifestations of joy.

The method of the "trance," for instance a trance of beauty, a trance of joy and laughter, a trance of beatitude, was to see that quality in everything throughout the entire days and nights of a given period. In the trance of Beauty, one sees beauty in everything that touches one's consciousness, allowing no feeling or idea of ugliness to enter. In the trance of Laughter, one should imagine, feel and see life and living as a Divine Comedy without intrusion of any element of the Divine Tragedy. In the trance of Beatitude, the breeze caresses one, the birds sing to one, every person that crosses one's path has a most friendly glance or smile for one, etc.

"Lust not for result." This is an admonition that seems almost contrary to what you expect. The point is that your goals must be established before the Work begins, and during the ritual focus only on the Work, not the goal.

The 'lust for result' refers to the fact that pure will is expressed in a love of doing rather than looking for rewards or consequences. Both Wagner and Shakespeare expressed their true genius purely for the love of expressing it, and with no pressing motive of gain or "lust of result." Those possessed by the lust of result are rendered desperate and impatient; and they wind up in disillusionment.

Magical Name. It is common practice with magical orders as well as Wiccan, neo-Pagan, and other "secret" groups that members will adopt a magical name or motto for use within the group. In many magical groups, the name is in Greek or Latin, whereas in others it may be a name derived from mythology, folklore, Sanskrit, various African languages, etc. The purpose is both secretive and a declaration about one's personal goals or sense of inner identity.

The meaning of C. F. Russell's Hebrew name, *Genesthai,* is somewhat confusing in the absence of a statement from him. It is generally interpreted to mean "To cause to be" or "to become," or even "to become again." From a purely magical perspective, I suggest that it is "to become" as a statement of intent to be transformed.

Magical Oaths. The two oaths taken by the GBG members can be seen as being used to describe the importance of understanding the true nature of a magical oath—which is to establish a new relationship with your Higher Self that puts meaning into life.

I swear to tell myself the truth.

I swear to regard every event (or condition) as a particular dealing between myself and the Holy Guardian Angel.

Truth is generally a *relative* term for the simple reason that we can never know all the facts around any situation. At the same time, in a legal sense an oath is binding to honestly answer every question and perform every duty to the best of your ability.

A magical oath is different. It requires that you continuously tell yourself the truth, which may mean thinking over what you previously thought to be true and then telling yourself a new truth. It isn't honesty before the Law, but honesty before your own Higher Self.

An "event" isn't really *every* event, but those which take on a special kind of "halo effect" of calling itself to your attention. It must arise within your own personal sphere of awareness. It may be a completely ordinary event, but suddenly it stands out as if speaking to you. Yet to regard, or rather to believe, that everything which a person sees, feels, or hears is an omen or message, is a psychopathic condition.

The main point is that one must maintain a sense of keen awareness. When this is done, the way is open for one's intuition or inspiration to inform one on any possible oracular import. As part of a devoted program of relating to one's Higher Self, then one can get much symbology and "conversation" concerning his or her Great Work in the many things that touch his or her life. As you progress, both the events and their messages are greatly increased—those that are of value.

Under this Oath, the budding magician stands between two extremes. On the one side is the near-psychopath who regards everything that touches the eye and ear as a particular secret personal message. On the other side is the impervious one who sees no soul message in anything. Here, the neophyte stands in the middle ground, with open eye and ear to heed anything that may be relevant to his Great Work.

Magical Rituals. There are many kinds of rituals from the most ornate and complex to the pure and simple, but they all break down to common purpose: They are "planting seeds" for something desired to be grown and developed in consciousness.

Consciously performing actions with goals in mind are rituals. Planting seeds in a garden can become a ritual, and it is an example of a ritual designed to produce future results. Weeding the garden can be made into a ritual and would be a ritual of weeding out the undesirable and giving a better chance for the growth of the desirable.

One can readily see that many activities are eminently suitable as little magical rituals. Other rituals can be designed to produce effects in improving health, becoming more successful in daily life, building relationships, attaining psychic powers, transforming the self, and in achieving the Conversation with one's Holy Guardian Angel.

Magical Voice. There is lot to be said about how one speaks the words of ritual. Some words, particularly those in languages other than your native tongue, should be spoken in a special manner—in a slow, sonorous, or deep and resonating, voice. Think of the deep sounds emitted from a church pipe organ!

Culling makes the point that you should feel stimulated as you intone these words so that you have "goose-pimples running up and down the spine."

He also suggests that one should imagine "that the magickal power of the words derives from the many magicians of centuries past who have used these same words."

Others have suggested using your imagination to see the words projected out into the universe, awakening whatever it is you are calling. In the case of the barbarous words for the five elements, you want to sense that you are awakening these powers to respond to your call, and that you are being filled with them.

These words you speak in your Individual Rituals are for you, alone. You are not performing before an audience, *not even an invisible one!* This is important—it is easy to get carried away by your own voice, resulting in an inflated ego, which is the antithesis of what you need.

The inflated ego of the magician, the religious preacher, the politician, or anyone speaking or reading aloud, can create a barrier separating you from your Higher Self and decreasing your psychic and occult abilities even to the point that you will be misled by them.

Magick. Readers familiar with the writings of Aleister Crowley will recognize the somewhat unusual spelling of the word "MAGICK." Crowley did this to distinguish *Occult* "Magick" from the "magic" of *legerdemain,* and also to separate the new Occult Magick from that of the old which was often sadly loaded with useless junk! It may also be seen that the Qabalistic value of "Magick" comes to 83, and $8 + 3 = 11$. From *Liber Legis*— "My number is 11 as all their numbers who are of us." The number 11 stands for the Great Work accomplished—ABRACADABRA.

Magick Wand. The extended right thumb between clenched fingers as the Magick Wand is, to my knowledge, unique to the GBG. Other common substitutes for this tool are the right, or even the 'power' index finger if left-handed, and the thumb and first two fingers clenched together and pointed.

The non-use of traditional magickal tools—like daggers, swords, chalices—is also fairly unique to the GBG and is intended to keep the emphasis on the person and the Great Work and not on accessories. In some groups, the equipment can become quite expensive, sometimes with individuals trying to outdo each other with gold and jewels, fancy robes and crowns, etc. Or, at another extreme, the tradition may require that each person make their equipment: forging a sword, carving a wand in particular wood, and so on.

There is empowering magical validity to this, but again it is a distraction from the Great Work itself—the integration of personality with the Higher Self.

The question is the role of Magick in your life: If your goal is the Great Work of Self-Initiation, then focus on the "end" suggests simplicity of the tools and accessories. If the goal is to become a "professional" magician, then the focus on the "means" suggests great tools and accessories.

Magickal Identity. The instruction in the GBG was for the student to get a blank book and name it "Magickal Identity." Every evening, perhaps during your daily review, you are to concentrate on what you want to be—not what you want to do. You are discovering who you really are, the person you are coming to be.

Magickal Imagination. One should have good respect for this thing called "Imagination"—the *Imago* is a manifestation of the force of Spirit. To those having proper respect for the word 'imagination,' it can be told that the Magickal Imagination may well be over 50 percent of the total of Magick itself. Naturally, it is meant that kind of Imagination that is brought to a point of *Subjective Reality* and most certainly never the non-willed and uncontrolled ramblings of what can hardly be called "mind" in the undisciplined person.

The imagination is one of the most powerful tools that a human has. Through the imagination we can see what is not yet existent, and can change one thing into another. We can fly without wings, see with our eyes closed, hear sounds beyond sounds or silence in place of sound. We can test things in our imagination and work out any problems.

Tesla, the great electrical genius, is said to have been able to design a motor in his imagination, set it running, and then come back to it at a later time and check for wear on the bearings and other parts so he could make improvements in the design.

The Magickal Imagination is a major factor in Magick itself—to the point where "Subjective Reality" is equal to "Normal Reality." At some point, *Inner* can be substituted for *Outer,* and *that which is imaged happens!* With new understanding of Quantum Theory, "Subjective Reality" finds new expression in Magickal practice.

Imago is an idealized mental picture that can be recalled in its perfection at any time. While still in the realm of the Imagination, it is a manifestation of the *Force of Spirit*, taking it beyond ordinary imaginary images. To illustrate, the *Imago* was the name of the death mask worn in a special ritual on behalf of the deceased in Ancient Rome to establish his immortality. Similarly, I once had a dream about a "Life Mask" to be molded when a person was at their peak, and then worn ritually to enforce that image of youth, strength, and beauty.

The Magickal Imagination is that process at work—an *Imago* of perfection imposed to change ordinary reality into the ideal.

This is demonstrated well in Sex Magick where it is the careful role-playing of the imagination that allows the partners to exchange one reality with another. In your ritual, you submerge the personality of your partner into the imagined identity of a god or goddess. It isn't illusion, for the more often this is done, the more attributes of the god or goddess will manifest into the old personality.

The skill of the magician is enhanced by the skilled use of correspondences so that the imagined identity is supported by the established attributes associated with the god or goddess. This is why it is important to memorize and know the various appropriate correspondences.

Magickal Powers. Nearly all esoteric groups and teachers make the point that the attainment of psychic and magical powers can be an impediment to real spiritual growth. But, *is that really true?* If the object of the Great Work is integration with the Higher Self to become more than we are, we have to presume the accompaniment of such powers and skill as natural to the Whole Person.

Jesus said "ye are Gods . . . these things I do ye shall do and even greater." To me, that reads as both prophecy and promise; He doesn't say we will become gods but that we *are* gods who will do miracles. As we grow in Wholeness, our latent powers become skills we can perform at will. We refer to this as "Self-Empowerment" because it is not given to us by others, nor do we have to be Christian for this to happen. On the other hand, merely having psychic powers does not make us a *spiritually powerful* person who has become Whole.

"A Shortcut to Initiation" is a program of psychological and spiritual integration leading to Self-Empowerment. It isn't the only way, but it is one way.

Magickal Ritual Goals. Remember that the purpose of the rituals you compose in the practice of High Magick is psychological integration, otherwise known as Initiation. Your goal is to awaken, develop, cleanse and unite your many parts into the Whole Person that is your potential.

Nothing in this book can be said to directly instruct you in the practical magic involved in Self-Help practices—the matters of "Money, Sex, and Power" as one occultist put it. You can expand those categories as you need: "Money" becomes questions of career, training, financing, contracts, success, buying a house, etc., while "Sex" includes romance, love, relationships, marriage, children, and so on, and "Power" is really the ability to be who you are.

Yet, all the elements are here. There is no absolute conflict between the realities of the *outer* world and those of the *inner* world. We are spiritual beings incarnated and living in a material world. We have the obligations of being *co-creators* to "make the world a better place." We're partners with the world spirit, and brothers and sisters to all living beings.

We are "gods in the making" and need to think of that as *our life purpose* without letting ego inflation hinder our ability to "listen" to not only our brothers and sisters walking this same path, but to the "whispers from eternity." You don't need an intermediary between the divinity within and the Divine itself so long as ego is kept in its proper place.

McMurtry, Grady. (1918–1985) A student of Aleister Crowley, he was largely responsible for giving new life to the OTO which he headed from 1971 until his death.

He studied engineering at Pasadena Junior College and met Jack Parsons at nearby CalTech through their mutual enthusiasm for science fiction. In 1941 he was initiated into the OTO. In 1942, as a member of R.O.T.C. he was called to active duty, and took part in the Normandy invasion. He was recalled to active duty in the Korean War and retired as a Lieutenant Colonel.

Stationed in England in 1943–1944, he was a personal student of Crowley. Back in California after WWII, Crowley appointed him OTO representative for the United States, subject only to Karl Germer. When Crowley died in 1947, Germer became head of the OTO. McMurty ended his involvement with the OTO in 1961 over disputes with Germer and moved to Washington DC.

Germer died in 1962 and in 1969 McMurty returned to California to take charge of the OTO. By 1985, there were over 700 members in several countries. Since his death, the OTO has continued to grow to several thousand active members in over fifty countries.

Menstruum. The "menstruum" is the "solvent of the White Eagle" in the retort.

Messages. It can be "psychopathic" to believe that all the ideas sometimes inspired when we're in the presence of a tree or a garden, an animal or bird, or the night sky or a glorious dawn, are personal messages whispered to our ears alone. But, the source of inspiration knows no boundaries, and our openness to such stimulation is healthy and vastly different than pathology. And like symbols in dreams, our Higher Self may alert us to some needed idea by awakening our interest to something happening in our environment.

While not exactly the same thing, it is fascinating to let things "speak" to you in divination. Rather than following other people's interpretations, let the cards, crystals, shells, bones, stones, coins, sticks, or whatever, speak through your touch and gaze. Let yourself slide into a mild trance, and "let your fingers do the talking" as they manipulate the chosen objects.

Don't impose a *left brain* rigidity of rules on what is essentially a *right brain* work of creative response. Patterns found in a tea cup may seem to say things, but the wisdom is in yourself and not the bottom of the cup.

Muladhara. The root chakra located at the base of the spine, color red, associated planet Saturn, associated Sephirah Malkuth. It is home to Kundalini, and sexual energy.

Nature Magick. In the World of Nature there are many natural powers and natural remedies. At the same time, through the Natural World there are intelligences at work—from the "animal spirits" of the group minds to the Nature Spirits of Element Forces that can be both invoked

and evoked, and on to the Earthern Energies that can be called into the
Magician's Body and Mind.

Nature Magick is a class of magick unto itself, residing between
Folk Magic, Practical Magic, and Ceremonial Magick, while the World
of Nature is a resource for all kinds of magic.

Nemyss. The familiar Egyptian head-dress that somewhat resembles a
'page-boy' hair styling. The colors and designs all have meanings, and
additional meanings beyond the traditional associations make the nemyss in different colors and patterns a convenient ceremonial garment
to distinguish ritualists from one another, and signifying their ceremonial function.

New Aeon of Horus. *Is this the same as "the New Age" or "the Age of Aquarius?"* Perhaps yes, perhaps no. Crowley predicted the coming of *the
"New Aeon of Horus" when Every Person is a Star moving by his own inner
light and will.* Sincere followers of Crowley would likely say there's no
connection. Astrologers are just as likely to say that the zodiacal entry
into Aquarius has little connection to either, while maintaining that
Aquarius does embody much that is claimed for the New Age and for
the New Aeon.

My own inclination is to believe they are all manifestations of the
same thing—that we are indeed in a New Age opening up opportunities for growth and development of the Whole Person. Maybe the as-
tronomical/astrological precession triggers a more *Aquarian perception*
in all of us, leaving behind what has been claimed as repressive in the
Age of Pisces. And maybe this is the same as the New Aeon of Horus.
Why not?

I believe we are in a new *era* (to substitute those three loaded concepts with a neutral word for purposes of discussion) in which there
has been a shift of energies allowing more people to open up to new
ideas and to respond to new ideas. And, yes, it is likely that the transition from Piscean to Aquarian energies facilitates this. Again: *Why not?*

Regardless, any study of history will demonstrate that we have
more intellectual freedom and opportunity today than in any previous
era we know anything about. Myth may claim that in some ancient

past, perhaps in some Atlantean civilization, we had a similar situation that led to abuse of knowledge by the few to the detriment of all.

Crowley tells us that this new age brings us the freedom and the *impetus*—a "call" urging to step ahead of the external regimentation. Individually, we have to make the effort while the energies of the age make it possible to succeed. Magick is no longer for the few, the elite priesthood of the secret lodge, but for everybody who makes the effort. Magick is the technology for self-transformation and self-empowerment. Every Man and every woman can become a Star by employing the esoteric technology now available to everyone.

Myth always contains some kind of truth, and perhaps this warns us of needs for awareness of potential hazards as more people are enabled to develop their psychic powers and to more easily gain deeper understanding of the human psyche and of quantum theory.

"New Thought." The name given the philosophy of Phineas Quimby which can be summed up: "The infinitude of the Supreme One; the Divinity of man and his infinite possibilities through the creative power of constructive thinking and obedience to the voice of the indwelling Presence, which is our source of Inspiration, Power, Health and Prosperity."

It's a beautiful philosophy, and was an inspiration in the development of Mary Baker Eddy's Christian Science religion with the belief that the physical is not truly real, and that healing of disease occurs by virtue of the presence of Truth.

In addition to Christian Science, the New Thought is influential in three major, but distinct, religious denominations within the American New Thought movement: Unity Church, Science of Mind, and the Church of Divine Science.

The difference between Magick as practiced by the GBG and other groups, and more importantly by individual magicians, and religious groups is less a distinction in philosophy than in practice. A *Shortcut to Initiation* is a promise of individual accelerated evolution, of self-transformation and integration of personality with the Higher Self leading to Self-Empowerment. There is no intermediary—teacher, priest, practitioner, swami or other person—doing the Work that only you can do for yourself.

As sources of inspiration and knowledge, all of these movements have great value but they are not in themselves practical programs or self-transformation leading to that integration of personality with the Higher Self.

Nuit. (Also Nut) The Egyptian sky goddess whom we see as arched as the sky overhead with only finger tips and toes touching the Holy Earth - who is also Geb, her husband. Beneath Nuit, Geb is often shown with an erect penis for it is through their union that all is born. Geb is also her brother, and Nuit and Geb are the parents of Isis, Osiris, Nephthys, and Set. (Note: "Incestuous" relationships are common in all mythology and that has no pertinence to humanity. Myth's pertinence is to the inner understanding of cosmic energies.)

Nuit is also matter, and Hadit (also her husband, or masculine counterpart) is motion. Nuit is an infinite Circle, while Hadit is the infinitely small point at the core of everything.

Oaths. Oaths are common in magickal work. If you are a member of an active coven or lodge you may be expected to swear to secrecy of the group name and the names—magick and mundane—of the members, you may be required not to reveal the teachings of the group, and in particular the names of the gods evoked in group work.

There are two primary reasons for such oaths: (1) to establish a feeling of respect for magick itself, and (2) to protect the members' identities. When you take an oath, you do so because of the perceived value and importance of those identities, and the wishes of the people involved.

A third reason for secrecy is to isolate and contain the energies involved with magickal work, including the particular egregor, or thought form that is the magickal identity of the particular group or even of the individual.

Oaths are best chosen and understood as important to the project and not as part of the pageantry of the group. Think of your oath, and of secrecy itself as an internalizing. Your own magickal name takes on a greater psychological and spiritual importance by being held secret, and the oath feeds energy to the process.

Order of Palladians. A French magical order of the late 1800s created by Leo Taxil (pen name of Gabriel Jorgand-Pages), apparently, as a total fraud. In books and articles, Taxil described dramatic sexual scenes in magickal settings, later admitted to being fictional.

However, that doesn't mean that the sexual teachings were erroneous. Rather, they were the inspiration for the scheme.

O. T. A. (Ordo Templi Astartes) founded in 1970 by Carroll (Poke) Runyon (Frater Thabion) following a near-death experience and mystic vision. "The O.T. A. is now America's oldest continually operating Ritual magick Lodge. We are first and foremost a working lodge. Our Emphasis is on doing magick—and by that we mean good old fashioned wizardry: summoning spirits to visible appearance in the Dark Mirror and bringing down Gods, Goddesses and Angels to illuminate our crystal orb so that we can communicate with them. We use powerful hypnotic and yoga techniques that we have developed and perfected in over a quarter century of practice. The O.T.A. is the oldest continually practicing ritual lodge in the U.S. We are the recognized leaders in the art of evocation (conjuration to visible appearance in the dark mirror) and our Pathworking System combines the best aspects of Eastern technique with Western symbolism. Classes are offered on these unique techniques, as well as on the history of the origin of our Hermetic Tradition, at our Rivendell Lodge in Silverado, CA. For more information, Please contact Frater Thabion, Archmage at: Kingsword@ aol.com."

O.T.O.—O.∴T.∴O.∴. (Ordo Templi Orientis—The "Order of the Temple of the East") The OTO was or is (depending on how you look at it) a magickal order founded by Karl Kellner (1851–1905) in 1890. Upon Kellner's passing in 1905, the leadership passed to Theodore Reuss (1855–1923) and then to Aleister Crowley in 1922.

Currently there are (or were) two OTO organizations: One in England headed by Kenneth Grant and the other headed by successors to Grady McMurtry.

The distinguishing characteristic of OTO rituals is their overt intention to arouse and direct sexual energy. Kellner claimed to have been given secrets of a sexual yoga during travels in the Middle East and India, and he believed that the Knights Templar had this same knowledge.

Per their website, the "O.T.O. is dedicated to the high purpose of securing the Liberty of the Individual and his or her advancement in Light, Wisdom, Understanding, Knowledge, and Power through Beauty, Courage, and Wit, on the Foundation of Universal Brotherhood. U.S. Grand Lodge is the governing body of O.T.O. in the United States. It is the most populous and active branch of O.T.O., with 44 local bodies in 26 states as of March 2009. If you are interested in becoming a member of Ordo Templi Orientis, see the membership page for more information. To find an O.T.O. body near you, consult our list of local bodies. Our FAQ answers many common questions about O.T.O. and Thelema." www.oto-usa.org

Pa Kua. Eight trigrams, the eight signs which form the basis of I Ching, and from which the sixty-four hexagrams are constructed.

The Pa Kua is also used in various decorative and religious motifs incorporating the eight trigrams of I Ching; *specifically* in a circle around the yin-yang symbol.

Though the origin of the Pa Kua, and hence of the I Ching, is often attributed to Fu Hsi, the legendary Chinese emperor thought to have ruled at the beginning of the millennium BC, the eight trigrams used for divination were not invented until about 1000 BC. Fundamental to their divinatory usage, these three-lined figures, in their sixty-four combinations, form the basis of Chinese cosmological speculation.

Pan. The Greek god of nature with a human head and torso and the hind legs, ears, and horns of a goat. Also symbolic of the male sexual drive.

Parrott, Wanda Sue. Founder of the Amy Kitchener's Angels Without Wings Foundation, Wanda was born in 1935 in Kansas City, Missouri, but was raised and educated in Southern California. She returned to Missouri in 1988 where she has been president of Springfield Writers' Guild, honorary life member of Missouri State Poetry Society, and founder of Springfield Writers Workshop, which has been meeting in Springfield-Greene County Library since 1992. More recently she has returned to California.

She was an investigative reporter with the Los Angeles Herald-Examiner, syndicated feature writer with Ozarks Senior Living newspapers, and holds many awards for poetry and short fiction, as well as newspaper columns and features. She won several "Best Feature" awards in the Hearst Corporation's chain of newspapers. In 2002 she was honored recipient of the Alumnus of the Year Award from her alma mater, Citrus College in Glendora, California, where she served as president of the Associated Women Students in 1953–1954. In 2004 her sci-fi story "Power Lunches" won first place in the Writer's Challenge Literary Association's transcendental tales contest. She won the 2007 Mistress of Mayhem Award from Sleuth's Ink Mystery Writers for her short story "Elfinetta's ETs."

She has published under eighteen pen names, including Prairie Flower and Edgar Allan Philpott. As Diogenes Rosenberg, she invented the Pissonnet in 1997; the world's shortest sonnet form is now in public domain and she has admitted being its inventor. She is co-founder and sponsor of the National Annual Senior Poets Laureate Poetry Competition for American poets age fifty and older, now in its seventeenth year. Visit her website: http://www.amykitchenerfdn.org

Parsons, Jack. (1914–1952) Parsons was a rocket propulsion researcher at CalTech and co-founder of the Jet Propulsion Laboratory and of Aerojet Corp. He was an early devotee of Aleister Crowley and a member of the O.T.O.

Crowley said that Parsons and L. Ron Hubbard practiced ritual magick and worked sex magick with Parsons' girl friend. Later Parsons accused Hubbard of stealing both his money and girl friend.

Parsons died in an explosion in his home laboratory.

Pentagram. A five-pointed star.

Postures, and Movements, East and West. "Postures" generally refer to Eastern yogic postures along with controlled breathing, and our familiar Western postures of standing and sitting. In addition, postures in-

volve intentional movement—even if just sitting with grace and awareness of energy flow.

There are, of course, other postures: those of the martial arts in
China and Japan, belly and dervish dances in the Middle East, Hula
from Hawaii, and much more. Any movement and posture that involves energy probably has an associated shamanic or sacred tradition.

The Western Esoteric Tradition has adopted the Egyptian God postures as seen in paintings on tomb and temple walls. Whether standing, moving, or seated, these show positions of dignity and energy restraint. You can sense power that would be released in a simple gesture.

Psychic Self-Defense. Techniques and practices to build psychic defenses
against psychic predators, skilled advertisers and sales people, emotional manipulators, and psychic attack.

Suggested Reading:

Denning & Phillips: *Practical Guide to Psychic Self-Defense: Strengthen
Your Aura*

Penczak: *The Witch's Shield, Protection Magick and Psychic Self-Defense*

Ptah. In the ancient Egyptian pantheon, the first of the gods and the primal creator of the entire world and all in it. He is the primal matter
itself. He appears as a bearded man wrapped up like a mummy with
his hands free to hold a staff made up of the symbols for life, stability,
and power. He is the patron of craftsmen and artisans, of all things
creative.

Qabala. There are various alternative spelling of the words *Qabala* and
Qabalistic. The most common is "Kabbalah" and "Kabalistic;" another
is "Kabala, and then "Cabala" and "Cabalistic." All are transliterations
of the Hebrew word QBLH meaning "an unwritten tradition transmitted orally from teacher to student." "Kabbalah" and "Kabala" generally
refer to the original Jewish version, "Cabala" refers the Christian version, and "Qabala" and Qabalah" for the magical or Hermetic version.

The Kabbalah—no matter how spelled—is probably the most
complete purview of the world as perceived and experienced through
spiritual vision that we have. It is a systematic organization of spiritual

reality into a manageable formula for human study along with a methodology of "correspondences" to organize all of human knowledge.

It is a treasure trove for practicing magicians and the most expert self-study program of progressive mediation the world has ever seen.

Qodosh. In the Third Degree of Sex Magick in the GBG. Physical ecstasy must become psychic ecstasy that in turns 'fires' the Magickal Imagination. In the now empowered imagination we aim for realization of the objective of the operation. All the while, the chosen objective is the central focus of the concentration and imagining from beginning to end of the sexual union.

If the objective of the operation is a quality, such as the vision of Beauty, then the experience, the trance, may continue on for a week or even more. And if the operation is repeated, the experience extends more and more, and becomes Reality.

Even though the objective may seem "external," the effect on the two partners is internally transforming. It bears a lot of thought.

Quintessence. The transmuted sexual fluids are held in the mouth, and used for magickal operations.

Ra. Egyptian king of the gods who watches over the world from the sky as the sun. See *Ra-Hoor-Khuit*.

Ra-Hoor-Khuit. Ra is the sun god of the ancient Egyptian religion, and was carried on the back of Nuit, the sky goddess. Ra is the god of birth and of rebirth as he appears to be reborn at the dawn of each new day. Ra-Hoor-Khuit is a form of Horus and symbolic of the Solar Sexual Energies that are part of Crowley's sexual magick.

Red Lion. The male of the magickal sex rite.

Reduction. In the practice of numerology, larger numbers are—for the most part—*reduced* to single digit numbers. Thus 12 becomes $1 + 2 = 3$.

Regardie, Dr. Francis Israel. (1907–1985) A widely respected authority on magic and Kabbalah, once personal secretary to Aleister Crowley and member of the Golden Dawn. His *The Golden Dawn* is a principal resource of western magic. His *Tree of Life, The Middle Pillar,* and *A Garden of Pomegranates* are considered modern classics.

Regularity. The need for and value of regular and consistent practice will be emphasized again and again. It is *regularity* and *recording* that are the foundations of *process.* These are the practices that are compared to *gardening,* for the consistency of these basic practices is what nurtures the transformation of personality into the Higher Self. The rule of regularity is not unique to Magick, but is the proven key to every program for the attainment of knowledge and skill. It is necessary because every practice builds upon the previous one. You are building skills the same way that you build muscles—by practice and use. Any system of knowledge is accumulative, and regularity of study is like laying bricks to build a building—it is a continuous process, and if stopped the lower layers are exposed to weather and loss. Set up a schedule for what can be done within your other obligations, and stick to it. If you are interrupted for any reason, start over from the beginning.

Regularity of practice is reinforced through the use of a daily Journal—whether called a *Magical Diary* or *Book of Shadows* or *Dream Book* or some other name of your choice. It is here that you should record not only your magical study and practice, but your insights and record your dreams.

One of the key teachings of the GBG was to "regard every event whatsoever as a particular dealing between myself and my daemon." This is, of course, a factual impossibility, but Lou went on to explain it with an example. If you are driving down the highway, and *something* calls your attention to the mileage on your odometer, then that is an "event" by which your higher self is sending you an important message. In this example, the mileage is a number to be interpreted through numerology. And this event and your interpretation should be recorded in your diary. (See Magical Oaths)

Retirement Ritual. A "retirement ritual" or "retreat" is common to many magical, shamanic, and spiritual systems. As a time of isolation and self-deprivation, it involves a challenge to one's self-identity and an opening to the Higher Self whether conceived as the Holy Guardian Angel or God.

A familiar task of the retirement ritual is to record one's visions and realizations in a diary, and/or to discuss the experiences with the shaman or teacher, and to return to that record in future times to review those insights from an evolving perspective.

Retirement rituals, retreats, vision quests, wilderness journeys, periods of silence, etc., are all common to Initiatory Practices. Each tradition has its own unique practices, many symbolic and dramatic, and intended to "shake the foundations" and "stir the pot." The intention is to mark the ending of one part of your life and to mark the beginning of another. All involve a "change of pace" during which things can happen.

Some may demand a life-changing accomplishment at their culmination—a "Big Dream," the finding of an amulet, the making of a talisman, a substantial fasting and purging, the killing of an animal that then becomes one's totem, and other ways to establish a transition from one phase of life to another.

Aside from the Retirement Retreat, there is proven value to periodic retreats, even annually, to encourage review and communication with the Higher Self, the Holy Guardian Angel. Various businesses and organizations, churches and other groups provide for such retreats for their own purposes—*shouldn't you do the same for the most important personal purpose of all?*

It doesn't demand much on your time and resources, and can be combined—as long as you are honest and disciplined about it—with a family vacation. But, you don't really have to go somewhere beyond your own home for a weekend retreat or personal vacation. The advantage of a change of place is the same as for a change of pace—you plan the time and environment to get the most out of your reflection time.

The only equipment you need is your journal and a pen, or your laptop computer provided you use it only for your journaling purpose. No e-mails, no online searches, just your journal. Your *ideal* program should call for three periods of meditation, 30 to 60 minutes each, followed by one to two hours of writing. That's it, a maximum of nine hours over two days once a year for the most important endeavor of your life. But, even as an ideal it may be too much. Adjust it if necessary.

If you have BIG questions about your spiritual progress, write them down and start your morning meditation with them. If you have no questions, just ask your Higher Self to communicate with you, and patiently *listen*. Make no demands; just be open to your Holy Guardian Angel.

Expect nothing specifically. You do not know your own self-created necessity in relation to the Angel or Daemon. You can in no way command your Daemon! You may have an energized feeling of freedom or of being rejuvenated, and it may last for many weeks. You may have a completely empty feeling that absolutely nothing has taken place—and this is a sure sign that something of no value has been taken from you, which you will later realize. On the other hand, something outstanding may manifest almost immediately. Above all things, as an aspiring magician you must learn in your aspiration to "Lust not for result." To lust for result is anathema in Magick.

Of course, you can do lesser meditations for this sort anytime, but there is value to this larger, weekend retreat that will pay unlimited dividends.

Retort. The vagina is the vessel that receives the ejaculated semen, i.e., the essence of the male orgasm, also called "the blood of the Red Lion."

Rite of Diana. A sex magick ritual bringing one or both partners into the Borderland State and the the imagination subjectively real, during one Dianism congrex lasting for hours without break.

Rite of Transubstantiation. The Rite of "Transubstantiation" is the alchemical transformation of the shared sexual fluids. In the Christian churches the consecrated wine and wafer is declared to be the body and blood of Jesus Christ. The only difference in the herein described magick rite is that there is an actual vital spiritualized substance that is consecrated.

Ritual Record Book. The importance of a record book—whether as a Magical Diary, Book of Shadows, or other name—has previously been mentioned. I repeat that this is one of the most important actions that are undertaken by the magician. And, it is just as important in any activity, whether as student or professional, as wife or husband, etc. The act of recording is the act of self-observation and the opportunity for self-evaluation. Keeping in mind whatever the goal of your procedure, writing down what you did and how it affected you becomes a measure of your work.

Rosicrucian (AMORC) Order. AMORC has been operating since 1915, and has affiliated lodges and chapters all over the world. The Rosicrucian system is unique—it provides a foundation tying together all of the different aspects of metaphysical study, and demonstrates their interconnectedness. Contact them at www.rosicrucian.org/ for more information.

Rosicrucian Fellowship. Founded by Max Heindel with its main teaching presented his book *The Rosicrucian Cosmo-Conception*. This Christian Mystic Philosophy presents deep insights into the Christian Mysteries and establishes a meeting ground for Art, Religion, and Science. Max Heindel was selected by the Elder Brothers of the Rose Cross to publicly give out the Western Wisdom Teachings in order to help prepare mankind for the coming age of Universal Brotherhood, the Age of Aquarius. Although the Rosicrucian Fellowship books are sold, the services of their Healing Department, the Correspondence Courses, and the various School activities continue to be offered on a free-will love-offering basis. www.rosicrucian.com/

Russell, C. F. Cecil Frederick Russell. (1897–1987) Russell wrote in 1922: "Magick is aptly defined as the science and art of doing one's Wil—achieving one's purpose, fulfilling the Law of THELEMA. Thus theoretical magick is the art of perfecting mental processes, and practical magick the art of perfecting volitional processes. These definitions are hardly conclusive, but they are scholarly enough for practical purposes, I think. I think that every member should be drilled in ceremonial magick until he subconsciously acquires the attitude of doing the right thing at the right moment with omnipotence at his command and eternity at his disposal. The ideas that dissolve the sin complex, viz that nothing really matters, that it is impossible to make a mistake, etc., cannot be rooted in the organism by any other method."

Russell was a member of the A∴A∴ & O.T.O. (Fr. Genesthai) and was secretary to Aleister Crowley during the (in) famous 1920s' Cefalu period. Some speculation suggests that Russell's experiences on "the Rock" during this period at Thelema Abbey subsequently led to his establishment of the Gnostic Body of God (G∴B∴G∴) and his personal magickal explorations into the fields of mathematics and logic. More can be found at the website: www.cfrussell.homestead.com/.

(Note that there is some dispute as to the meaning of the acronym G∴B∴G∴. Culling says it means the "Great Brotherhood of God," but the above description says it means the "Gnostic Body of God." Both Russell and Culling are no longer with us, so let's just stick with "GBG.")

Self-superhumerated. "The Old, the Patriarchal Aeon has taught man not to live and think by his own individual Light, but instead to live by the dicta of a self-superhumerated, regimenting, all-powerful intelligentsia. Crowley was the arch-rebel against this."

Louis Culling wrote: "'Humerate' (if there were such a word) would mean metaphorically to take upon oneself a task or position. Hence 'superhumerate' is a favorite nasty word of mine which means, for illustration, one poses that the mantle of Elijah has been cast upon his shoulders—making a pretense of greatness or authority."

Sex Magick. Sex Magick is the whole thing—the persisted application of all that has been learned and gained as skills in the training of Alphaism, Dianism, Qodosh, the exercise of the Magickal Imagination, the memorization of correspondences, the learning of concentration and visualization, and the glory of union.

For I am divided for love's sake, for the chance of union.

What is "Sex Magick?"

Hey Baby, want to get together and do some Sex Magick?

NO!

At least, I hope she says "no" to that proposition because what he's after is not what we call "Sex Magick." Nor are we proposing "the magic of sex." And to clarify, romance and relationship are not fundamental to Sex Magick. You will find out why as we progress in this discussion.

Every man thinks he's an expert on sex, and most women know that he's not. He does know how to make babies, but he doesn't necessarily know how to make love, or to make magic. Women instinctively know how to make magic but both men and women need to learn Sex Magick.

The simple truth is that men simply get an *itch* in their penis, and want it scratched—preferably by a woman. Women yearn for something more complex: they want to be attractive and desirable; gathering men like honey gathers flies. The want to feel adored and they want to know that they cause a man to have an erection and desire sex. And they want romance and intimacy, to feel that they are the only one in his life. They want to be held and kissed, and to have lots of slow foreplay.

Women's pleasure is the key, and orgasm is not the biggest part of it. Prolonged intercourse, with or without her orgasm, is vital to create the energy field needed for the transformation of consciousness fundamental to Sex Magick. Women are the *engines* that power-up the field whereas men are just the mechanics and the best of them learn how to carefully manage the process while she just swoons in enjoyment.

Every woman should feel herself as a goddess incarnate in the lead-up to sex, during sex, and after sex. His role as a god is a secret—else his ego inflates and robs the mission. She should become filled with energy, but her energy is 'magnetic' while his is 'electric.' They should both enter into the "Borderland" state of consciousness where there is only pleasure but no climax, and hold that state for two or more hours. When the "moment is right," her magnetism should simple draw his electricity into her person, body and soul, with or without his sperm which is of no particular interest to the Sex Magick operation.

And when the "moment" comes, he projects his special intention, the magickal goal of the operation, right along with his electricity and semen. His role is primarily that of the Magician who projects the imaged goal with the release of his power into her. She receives, transmutes, and makes it happen in dimensions beyond the physical and mostly beyond her awareness. Some women claim to know when they're impregnated, but it's not likely and not necessary. Instead of a physical child, here there is a "magickal childe."

In Giving and Receiving there is Magick, and Love

Yes, all this does require preparation, discipline, and restraint. And the importance of preparation precedes foreplay and should include the planning and execution of drama to elevate the feeling of importance of the ritual and the roles of the players. Sex Magick evolves from Dramatic Ritual with the staging of place, costuming, incense or aromatic oils, soft lighting, music possibly romantic or with a stimulating base beat, and possibly a non-intrusive script leading to awareness of the intended result.

In this case of a Magickal Curriculum, it is the Knowledge and Conversation with the Holy Guardian Angel. It can be the objective for either partner, or both.

It calls upon the Magickal Imagination to see the partner as god or goddess, or as Holy Guardian Angel. *What does the god or goddess or Holy Guardian Angel look like? Do they move? Do they speak?* Some answers can be found in reference works in religion and mythology, while others will arise from your subconsciousness.

Do what thou Wilt. Love is the Law; Love under Will

In your planning, let awareness of pleasure and arousal be your guide. Don't neglect the possible role of fantasy roll playing and fetishes in costuming. Goddesses wear anything they want, and what they want includes knowing and witnessing the arousal and lust of their partner. The challenge remains the required discipline and restraint, especially on the part of the man so that you can remain engaged for two or more hours. Even though the emphasis in a Sex Magick operation does not call for the partners to be an established couple, knowledge and understanding of each other's needs and 'turn-ons' is helpful in holding the man back from orgasm and leading the woman to the edge, and then pushing that edge beyond previous limits. The edge should not be a cliff to fall down but the start of a spiral upward to heaven. An important side note: fantasies and fetishes should be her choices, not his. We have been conditioned to think that only men have fetishes and sexual fantasies, but that's not accurate. Hers are more subjective and his more objective but in Sex Magick it is "She who must be obeyed." An important book is *She Comes First,* by Ian Kerner.

See yourselves enjoying the extended bliss of the Borderland state rather than the immediacy of satisfaction. Make Love for an Eternity! You will find that extended bliss is healthful, will rejuvenate you; will lower blood pressure, bathing your inner bodies with health-giving energies and secretions.

Love is the Law

Suggested Reading:

Kerner, Ian: *She Comes First: The thinking man's guide to pleasuring a woman,* 2004, Collins.

Kraig, Donald Michael: *Modern Sex Magick: Secrets of Erotic Spirituality—Learn to control and direct sexual power when it's most intense— during arousal. Increase your pleasure and enhance your relationships.* 2002, Llewellyn.

Shells. Shells are a Kabalistic concept, and are known by the Hebrew *Qlippoth.* They are the negative side of existence, the leftovers after creation. In many ways, the idea of a shell is appropriate for it is a container for the positive aspect, the inner goodness, the seed of life. Think of a walnut, and crack the shell to get the edible 'meat' out. The shell is discarded, yet it has some residual value—perhaps as fuel, compost materials for your garden, etc. In the process of life, the buried walnut would come to life, bursting out of the shell and growing into a new tree. The shell is waste debris having served its purpose.

In some philosophical perspectives, the Klippoth (alternate spelling of Qlippoth) are seen as evil because they limit the life force within. In our analogy, if the walnut shell is too thick, the seed won't be able to burst into life. Or think of a chicken egg with a shell so thick and hard that the baby chick is unable to peck through and become the chicken intended.

Now, let's extend our story of the Chicken and the Egg another step, and agree that the egg comes first. But, before there is a real egg the shell is formed. That shell has a purpose of its own in containing and limiting the growing embryo. If it has a consciousness, it is fighting to contain the embryo. On a cosmic scale, there are such "forms without force" left over from the descent of life and consciousness into matter. As such, they are evil and demonic. If fed with the energies of hate, greed, and desire to return to the past (as in some religions' hatred of modernism), they may become true demons with enough consciousness to act on their own.

Basically, however, we can think of the qlippoth as the opposite of the Sephiroth on the Tree of Life as in the following table:

Sephiroth	Qlippoth
Kether	Futility
Chokmah	Arbitrariness
Binah	Fatalism
Chesed	Ideology
Geburah	Bureaucracy
Tiphareth	Emptiness
Netzach	Repetitiveness
Hod	Order regardless of purpose
Yesod	Form without Life
Malkuth	Stasis

Shortcut to Initiation. A shortcut obviously contrasts with the longer route. Often a shortcut is a rougher road; one with particular hazards and without some common comforts and resources, and sometimes it doesn't even show up on the official map. But there are reasons to take the shortcut: it is more efficient, often both shorter and faster, and sometimes more adventurous.

A shortcut may go through dangerous territory, and sometimes it may leave the paved road completely and take you cross country through which you have to make your own trail. There may be no rest areas or food stops or gas stations—so you have to plan ahead and be able to take some risks. There's no guide to lead you. *You are on your own!*

But, ultimately, you are always 'on your own.' The work can't be done for you—so whether you take the 'high road' or the 'low road,' the better mapped route or the shortcut across country—you are the one! You will learn more because you are your own guide, your own resource. Instead of a teacher watching over you, you have only your own Higher Self *who will respond to your need!*

Initiation is one of those ambiguous words that are used variously. In esoteric practice, it sometimes seems to mark one's "graduation" for the completion of *under-graduate studies*. But 'to initiate' also means to start a process.

In our magickal curriculum it means both. The goal is to make you a Whole Person so that you can become a Greater Being. Like the good Scout, the Initiate is prepared because of the work he has completed. The Initiate is ready for the Great Adventure leading to God.

The only mysteries are the Inner Mysteries.

Signs. As used in ritual, these are the movements and postures, accompanied by gestures that function in unity with the voiced expressions, chants, invocations, evocations, and mental visualization and astral extensions.

Silver Cone. Also known as a "cone of power." A cone is commonly visualized as a three-dimensional extension of the Magick Circle to function as a container of inner strength and purpose and as a barrier against external disturbance. In addition, the "cone" can be directed to deliver magical force to an intended target for healing and other purposes.

Simon Magus. Also known as **Simon the Sorcerer,** he was a native of Gitta. Possessing great magical powers, he described himself as a 'son of God,' and that we were all gods in the making imprisoned in matter. In this sense, he is considered the founder of Gnosticism.

There were accusations by Christians that he was a demon in human form, and he was specifically said to possess the ability to levitate and fly at will. The fantastic stories of Simon the magician persisted into the Middle Ages, and were possibly inspiration for Goethe's Faust.

He was the Emperor Nero's Court Magician for whom he did many demonstrations, among them the moving about of heavy furniture untouched by human hands. Legend has it that while performing magic, he levitated to prove himself a god. St. Peter prayed to God to stop his flying, and Simon fell to the ground, and later died of his wounds.

His constant companion was a woman he called Helen of Troy. Within Helen was the Spirit of God, leading to the Gnostic belief that the true God has a feminine part called Spirit. The Gnostics further held that God the father was accompanied by God the mother, sometimes called Sophia, or the Wisdom of God. In the Old Testament written in Hebrew the Spirit of God is referred to as *Ruach* having a feminine gender.

Society of the Inner Light. A Mystery School within the Western Esoteric Tradition, founded by Dion Fortune. The Society accepts students for both a Supervised Study Course and an Unsupervised Study Course. More information through their website, www.innerlight.org.uk/.

Solitary. A practitioner of Magic working alone rather than in a group.

Star, The. The seven-pointed star is the sigil of the Goddess Babalon. In the Tarot, the Star is the 17th Major Arcanum—image: a bright star overhead and most commonly a naked woman kneeling at the edge of a body of water pouring water from two vessels, sometimes one onto the ground but other times both into the water; Hebrew letter: Tzaddi; Divinatory meaning: spiritual guidance, hope, help; the 28th path on the Tree of Life connecting Yesod to Netzach.

Sufi Magick of Eros—**the Ecstatic School.** Sufi Mysticism and Sex Magick, with ecstatic dancing and other shamanic practices.

Tahuti. An alternate name for Thoth.

Tarot. A vast system of Archetypal Knowledge condensed into a system of 78 images on cards that can be finger-manipulated and then laid out in systematic patterns to answer specific questions or provide guidance to the solution of problems. While it is a form of divination, it is one of the most sophisticated and carefully developed systems of images and relationships following the structure of the Kabbalah's Tree of Life. Going beyond divination, it is also a system to access the Unconscious, and to structure magical ritual. It's a powerful Western esoteric system comparable to the Eastern I Ching.

The concepts of the Tarot cards have kept pace with the evolution of advancing knowledge, with the concepts and psychology of the European peoples. This is a very important point for it is fairly unique among occult divinatory systems for such evolution to take place. While interpretations of such systems as the I Ching will have some evolutionary change, the system and its physical representation in the 64 Hexagrams has remained static. The Tarot, in contrast, has changed, been modified, and evolved in physical form and structure, and in interpretation and application.

And there is interchange between the Tarot deck and the person using the deck, facilitated by the artwork that—in my opinion—a positive aspect no other system has. The reader is *invited* to communicate with the cards, and that's one among many reasons that there are so many Tarot decks—over a thousand—to choose from.

Suggested Reading:

Amber K & Azrael Arynn K: *Heart of Tarot, an Intuitive Approach,* Llewellyn

Ferguson: *The Llewellyn Tarot.* 78-card deck and 288 page book, Llewellyn

Cicero, Chic & Tabatha: *The New Golden Dawn Ritual Tarot—Keys to the Rituals, Symbolism, Magic & Divination,* Llewellyn

Hollander: *Tarot for Beginners—An Easy Guide to Understanding & Interpreting the Tarot,* Llewellyn

Kraig: *Tarot & Magic—How to use the Tarot to do magic on a practical level, with Tarot Spells, Talismans, working on the Astral Plane, etc.,* Llewellyn

Louis: *Tarot Plain and Simple—A self-study program to do readings for yourself and others,* Llewellyn. Written by a psychiatrist, with a Jungian approach to understanding human nature and psychological conflict.

Sterling: *Tarot Awareness: Exploring the Spiritual Path,* Llewellyn. How the Tarot can be a gateway toward spiritual development by unlocking a vibrant communication with the divine.

Technic. Technic is not another word for technique. It means rather *the applied science of this field of knowledge.* It is not theoretical science, but science applied to obtain specific and practical ends. I prefer to think of Technic as technology applied with scientific understanding.

Templars. The Order of the Temple of Jerusalem founded in 1118 to protect pilgrims travelling to the Holy Land. Originally poor, they became rich with gifts from King Alfonso of Aragon. Folk lore claims their wealth was derived from alchemy, from the practice of the magic of "attraction," and the discovery of King Solomon's Treasure. With their wealth, the Order grew to 30,000 members, a very powerful force. King Phillip IV of France was jealous and instigated the accusation of heresy in which they were accused of denying Christ, of worshipping the devil, and of engaging in "unnatural sex acts." Confessions were extracted by torture and many were burned to death. An investigation by Pope Clement V found no evidence of heresy. Their real crime may have been their interest in Gnosticism and the esoteric traditions of Manichaeism. In addition, some claim that the Templars were involved in practices of sex magick and Sufi mysticism.

"The seer cannot be, at the same time, the seen." As Culling points out, it is much easier to make observations in another person in their outer and visible character than in oneself. However, one's inner relations with one's HGA is quite another matter—unknown to the outsider. An outsider is outside this inner relationship and, at best, can only encourage you in the Great Work.

The "testing" of various intelligences. It has been a standard practice among astral traveling magicians to "test" the beings encountered by checking their names by their Qabalistic values.

C. F. Russell is quoted in *The Complete Magick Curriculum of the Secret Order G.·.B.·.G.·.* by Louis T. Culling as saying, "As long as you are an active, loyal, sincere aspirant to the Knowledge and Conversation of the Higher Guardian Angel, and using the oracle of the Yi, you cannot be a victim of 'alien' intelligences." Self-confident and "Knowing that there is nothing outside of yourself that is not also within yourself (and which you are daily facing), is enough to keep you sincerely and correctly on the path of the Great Work."

It's another way of saying "If your purpose be noble, and you're honest to yourself, you'll be OK." Or, "You have nothing to fear but fear itself." So, don't be afraid, and don't be seduced, stay with the purpose of your operation.

Thelema. (Will, in Greek) This is one's True Will, which can be discovered through the sincere practice of Magick. Crowley constructed this into his axiom: "Do what thou wilt shall be the whole of the law." The word of the Law is Thelema.

In the original writing of the *Book of the Law,* the word Thelema is in Greek letters; and by Greek gematria, the letters total the number 93. Thelema and 93 are synonymous with PURE WILL.

Thelema implies drawing closer and closer to the consciousness of one's real Individuality (the Khabs), in contradistinction to the active conscious Personality (the Khu). It then becomes the aim of the aspirant to be and to express one's True Individuality as much as possible, instead of being submerged in the Personality.

The key to the cryptic word "Thelema"—Will—is to recognize and DO THE TRUE WILL in conformity with the Conversation of the H G A, the Daemon.

Theosophical Society. The Theosophical Society was founded in New York City in 1875 by H.P. Blavatsky, Henry Steel Olcott, William Quan Judge and others. Its initial objective was the investigation, study and explanation of mediumistic phenomena. After a few years Olcott and Blavatsky moved to India and established the International Headquarters at Adyar, Madras (Chennai). There, they also became interested in studying Eastern religions, and these were included in the Society's agenda.

The Theosophical Society in America is a branch of the world fellowship and membership organization dedicated to promoting the unity of humanity and encouraging the study of religion, philosophy and science so that we may better understand ourselves and our relationships within this multidimensional universe. The Society stands for complete freedom of individual search and belief. There are lodges in most cities. More information at their website, www.theosophical .org/.

Totem Animal. The totem is deity in animal form. The selection of a totem is emblematic in a near archetypal way. Major animals, such as bear, lion, eagle, horse, etc., stir an instinctual emotional response. Your particular totem can be determined in response to the simple question: *"What animal would you like to be, and why?"*

A careful study of the answer can reveal a great deal about your preferred self-image, about the person you'd like to be, or—rather—the *persona* or mask you would like to present as your public image. At the same time, you will converse with totem. The technique of conversing with a God is well described in that classic, "The Invocation of Thoth" which is to be found in Crowley's *Equinox, Volume I, Number VI,* under the title of "The Rite of Mercury." It is also in Israel Regardie's magnum opus, *The Golden Dawn.*

Some ritualists do wear totem masks, and adopt it as an astral mask.

Think, for example, of what it would be like to choose the Eagle as your totem. *What is so admirable about the Eagle?* The Eagle has the true 'bird's eye view,' a perspective that sees the Big Picture, and yet the Eagle can focus on the minutest detail and descend from the sky to extract it. The Eagle soars effortlessly on updrafts, *going with the flow* until it is time for meaningful action. The Eagle wastes nothing, mates for life, returns to the nest season after season, building it stronger and stronger. The Bald Eagle is the American Emblem, fierce and protective, "Don't mess with me!"

As you adopt the totem's point of view, you learn lessons of life that called to you in response to your unconscious needs.

The basic procedure is to invoke the Totem Deity, and then to converse with the god following a very similar mental pattern. At the outset, one should have a clear, concise picture of the God and His Nature, and the imagined conversation should be on lines consonant with the God's Nature. One should not expect the God to converse a great deal at the beginning, except perhaps superficially. It is the magician who is active in initiating the conversation.

Presently, as in the second section of the Invocation, the magician should become passive and receptive. He may imagine that he is receiving conversation from the God even though he knows consciously that it is his own thoughts that he is tearing.

He progresses to the third stage wherein "He is in me and I in Him," and now there should be a strong feeling that the God is directing the conversation. Since the two are one, they now speak as one.

In the fourth section, if the invocation has been successful, the magician knows that he is no longer forming the words and the ideas. Unique concepts develop and the ideas produced are such as have never been before in the magician's conscious mind.

It is not advisable that this *conversation* be held with anyone other than a God or demi-god—never with a human being. No matter what God one converses with, it is assumed that the particular God is a part of the psyche of every human being, in spite of the fact that the conversation appears to be with a stranger. The Great Unconscious is a stranger to one's conscious mind unless and until the great union has been achieved, and even then there is the strange element.

Suggesting Reading:

Regardie, Israel: *The Golden Dawn,* Llewellyn

Transmuted. To be *transmuted* is to be changed in an evolutionary manner. Just as the alchemist sought to transmute base metal into gold, the goal of the Great Work is to transmute the lower self into the higher. As magicians, as workers, we are committed to a process of alchemical transformation of our own selves.

Trigrams. A trigram is a block of three parallel straight lines, each line being either complete (unbroken) or broken. See Pa Kua and I Ching for more details.

Vaughan, Thomas. (1622–1665) Welsh alchemist, Qabalist and mystic— "the spirit of man is itself the spirit of the Living God"—as Above, so Below. He translated many alchemical works, including the *Fama Fraternitatis* and *Confessio Fraternitatis* into English and wrote a number of important magical and alchemical works under the pseudonym "Eugenius Philalethes." His works include *Anthrosophia Theomagia, a Discourse of the Nature of Man and his State after Death* (1650), *Anima Magia Abscondita, a Discourse of the Universal Spirit of Nature* (1650), *Ma-*

gia Adamica, the Antiquity of Magic (1650), *Coelum Terrae, the Magician's Heavenly Chaos, Unfolding a Doctrine Concerning the Terrestrial Heaven* (1650), *Lumen de Lumine, a New Magical Light* (1651), *Aula Lucis, the House of Light* (1651), *The Fame and Confession of the Fraternity of the Rose Cross* (1652), and *Euphrates, the Waters of the East* (1655).

He was killed in an explosion during an alchemical experiment.

Wagner, Richard. (1813–1883) regarded himself as "the most German of men" who projected "the German spirit" in his thirteen operas and other compositions. He is best known for 'the Wedding March' familiar to most married couples. He was also a vociferous writer of about 230 books and articles. He was a vegetarian and a socialist, and has been called an anarchist, a nationalist, and even a fascist and anti-Semite. Hitler adored Wagner, and was often heard humming his operas.

Western Magick. *In this now global civilization, is there a distinction between eastern and western magick?* Yes, but it is less a distinction than so sincerely proclaimed when it was assumed that the eastern mind was different than the western. We can understand that various esoteric methods have a cultural history without saying that yoga is only for people born in India just as we've learned that computer science is not the sole province of Americans.

Western Magick has a distinctive system of knowledge and application, just as does Indian Tantra and Chinese Alchemy, but anyone can learn and apply these techniques without limitation.

Western Magick is largely founded on the Kabbalah and today includes Tarot and Ritual Magick. At the same time, there are differences in different traditions as to the understanding of various correspondences and symbols. At the practical levels, one system is not necessarily enriched by another. Learn the basic correspondences and symbols of the system you practice.

When a Word is more than a word. Some words have meanings that have evolved through their usage; others are attached purely through the emotions projected as they are spoken. There can be powerful effects through relatively minor nuances in pronunciation that should be carefully observed and used to effect.

Beyond that, words can be spoken to be heard like music, as indeed is the case with some poetry. The power of the words spoken in rhythm and rhyme have an almost hallucinogenic effect. They can lift you off your seat as if levitating.

White Eagle. The female of the magickal sex rite.

Will. (Kabbalah) Will is found in Geburah as part of Ruach, the Conscious Self. It is that part that decides on action and what that action will be, channeling all our energies towards a specific goal.

Suggested Reading: Regardie, with the Ciceros: *The Tree of Life—An Illustrated Study in Magic*

Yi King. See I Ching.

You're the Captain of your own Ship! Magick is generally perceived as a group function, but like the journey of The Fool in the Tarot deck, the esoteric path is ultimately personal and solitary.

On the solitary path, you are the one in charge, you are the one responsible, and you are the lone actor on the stage of life even though it is the same path and the same stage we all eventually traverse. You don't have a teacher to lean on, you are not apprenticed to a 'master,' and your only True Guide is your own Higher Self—*your own Holy Guardian Angel!*

Of course you have resources—books, courses, lectures and online information—to draw upon that were previously unavailable to sincere students. There was a time when only the teacher/student relationship was the reliable way to go, but that is no longer true. There are hazards you will encounter, and you alone will meet and defeat the challenges to your success. Even with the help and guidance of others, you alone must crown yourself, just as Napoleon crowned himself emperor of the French empire.

Suggested Reading & Reference Library:
A *Selection of Helpful Texts*

Andrews, Ted. *Simplified Qabala Magic*. Easy-to-follow techniques for utilizing the transformative energies of the Qabala—including meditation, pathworking, the Qabalist Cross and Middle Pillar, and more.

Brennan, J. H. *The Magical I Ching*. While providing strikingly accurate divination, the I Ching also provides links to the astral plane and the spirit world. Use in ritual and pathworking, an astral doorway, and a spirit guide.

Buckland, Raymond. *Signs, Symbols & Omens*. Describes the meaning of over 800 symbols from ancient and modern religions, magical traditions, and indigenous cultures around the world.

Christopher, Lyam Thomas. *Kabbalah, Magic and the Great Work of Self-Transformation*. Based on the Order of the Golden Dawn, a step-by-step program toward spiritual attainment.

Cicero, Chic, and Sandra Tabitha Cicero. *The Essential Golden Dawn: An Introduction to High Magic*. Explores the origins of Hermeticism and the Western Esoteric Tradition, the laws of magick, and magickal philosophy, and different areas of magickal knowledge.

———. *Self-Initiation into the Golden Dawn Tradition*. Become a practicing Golden Dawn magician with essential knowledge of Qabalah, astrology, Tarot, geomancy, and spiritual alchemy.

Denning, Melita, and Osborne Phillips. *Mysteria Magica: Fundamental Techniques of High Magick*. Essential and advanced teachings, potent techniques and rituals for self-training, constructing magickal defenses, consecrating magickal implements, and tables of essential information.

———. *The Sword & Serpent: The Two-fold Qabalistic Universe.* The philosophy of ceremonial magick and its relationship to the Qabalah.

Frater U.˙.D.˙.. *High Magic I: Theory and Practice.* Basic magickal exercises and practices in a consistent program of development with tables and charts to simplify the learning process. Encyclopedic in depth, even including chaos and cyber magick.

———. *High Magic II: Expanded Theory and Practice.* Mirror magick, mudras, sigil magick, shamanism, magickal orders, folk magick, demonic magick, divination and letter magick, magick and yoga, magick in the Bible, the practical Kabbalah, forms of Initiation, and the magick of ancient Egypt.

Greer, John Michael. *Inside a Magical Lodge: Group Ritual in the Western Tradition.* What happens inside a magickal lodge, including floor layout and responsibilities of the officers, Initiation and rituals, along with rites for cleansing, sealing the aura, invisibility, and more. Also how to set up a lodge as a corporation.

Hollander, P. Scott. *Tarot for Beginners: An Easy Guide to Understanding & Interpreting the Tarot.* Provides a road to self-discovery, and shows how to use the cards in divination, meditation, and self-enlightenment.

Hulse, David Allen. *The Western Mysteries.* Catalogs and distills—in hundreds of tables of secret symbolism—the true alphabet of magick of every Western magickal tradition.

Konstantinos. *Summoning Spirits: The Art of Magical Evocation.* One of the most powerful and beneficial magickal techniques. Obtain mystical abilities, locate hidden treasure, command a spirit army to protect your home, etc.

Kraig, Donald Michael. *Modern Magick: Eleven Lessons in the High Magickal Arts.* How to evoke entities to physical appearance, how to use the Greater and Lesser Keys of Solomon, how to make and use talismans and amulets, a magick mirror, and how to do Sex Magick.

————. *Modern Sex Magick: Secrets of Erotic Spirituality.* Learn to control and direct sexual power when it's most intense—during arousal. Increase your pleasure and enhance your relationships.

————. *Tarot & Magic.* How to use the Tarot to do magick on a practical level, with Tarot spells, talismans, working on the astral plane, etc.

Leitch, Aaron. *Secrets of the Magickal Grimoires: The Classical Texts of Magick Deciphered.* A comprehensive reference of magickal practices and shamanic methods of working with the spirit world.

Louis, Anthony. *Tarot Plain and Simple.* A self-study program to do readings for yourself and others. Written by a psychiatrist, with a Jungian approach to understanding human nature and psychological conflict.

Regardie, Israel. *The Golden Dawn: The Original Account of the Teachings, Rites & Ceremonies of the Hermetic Order.* Initiation, consecration, invocation, meditation, Tarot, Qabalistic correspondences, etc. An in-depth encyclopedia and study program from the foundations of the Western Esoteric System.

Regardie, Israel, Chic Cicero, and Tabitha Cicero. *A Garden of Pomegranates: Skrying on the Tree of Life.* The classic guidebook to the Hermetic Qabalah and its symbolism with full commentary and explanatory notes.

————. *The Middle Pillar: The Balance Between Mind and Magic.* Breaking the barrier between conscious and unconscious through the Middle Pillar exercise working as a bridge into magick, chakra work, and psychology.

————. *The Tree of Life: An Illustrated Study in Magic.* Combining ancient wisdom with modern magickal practice, and developing the principles of magick that cut across boundaries of time, religion, and culture.

Skinner, Stephen. *The Complete Magician's Tables.* The most complete collection of magician's tables available, documenting thousands of magickal links, pagan pantheons, Kabbalah, astrology, Tarot, I Ching, angels, demons, herbs, perfumes, and more, and how it's all connected together.

Skinner, Stephen, and David Rankine. *The Veritable Key of Solomon*. Never before published material and based on one of the best-known grimoires of the Western world, this is a complete and workable system of high magick with over 160 illustrations.

Sterling, Stephen Walter. *Tarot Awareness: Exploring the Spiritual Path*. How the Tarot can be a gateway toward spiritual development by unlocking a vibrant communication with the divine.

Tyson, Donald. *Familiar Spirits: A Practical Guide for Witches & Magicians*. A revolutionary system for safely summoning, directing, and dismissing a familiar without expertise in formal ritual, astrology, or the Kabbalah.

———. *Ritual Magic: What It Is & How to Do It*. What magick can do for you, and what it can't, the differences among various magickal paths, and instructions for two rituals.

Whitcomb, Bill: *The Magician's Companion: A Practical and Encyclopedic Guide to Magical and Religious Symbolism*. The theory and practice of magick and ritual with over thirty-five magickal models, and tables and data on runes, the Tree of Life, yoga, Enochian Magick, the I Ching, symbology, magickal alphabets, the chakras, planetary spirits, Hindu Tattwas, the Wheel of the Year, eight psychic channels, geomancy, the Tarot, astral travel, the body of light, magickal squares and sigils, descriptions of major deities, and much more.

Index

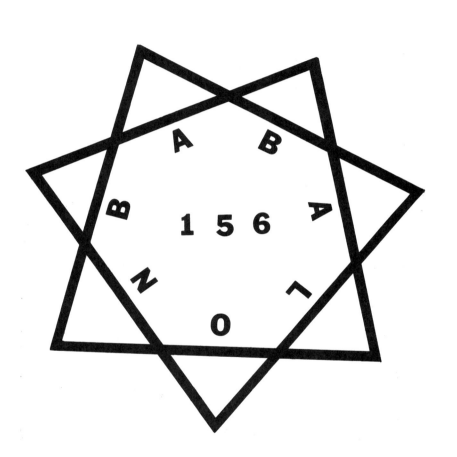

To Write to the Author

If you wish to contact the author or would like more information about this book, please write to the author in care of Llewellyn Worldwide and we will forward your request. Both the author and publisher appreciate hearing from you and learning of your enjoyment of this book and how it has helped you. Llewellyn Worldwide cannot guarantee that every letter written to the author can be answered, but all will be forwarded. Please write to:

Carl Llewellyn Weschcke
℅ Llewellyn Worldwide
2143 Wooddale Drive
Woodbury, MN 55125-2989

Please enclose a self-addressed stamped envelope for reply,
or $1.00 to cover costs. If outside the USA, enclose
an international postal reply coupon.

Many of Llewellyn's authors have websites with additional information and resources. For more information, please visit our website at http://www.llewellyn.com.

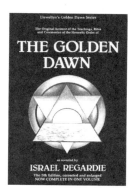

The Golden Dawn

The Original Account of the Teachings, Rites & Ceremonies
of the Hermetic Order as Revealed by Israel Regardie

Originally published in four bulky volumes of some 1,200 pages, this complete 6th revised and enlarged edition is compiled in one volume! It includes additional notes—by Regardie, Cris Monnastre, and others—and an index of more than 100 pages! All of the original pagination is retained in marginal notations for reference.

Also included are Initiation Ceremonies, important rituals for consecration and invocation, methods of meditation and magical working based on the Enochian Tablets, studies in the Tarot, and the system of Qabalistic Correspondences that unite the world's religions and magical traditions into a comprehensive and practical whole.

This volume is designed as a study and practice curriculum suited to both group and private practice. The 6th edition of *The Golden Dawn* is a complete reference encyclopedia of Western Magick.

978-0-87542-663-1, 844 pp., 6 x 9   **$37.95**

To order, call 1-877-NEW-WRLD
Prices subject to change without notice
Order at Llewellyn.com 24 hours a day, 7 days a week!

A Garden of Pomegranates

Skrying on the Tree of Life

ISRAEL REGARDIE

ED. CHIC CICERO AND SANDRA TABATHA CICERO

(Annotated with new material.)

When Israel Regardie wrote *A Garden of Pomegranates* in 1932, he designed it to be a simple yet comprehensive guidebook outlining the complex system of the Qabalah and providing a key to its symbolism. Since then it has achieved the status of a classic among texts on the Hermetic Qabalah. It stands as the best single introductory guide for magicians on this complex system, with an emphasis on direct experience through meditation on the twenty-two paths.

Now, Chic Cicero and Sandra Tabatha Cicero—Golden Dawn adepts and personal friends of the late Regardie—have made the book even more useful for today's occult students with full annotations, critical commentary, and explanatory notes. They've added practical material in the form of pathworkings, suggested exercises, and daily affirmations—one for each Sephirah and each path. Brief rituals, meditations, and Qabalistic mantras complement Regardie's section on gematria and other forms of numerical Qabalah.

978-1-56718-141-8, 552 pp., 6 x 9 $21.95

To order, call 1-877-NEW-WRLD
Prices subject to change without notice
Order at Llewellyn.com 24 hours a day, 7 days a week!

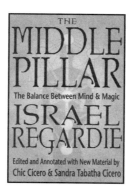

Middle Pillar

The Balance Between Mind & Magic

ISRAEL REGARDIE

ED. CHIC CICERO AND SANDRA TABATHA CICERO

Break the barrier between the conscious and unconscious mind through the Middle Pillar exercise, a technique that serves as a bridge into magic, chakra work, and psychology. This classic work introduces a psychological perspective on magic and occultism while giving clear directions on how to perform the Qabalistic Cross, The Lesser Banishing Ritual of the Pentagram, the Middle Pillar exercise, along with its accompanying methods of circulating the light, the Vibratory Formula, and the building up of the Tree of Life in the aura.

The Ciceros, who knew Regardie personally, have made his book much more accessible by adding an extensive and useful set of notes, along with chapters that explain Regardie's work in depth. They expand upon it by carrying it into a realm of new techniques that are directly related to Regardie's core material. Especially valuable is the chapter on psychology, which provides a solid frame of reference for Regardie's numerous remarks on this subject.

978-1-56718-140-1, 312pp., 6 x 9   **$17.95**

To order, call 1-877-NEW-WRLD
Prices subject to change without notice
Order at Llewellyn.com 24 hours a day, 7 days a week!

The Tree of Life

An Illustrated Study in Magic

ISRAEL REGARDIE

EDITED AND ANNOTATED BY

CHIC CICERO AND SANDRA TABATHA CICERO

In 1932, when magic was a "forbidden subject," Israel Regardie wrote *The Tree of Life* at the age of 24. He believed that magic was a precise scientific discipline as well as a highly spiritual way of life, and he took on the enormous task of making it accessible to a wide audience of eager spiritual seekers. The result was this book, which adroitly presents a massive amount of diverse material in a remarkably unified whole.

From the day it was first published, *The Tree of Life* has remained in high demand by ceremonial magicians for its skillful combination of ancient wisdom and modern magical experience. It was Regardie's primary desire to point out the principles of magic that cut across all boundaries of time, religion, and culture—those fundamental principles common to all magic, regardless of any specific tradition or spiritual path.

978-1-56718-132-6, 552 pp., 6 x 9   **$24.95**